London

· Central London · South West
· South East · North
· West · East
· Kids' Rides

By Nick Woodford

BA Press
36 Wentworth Street,
Port Kembla NSW, 2505
Australia
ABN: 67 008 273 827

Email: mail@bicyclingaustralia.com
Tel: (02) 4274 4884 - Fax: (02) 4274 0988 - www.bicyclingaustralia.com

First published in Australia in 2010 by BA Press.

The Cycling Kangaroo logo is a trademark of Lake Wangary Publishing Company Pty Ltd.
Bicycling Australia are proud sponsors of The World Bicycle Relief.

The National Library of Australia Cataloguing-in-Publication data

Author:	Woodford, Nick
Title:	Where to Ride London / Nick Woodford
ISBN:	9780980354690 (pbk.)
	9780980750232 (box set)
Dewey Number:	796.609421

1. Cycling - England - London - Guidebooks.
2. Bicycle trails - England - London - Guidebooks.
3. London (England) - Guidebooks.

Design and layout - Justine Powell
Advertising - Justine Powell
Photography - All photos taken by Nick Woodford unless otherwise specified.
Mapping - Mapping Specialists Ltd

Printed in China by RR Donnelley.
Cover Image: Nick Woodford

Bicycling Australia

About us...

Cycling has many health and environmental benefits, but apart from these it's a fun leisure time activity for all ages. Most of our small team are active cyclists; we love to ride and hope that we can, through interesting, exciting and timely information, make your cycling experience more enjoyable.

Founded 20 years ago by Phil and Catie Latz, Lake Wangary Publishing Company began with a single black and white road cycling magazine. We now publish four cycling magazines as well as the growing series of Where to Ride guides in Australia, America, New Zealand and now the UK.

We're committed to our vision of enhancing all aspects of cycling by providing information for all our customers. Whether through our magazines or books, we hope to make your riding experience as enjoyable as possible.

Look out for BA Press books and the 'cycling kangaroo' logos in newsagents and bookstores; it's your key to great cycling publications.

London

Contents

About Us 3
Author's Note 6
About the Author 7
Introduction 8
Ride Overview 10
How to Use This Book 12
What to Take 13
World Bicycle Relief 14
On the Road 16
Off the Road 18
You, Your Bike and Public Transport in London 21
Public Transport Maps 22-27
Getting You and Your Bike to London 26
Notes 251

Central London

Introduction 30
Ride 1 - The Big Three Parks Loop 32
Ride 2 - Rags to Riches Route 36
Ride 3 - Regents Canal East Trail 40
Ride 4 - Sunday in the City Loop 44
Ride 5 - The Thames City Loop 48
Ride 6 - Grey Day Museums 52
Ride 7 - City to Canary Wharf Loop 56
Ride 8 - Sunny Day Sights Route 60

South West

Introduction 66
Ride 9 - Epsom Countryside Loop 68
Ride 10 - Horton Country Park Loop 72
Ride 11 - South West Parks 76
Ride 12 - Hampton Court Trail 80
Ride 13 - Richmond Park Loop 84
Ride 14 - Syon Park and Kew Loop 88
Ride 15 - Wandle Trail Loop 92
Ride 16 - Ham House Loop 96
Ride 17 - Wimbledon Common 100
Ride 18 - Hampton Ferry Loop 104
Ride 19 - Kingston, Bushy Park Loop 108
Ride 20 - Battersea to Fulham Loop 112

South East

Introduction 116
Ride 21 - Bromley, Beckenham Loop 118
Ride 22 - Docks to Salt Marshes Trail 122
Ride 23 - Greenwich to Woolwich Trail 126
Ride 24 - Biggin Hill Loop 130
Ride 25 - Ravensbourne River Trail 134
Ride 26 - South East Parks Loop 138
Ride 27 - Southwark Sights Route 142
Ride 28 - Blackheath to Woolwich 146
Ride 29 - Two Thames Tunnels Loop 150

North

Introduction 154
Ride 30 - Hampstead Heath Loop 156
Ride 31 - Totteridge Common Loop 160
Ride 32 - Finsbury to Highgate Route 164
Ride 33 - Muswell Hill Loop 168
Ride 34 - Parkland Walk Trail 172
Ride 35 - War Museum to Ali Pali 176
Ride 36 - Hadley Common Loop 180

West

Introduction 184
Ride 37 - River Brent Route 186
Ride 38 - Hendon Parks Loop 190
Ride 39 - The Grand Union Canal Loop 194
Ride 40 - Barnes and Chiswick Loop 198
Ride 41 - Willesden to Kew Bridge Loop 202
Ride 42 - Camden to the Thames Route 206

East

Introduction 210
Ride 43 - Epping Forest Loop 212
Ride 44 - East London Greenway 216
Ride 45 - Hackney Parks Loop 220
Ride 46 - Lee Valley Regional Park Trail 224
Ride 47 - Olympic Greenway Loop 228
Ride 48 - River Lee South Trail 232
Ride 49 - Epping to Stratford Trail 236
Ride 50 - Woolwich to Isle of Dogs 240

Kids' Rides

Introduction 244
Ride 1 - Hyde Park 246
Ride 2 - Wimbledon Common 247
Ride 3 - Dulwich Park 248
Ride 4 - Hampstead Heath 249
Ride 5 - Victoria Park 250

Editor's Note

Despite living in London most my life, I only really got to know the city when I started cycling. Tired of the underground crush, I dusted off my childhood bike and joined in the pedal powered movement. I can best describe it as revelation and I am not alone, thousands of new cyclists throng onto London's streets every year. So what is the draw?

The cool, dry climate and flat terrain are a good start; then there are the mighty parks and treasured commons while thanks to its layers of history, the city also hides tranquil canal towpaths, riverside walks and disused railway lines, all of which make brilliant car free cycling routes. But this is just the start. In recent years the city authorities have invested in better provision for cyclists on the roads too. The introduction of cycle superhighways and the city's cycle hire scheme are both in addition to more parking stands, safe storage spaces, free maps and business development, encouraging companies to provide showers and changing rooms as well as subsidised cycle purchase.

However the greatest driver is the ever-increasing number of cyclists themselves. Some take it up as a way to beat the system and avoid the congested roads and public transport, others see it as a way of keeping fit, while some start for environmental reasons however most do it for fun. Whatever the motive it is generally, faster, cheaper, cleaner and nicer than any other mode of transport and it is perfectly suited to both London's multicentric geography and her particular immediacy and disorder. More cyclists mean more bike shops and cycle organisations. The London Cycle Campaign, Sustrans and CTC are just some of the groups promoting cycling in the capital and further a field. Many boroughs have their own clubs and groups for mountain biking, racing, touring and even commuting. However, it's not just London's cycling credentials that make it a great city to explore by bike;

it's the cafes, cultural sights and views it gives of every day London life from fishing to finance.

The 50 rides in this book are tailored to make the most of the city's car free cycling routes whilst tapping into her sights and areas of beauty. They range from road rides to tough muddy mountain bike tracks, from tranquil riverside paths to cultural odysseys weaving through the intense urban fabric. So no matter which cycle tribe you belong to, or if you haven't yet joined the velorution, there will be a ride for you. The guide has been broken down into six chapters and there is an easy to use rating scale so you know what to expect. We have made every effort to ensure the accuracy of these rides but it is worth noting that trails are regularly being improved. If you discover any errors or would like to comment on any of the rides in this book please email us at wheretoride@bicyclingaustralia.com.

So all that's left for me to say is have fun and enjoy the rides.

Nick Woodford
Author, Editor and Photographer

About the Author

Born and raised in London, Nick thought he had the city pretty well sussed, but creating this guide has been a voyage of discovery rekindling the excitement a first time visitor would feel. Nick has journeyed the world, writing and contributed to many other travel books including Rough Guides and Alastair Sawday's, but this is the first time he has had the chance to cover his own beloved city and in his words "there is no better way of doing it than by bike".

Acknowledgments

A huge thank you to all of you that joined the Where to Ride - Cycle Guide to London facebook group and accompanying me on various rides, you were beautiful models and you kept me company through urban jungle and on deserted trails. I would particularly like to thank my brothers Olly and Mark as well as Louise and Thabata and my Mum and Dad. I must also thank Joanne David for her hours of proofing, Justine Powell for project managing and the rest of the WTR team in Port Kembla for putting together such a great book. Finally thanks to Angelita Bradney and Chris Mullin for their 11th hour check of the whole book.

Introduction

" B y seeing London, I have seen as much of life as the world can show" Samuel Johnson

Love London. Embrace the good, humour the bad and avoid the ugly; then you can dispense with feeling like a stranger, after all no matter where you are from you can still call London home. At eight million people and stretching more than 30 miles at its broadest point, London is by far the largest metropolis in western Europe and though not one of the world's most populous cities it could arguably be the most diverse and culturally influential. History and geography mean the city's inhabitants come from all corners of the globe bringing with them their traditions and culture. The resulting exchange of ideas generates innovation, new trends are created, new ideas are traded and the buzz is palpable.

London is like a colourful urban patchwork quilt. There is no true centre but an amalgamation of towns and neighbourhoods each with their own distinct characteristics. For this reason, many Londoners struggle to leave their borough or neighbourhood, however London is everywhere and there is no better way to explore it than by bike.

So what's to see and do? There are four world heritage sites, world famous museums and art galleries, palaces, a parliament, churches, clocks and cathedrals; there is one mighty river, several smaller rivers and gentle canals; there are sporting events from rowing to football and the Olympics in 2012; there's modern and old architecture; wildlife reserves, world famous parks, royal forests with deer, ancient woodlands and public commons; there are libraries, botanical gardens, shopping and more shopping; cutting edge fashion, music venues big and small; markets for food, antiques, home wares and flowers; there are restaurants of every description, cocktail bars and sushi bars, old fashioned pubs and banging nightclubs; there is something for everyone and the best way of getting there is by bike.

So whether you're an eager, inquisitive visitor or a jaded analyst from Kensal Green, saddle up and explore the city from a fresh perspective. No longer stuck in traffic or fighting against elbows and armpits on a crowded train but able to whiz along as free as the breeze. Londoners can use these routes to piece together the islands of geography centred around tube stations, liberating yourself from the underground. While for those visiting the city these rides will allow you to do so much more than just scratch the surface that's provided by traditional guidebooks. Where to Ride London will take you to the lesser known, but just as worthwhile outer communities that make the city so unique.

Central London
30

South West
66

South East
116

North
154

West
184

East
210

Kids' Rides
244

Ride Overview

Central London

Page	Ride	Ride Name	Terrain	Distance (km)	Where to Ride Rating	Kid Friendly
32	1	The Big Three Parks Loop	Road	16.7	1	
36	2	Rags to Riches Route	Road	16.5	1	
40	3	Regents Canal East Trail	Path	9.1	1	✓
44	4	Sunday in the City Loop	Road	9.0	1	
48	5	The Thames City Loop	Road	7.9	1	
52	6	Grey Day Museums	Road	13.5	1	
56	7	City to Canary Wharf Loop	Road	9.9	1	✓
60	8	Sunny Day Sights Route	Road	10.2	1	

South West

Page	Ride	Ride Name	Terrain	Distance (km)	Where to Ride Rating	Kid Friendly
68	9	Epsom Countryside Loop	MTB	19.3	5	
72	10	Horton Country Park Loop	Off Road	12.4	4	
76	11	South West Parks	Road	15.6	1	
80	12	Hampton Court Trail	Path	5.3	1	✓
84	13	Richmond Park Loop	Off Road	11.8	2	✓
88	14	Syon Park and Kew Loop	Road	11.9	1	
92	15	Wandle Trail Loop	Path	28.6	3	
96	16	Ham House Loop	Path	9.8	1	✓
100	17	Wimbledon Common	Path	10.6	2	✓
104	18	Hampton Ferry Loop	Path	8.0	1	✓
108	19	Kingston, Bushy Park loop	Road	12.6	1	
112	20	Battersea to Fulham Loop	Road	13.9	1	

South East

Page	Ride	Ride Name	Terrain	Distance (km)	Where to Ride Rating	Kid Friendly
118	21	Bromley, Beckenham Loop	Road	34.9	3	
122	22	Docks to Salt Marshes Trail	Path	18.4	1	✓
126	23	Greenwich and Woolwich Trail	Path	8.2	1	✓
130	24	Biggin Hill Loop	MTB	32.0	5	
134	25	Ravensbourne River Trail	Road	14.5	1	✓

Page	Ride	Ride Name	Terrain	Distance (km)	Where to Ride Rating	Kid Friendly
138	26	South East Parks Loop	Road	11.4	1	✓
142	27	Southwark Sights Route	Road	15.4	1	
146	28	Blackheath to Woolwich	Road	11.7	1	
150	29	Two Thames Tunnels Loop	Road	15.4	1	

North

Page	Ride	Ride Name	Terrain	Distance (km)	Where to Ride Rating	Kid Friendly
156	30	Hampstead Heath Loop	Road	5.8	1	✓
160	31	Totteridge Common Loop	Off Road	16.0	3	
164	32	Finsbury to Highgate Route	Road	11.4	2	
168	33	Muswell Hill Loop	Road	15.7	1	
172	34	Parkland Walk Trail	Off Road	5.4	1	✓
176	35	War Museum to Ali Pali	Road	15.1	3	
180	36	Hadley Common Loop	Road	16.4	3	

West

Page	Ride	Ride Name	Terrain	Distance (km)	Where to Ride Rating	Kid Friendly
186	37	River Brent Route	Road	13.5	1	
190	38	Hendon Parks Loop	Off Road	9.6	2	✓
194	39	The Grand Union Canal Loop	Path	28.3	2	✓
198	40	Barnes and Chiswick Loop	Path	9.9	1	
202	41	Willesden to Kew Bridge Loop	Road	31.5	2	
206	42	Camden to the Thames Route	Road	13.5	1	

East

Page	Ride	Ride Name	Terrain	Distance (km)	Where to Ride Rating	Kid Friendly
212	43	Epping Forest Loop	MTB	19.5	5	
216	44	East London Greenway	Path	16.0	1	✓
220	45	Hackneys Park Loop	Road	10.2	1	✓
224	46	Lee Valley Regional Park Trail	Path	14.7	1	✓
228	47	Olympic Greenway Loop	Road	12.1	1	
232	48	River Lee South Trail	Path	11.0	1	✓
236	49	Epping to Stratford Trail	Off Road	13.3	4	
240	50	Woolwich to Isle of Dogs	Road	8.9	1	

How to Use This Book

In Where to Ride London, you have access to 50 great rides that explore the capital's sights and diversity.

The rides are broken down into six geographical regions. Central London covers Westminster and The City, the South West region stretches from Epsom and Kingston-Upon-Thames to Battersea including Richmond Park and Clapham Common. The South East runs from the South Bank to Woolwich with countryside rides around Biggin Hill and suburban rides through Crystal Palace, Beckenham, Blackheath and Camberwell. Suburban areas north of the river are divided into three chapters. North London includes Hampstead Heath and Totteridge Common, while highlights of West London include the Grand Union Canal and East London is home to Epping Forest, the Lea Valley and the developing Olympic Park. Each of these regions has been colour coded for easy reference. The last chapter has six children's rides; flat pleasant car-free routes that are great places to learn to ride. All the rides are categorised into either road or mountain bike. This should make the job of finding a bike ride that's right for you nice and simple!

Ride Scale

To help you understand each of the rides at a glance, we have rated them all using the Where to Ride rating scale. Each ride is awarded points based on the total distance covered, the total elevation gain of the ride and also the type of surface that the ride covers.

These tables and the levels within them should only be used as a guide. We do recommend that people new to the sport of cycling and those less fit should initially stick to Level 1 and 2 rides. As your fitness increases and experience improves, we hope you'll be able to enjoy the rest of the rides in the book, rated 3, 4 and 5. You can view the Where to Ride rating for each ride on its introductory page – just look for the Bicycling Australia kangaroo symbols.

Out on the ride, to make things easier, make sure you use the fold out map key from the inside front cover as a bookmark to keep you on the correct page.

While the maps have been produced with accurate GPS-collected data, there will be occasions when they do not show sufficient information to allow you to navigate using them. Make sure you are constantly referring to the detailed ride logs on the page opposite each map and before you set-out please pick-up the relevant TFL cycle map available free from libraries or online at www.tfl.gov.uk//roadusers/cycling/11682.aspx.

	1 pt	2 pts	3 pts	4 pts	5 pts
Distance –Rd (km)	<20	20-30	30-40	40-60	>60
Distance – MTB (km)	<10	10-15	15-25	25-40	>40
Climbing (m)	<150	150-300	300-450	450-600	>600
Surface	Sealed smooth	Sealed rough	Unsealed smooth	Unsealed moderate	Unsealed rough

Accumulated Points	Riding Level/Grade	Suggested Suitability
3	1	Beginner
4-5	2	
6-7	3	Moderately fit
8-9	4	
10+	5	Experienced cyclist

What to Take

On most of the rides in this book you're never far from civilisation but it's always important to make sure your bike is in good working order before you start out. It's also wise to ensure that you've got everything you need so there are no dramas in the event something does come unstuck.

It's a good idea to go through a checklist before you head out even if you are an experienced rider, and feel free to add to this list or modify it to suit. At the end of every ride, it's a good idea to give your bike a clean, lubricate the chain, and make any repairs that are required before your next trip. Make sure you re-stock too if you've used a spare tube or one of your tube patches.

Essentials
- Bicycle helmet with correctly adjusted straps
- Spare inner tube, tyre levers and possibly a puncture repair kit
- Bicycle pump or gas canister
- Multi-tool and any other tool specific to your bike for basic repairs
- Sunscreen
- Plenty of water; 1 litre per hour is an indication
- Food; a few snacks to keep your blood sugar levels OK
- Mobile phone and/or phone card
- A bike bell
- Identification
- Money

Optional Extras
- Light wet weather jacket
- Camera
- Binoculars
- Small First Aid kit
- Front and rear lights if you're likely to be out after dusk
- Bicycle lock

Before You Go

While the benefits of cycling as part of a healthy lifestyle and recreational pastime are well known, if you are starting out for the first time or after a lengthy lay-off, consult your doctor if you have any health concerns.

Make sure that your bicycle and equipment are in good working order and it's worth giving it a quick once over before you leave. Basic things to look for include:

- The tyres should be inflated to the suggested air pressure. It's wise to check the tyres carefully for damage and anything that might be embedded should be removed.
- The brake cables and pads should all be working and not worn.
- The gear cables should be nice and tight and you should be able to select every gear when pedalling.
- The chain should be clean and well lubricated and not stretched or worn out.

If you're unsure about any of these points, visit your local bike shop for advice or to arrange a regular service. Once you're ready to leave, it's wise to let somebody know where you're planning to ride and how long you're likely to be away.

WORLD BICYCLE RELIEF®

A bicycle is a powerful tool, one that can be used to get children to school, carry goods to market, commute to work or travel to a clinic for critical medical treatment; a bicycle gives a person power, freedom and increased livelihood opportunities.

MISSION

World Bicycle Relief is dedicated to providing access to independence and livelihood through the power of bicycles.

HISTORY

Founded by SRAM Corporation in 2005, World Bicycle Relief specializes in large-scale, comprehensive bicycle programs supporting poverty relief and disaster recovery initiatives. To date, World Bicycle Relief has provided over 60,000 bicycles in seven countries, including Sri Lanka, Zambia, Tanzania and Zimbabwe.

CAPACITY

Riding a bicycle increases a person's capacity to carry by 5 times

walking

riding a bike

DISTANCE

walking

Over equal units of time, a person can ride a bicycle over 4 times the distance as a person walking.

riding a bike

TIME

During a commuting day of 10 miles travelled, a bicycle saves 3 hours.

walking
2-1/2 miles per hour

3 extra hours per day to regain their livelihood.

bicycling
10 miles per hour

MEET TENDAI

Tendai lives in rural Zambia with her grandparents in Chillikwela village, nearly 5 miles from Chiyota Basic School where she is in 7th grade. She would like to go to teachers college.

Every morning, before going to school, she goes to fetch water.

Midday, she goes home to cook lunch for herself and her grandparents – and fetch more water.

Weekends, she goes to visit her mother and younger brothers in Susana, more than 12 miles away. She often carries vegetables to sell at market.

Tendai does not have an easy life, but her family supports her and wants her to do well in school.

In 2009, World Bicycle Relief's innovative Bicycles for Educational Empowerment Program provided students, teachers and administrators at Chiyota Basic School – including Tendai – with specially designed, locally assembled bikes. Her life has been changed by *The Power of Bicycles*®.

Help us provide *The Power of Bicycles*® for more students like Tendai.

These ideas can get you started:

- Visit our website at www.worldbicyclerelief.org to sign up for our newsletter, subscribe to our blog, follow us on Twitter or join our cause on Facebook.

- Request World Bicycle Relief postcards, posters and stickers for placement in a prominent area of your community.

- Host a World Bicycle Relief awareness event.

To learn more about World Bicycle Relief and how you can get involved, please visit our website at www.worldbicyclerelief.org **or email us at** info@worldbicyclerelief.org

On the Road
(Safety in City HGV Positioning)

We're all well aware of the growing popularity of bike riding in the UK; there are now an estimated 20 million, that's one in three adults. More people are commuting and it's no wonder – petrol prices are rising, obesity is the number one health problem, traffic congestion is prevalent in most of our major cities and we have a constant concern for the environment. The benefits of bike riding are becoming apparent to a greater portion of the population.

However, with this free, inclusive and liberating mode of transport comes vulnerability to other road users. Each year around 20 cyclists are killed and 300 seriously injured on London's roads. While many of these incidents do involve a motor vehicle, most of them are preventable.

As a bike rider you know that feeling of freedom when you're out riding, pedalling along past long queues of traffic on your way to work or enjoying the scenery and a coffee on a weekend ride. But as a legitimate road user, you also have an important role to play as an ambassador for the great sport of cycling. And it's easy! Simple things we can all do to make sure we arrive at our destination safely and build a harmonious relationship of shared respect with fellow road users.

All cyclists must abide by the road rules, just as motorists do. Here are some useful points to remember when heading out on the road. Cyclists must stop at red lights, not only is it the law but we're sure it's a good way to gain the respect of motorists. Wear a helmet, bright clothing and have lights on your bike. Be predictable and always indicate your intentions by using hand signals and make eye contact with drivers when changing direction.

Be aware of the main cycling hazards. Left-hand bends; vehicles turning left may not look or indicated and cut straight into your path. Gaps in lines of traffic are a sign of a motorist letting a car or pedestrian pass in front of them, slow down and be aware. When passing a row of parked cars be aware of car doors opening suddenly in your path. Always cycle away from the parked cars and look out for occupants in the vehicles. Finally the biggest danger to cyclists in the city and the reason for seven of 10 fatal accidents are articulated lorries and buses. When the driver of an HGV is turning he/she has a large blind spot and cannot see cyclists on the inside. Always stay well behind or well in front of hives at junctions. Make eye contact in the driver's mirrors and never, never undertake on the inside.

In return, as motorists we should be patient when overtaking and treat cyclists as equal partners; cycle

A red Routemaster bus is left behind a speeding cyclists as they whiz through Piccadilly Circus

traffic has the same rights and responsibilities as motor vehicle traffic. Look out for riders before opening car doors and making turns. Give people on bicycles at least one metre clearance, they may have to swing out to avoid hazards such as loose drain covers or glass. Bicycle lanes are for the exclusive use of cyclists to increase their safety, they can only be used when passing a right turning vehicle or to enter/leave a parking space.

Don't let London's heavy traffic put you off riding around the capital. With assertiveness, awareness and a tad of fitness, you can claim your space on the tarmac and enjoy being in control of your journey. There are bad careless drivers and good cyclists but the reverse is also true. Safety depends on two factors; awareness of potential hazards and how to avoid them and considerate cycling techniques designed to catch the attention of other drivers and help you to help them.

Finally don't get your bike nicked. The majority of thefts are opportunist so always lock your bike up even for a 30 second shop stop. Use a solid steel U-lock and secure to something immobile like a lamppost, railings or bike stand. Thread the lock through the frame and the back wheel and use a second type of lock to secure the front wheel. Take off anything that unclips: lights, pumps, water bottle and even your saddle if you think it is at risk. Even this is not infallible so insure your bike. Take a photo, note the frame number and get it coded at your local police station; thousand of bikes are recovered every year but cannot be traced to their owners.

Off the Road (Country Code)

Mountain biking is a great way of getting to know London's surprisingly extensive countryside, but it is amazing how quickly you can become lost along woodland bridleways and country trails often just a few hundred metres from suburban railway stations and main roads.

It will be important to have the right sort of bicycle if you intend to ride the MTB routes in this guide as there may be significant sections of rough and eroded trails where thin tyred road bikes would be susceptible to punctures.

MTB Code of Practice

We encourage the preservation of natural areas by fully and comprehensively endorsing a code of ethics for cycling in these areas. This code is based on mutual respect for other visitors and for the natural area itself. It supports the notion of all cyclists leaving natural areas in an undisturbed condition. It emphasizes responsible behaviour. Riding your mountain bike is as much about respect as anything else.

Respect for the Environment

• Ride only on trails open to mountain biking
• Cyclists must stay on the trails
• Stay off muddy trails after rain
• Always take out what you take in
• Leave all flora and fauna untouched
• Stay in control; trails are damaged when you skid

Respect for Others

• Respect other visitors to countryside
• Always expect that someone may be around the next corner
• Slow down as you approach others
• Pass others with care
• Control your speed

Respect for Yourself

• Ride within your ability
• Expect foreseeable risks
• Stay hydrated and protect yourself from the sun
• Plan your ride
• Enjoy your ride with others
• Carry tools and spares
• Take a mobile phone

Meeting Other Trail Users

It is important for all mountain bikers to be respectful of others. Most important is to manage your speed in areas which are known to be used by walkers and equestrians. Be courteous; the country code states - Bikers yield to horses and walkers. Walkers yield to horses. Rights of Way law forbids cycling on footpaths. However, section 30 of the 1968 Countryside act states that cycling is permitted on bridleways.

Walkers

Most of the issues between walkers and cyclists comes down to speed differential; the speed difference between walking (4kph) and cycling (15kph). Make your presence known well in advance, call out and make a noise or use your bell.

Pass walkers slowly and make sure they are aware what side you will pass on. Many walkers may be elderly or less agile so expect the unexpected.

Horses

Again, speed differential is a major issue with meeting horses out on a trail but a more important aspect is that horses have almost no vision behind their head and will react unpredictably if a fast moving strange object comes up behind them. Horses also feel the tension of their rider so you need to be doubly aware that horses may not be used to cyclists and that the rider may be feeling anxious about what their mount may react like and thus tense up causing the horse to be even more troubled. Horses also have very little vision above their eyes, so do not wave anything high and be aware if your bicycle has a flag. A startled horse is not only a risk to you as a cyclist it can also be very risky for the horse rider.

Make your presence known well ahead of time. Call out to the rider and make sure that the rider is expecting you and can settle the horse down. DO NOT use the bell, it can startle the horse. Talking as you approach helps settle the horse.

Pass very slowly. Make sure that the rider knows what side of the trail you will pass on and give the horse plenty of space. A horse has an enormous rear leg extension and will kick out as a protective measure if it feels threatened. Be aware that a horse will often spin around to face a perceived danger – make sure that you are well out of the danger zone.

If you are approaching a horse and rider consider stopping completely and talking to the rider. Use the horse's reaction to you to gauge what to do; always give way, and if there is any doubt, stop completely to let the horse and rider pass.

Canal Towpaths

British Waterway towpaths are not a public right of way for cyclists however the organisation gives out a free permit to cycle available to download from the internet - www.waterscape.com/things-to-do/cycling/permit. You will need to print it out and sign the permit. In signing the permit, you are agreeing to follow the rules for cycling on the towpaths.

- Give way to oncoming users at bridges, cyclists should slow down, ring with two tings and let other users through the bridge before continuing. Never pass a pedestrian or another cyclist underneath a bridge.
- Be extra careful at bends and entrances, be prepared to slow down, stop, or dismount if necessary.
- Consider other users and the local environment; the waterways and towpaths have many historic structures and important wildlife habitats for people to enjoy.
- Ring with two tings using a bell when approaching pedestrians, please be aware that some pedestrians may have visual or hearing impairments and might not hear.
- Pass people slowly. Give people space, slow down

Photo courtesy iStock Photo

when approaching pedestrians and only pass when it is safe to do so. Extra care should be taken when passing children, less able people and animals.
- Try to pass on the water side of the path. Pedestrians will tend to move to the back edge of the towpath to allow you to pass, be patient and courteous to pedestrians. Saying "thank you" to pedestrians who move to let you pass will make them more likely to move next time.
- Ride at a sensible speed, the towpath is never suitable for cycling fast as there are many other users, low bridges and narrow sections. If you are in a hurry, use an alternative route.

Taking heed of these simple rules will ensure a happy and positive cycling experience for yourself and all that you come in contact with. Certainly a result worth striving for.

High frequency services

Checking the TFL map at Kew

You, Your Bike and Public Transport in London

Public transport around London is generally bicycle friendly. This section lists what modes of transport bicycles are permitted on and when. Folding bicycles when fully folded are allowed on all public transport at any time and there is no extra cost for transporting your bike on any TFL or rail service where it is permitted.

Trains

Bicycles may be taken on London Overground and National Rail services outside rush hour periods (Rush hour periods are 07:00-10:00 and 16:30-19:00 on weekdays). Please bear in mind that there are often steps up and down from station platforms across the network. More stations are getting step free access but this is a slow process so be prepared for some lifting. Use the train doors where you see a bicycle symbol on the outside of the carriage. Most trains will only take two bikes in any one carriage so if you are travelling in a larger group you will have to split up.

Tube

Non-folded bicycles are allowed on certain sections of the underground system. Please refer to the attached map if you wish to make use of the underground or consult www.tfl.gov.uk.

Ferry Services

You can take any bicycle on any London boat service at any time.

Buses, Trams and DLR

Trams, buses and Docklands Light Railway trains only take folding bicycles - no container is required, although bicycles must be fully folded. No other bicycles are permitted on these services at any time.

Taxis

There is no hard and fast rule but most black cabs will NOT carry bicycles. Should your bike break and you need to get home you may have to use a minicab or recovery service. Alternatively try to get to a station and return by train.

TFL Cycle Hire Scheme

The public bicycle sharing scheme is designed for short journeys in and around central London. You can pick up a bicycle 24 hours a day, all year round. The 400 special docking stations are self-service and you can pick-up at one station and drop-off at another. You must be 14 or over and be able to use a bicycle without help.

Costs

To hire a bicycle you will need to pay:
- An access fee (gives you the right to use the scheme)
- A usage charge (based on the duration of the journey)

The first 30 minutes of each journey are free.

Access fee: 24-hour - £1; Seven-day access - £5; Annual access - £45 (members only)

If you'd like to cycle for longer than a couple of hours it might be cheaper for you to use a company that specialises in hiring bicycles.

Usage Charges

Up to 30 minutes is Free
Then…
- Up to 1 hour is £1
- Up to 1 hour and 30 minutes £4
- Up to 2 hours £6
- Up to 2 hours and 30 minutes £10
- Up to 3 hours £15
- Up to 6 hours £35
- Up to 24 hours (maximum usage fee) £50

Other charges...
- Late return charge is £150
- Damage charge is up to £300
- Non-return charge is £300

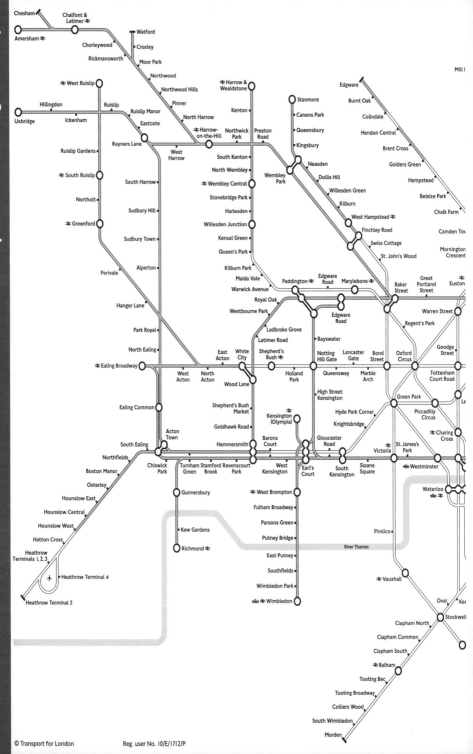

Bicycles on the Underground Map

© Transport for London   Reg. user No. 10/E/1712/P

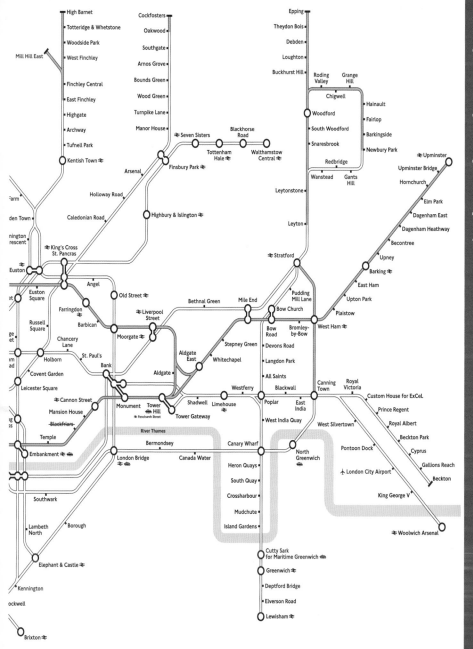

High Barnet
Totteridge & Whetstone
Woodside Park
West Finchley
Mill Hill East
Finchley Central
East Finchley
Highgate
Archway
Tufnell Park
Kentish Town

Cockfosters
Oakwood
Southgate
Arnos Grove
Bounds Green
Wood Green
Turnpike Lane
Manor House
Seven Sisters
Tottenham Hale
Finsbury Park
Arsenal

Blackhorse Road
Walthamstow Central

Epping
Theydon Bois
Debden
Loughton
Buckhurst Hill
Roding Valley
Grange Hill
Chigwell
Woodford
Hainault
South Woodford
Fairlop
Snaresbrook
Barkingside
Redbridge
Newbury Park
Wanstead
Gants Hill

Leytonstone
Leyton
Stratford

Upminster
Upminster Bridge
Hornchurch
Elm Park
Dagenham East
Dagenham Heathway
Becontree
Upney
Barking
East Ham
Upton Park
Plaistow
West Ham

Holloway Road
Caledonian Road
Highbury & Islington
King's Cross St. Pancras
Euston

Angel
Old Street
Euston Square
Farringdon
Russell Square
Barbican
Chancery Lane
Moorgate
Holborn
St. Paul's
Covent Garden
Bank
Leicester Square
Cannon Street
Mansion House
Monument
Tower Hill
Blackfriars
Tower Gateway
Temple
Embankment
London Bridge

farm
den Town
nington crescent
ge t
m ad
g ss

Bethnal Green
Mile End
Pudding Mill Lane
Bow Church
Bow Road
Bromley-by-Bow
Stepney Green
Devons Road
Aldgate East
Whitechapel
Langdon Park
Aldgate
All Saints
Westferry
Blackwall
Shadwell
Limehouse
Poplar
East India
West India Quay
Liverpool Street
Canning Town
Royal Victoria
Custom House for ExCeL
Prince Regent
Royal Albert
West Silvertown
Beckton Park
Cyprus
Pontoon Dock
Gallions Reach
Beckton
London City Airport
King George V

Bermondsey
River Thames
Canada Water
Canary Wharf
Heron Quays
South Quay
Crossharbour
Mudchute
Island Gardens
North Greenwich
Woolwich Arsenal

Southwark
Lambeth North
Borough
Elephant & Castle
Kennington
ockwell
Brixton

Cutty Sark for Maritime Greenwich
Greenwich
Deptford Bridge
Elverson Road
Lewisham

Fenchurch Street

Bicycles on the Underground

Bicycles may be taken free of charge on these sections, but not between 0730 and 0930 or 1600 and 1900 on Mondays to Fridays (except public holidays)

Sections where bicycles are not permitted

Correct at time of going to print

Oyster Rail Services Map

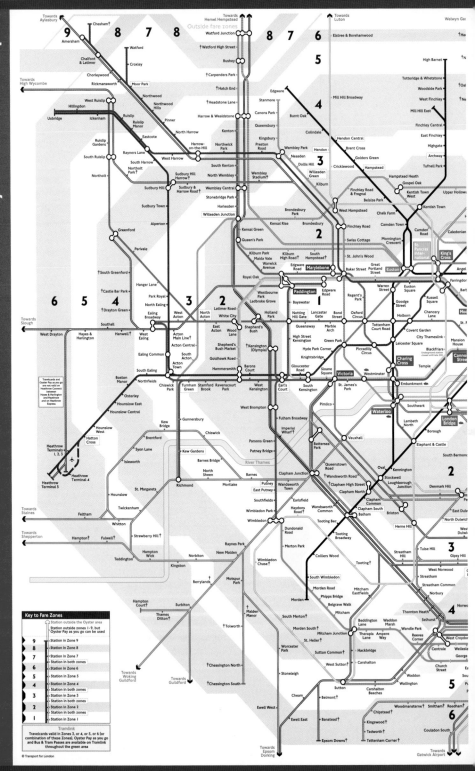

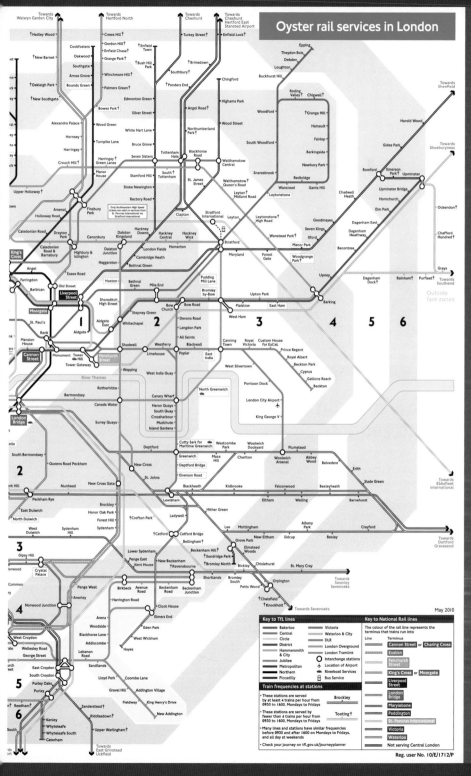

Oyster rail services in London

Oyster Rail Services Map

May 2010

Reg. user No. 10/E/1712/P

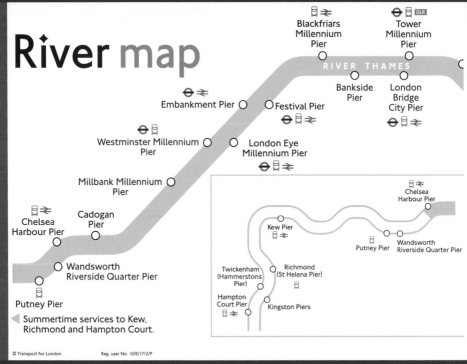

River map

Blackfriars Millennium Pier

Tower Millennium Pier

RIVER THAMES

Bankside Pier

London Bridge City Pier

Embankment Pier

Festival Pier

Westminster Millennium Pier

London Eye Millennium Pier

Millbank Millennium Pier

Chelsea Harbour Pier

Chelsea Harbour Pier

Cadogan Pier

Kew Pier

Wandsworth Riverside Quarter Pier

Putney Pier

Wandsworth Riverside Quarter Pier

Twickenham (Hammerstons Pier)

Richmond (St Helena Pier)

Putney Pier

Hampton Court Pier

Kingston Piers

Summertime services to Kew, Richmond and Hampton Court.

© Transport for London   Reg. user No. I0/E/I7I2/P

Getting You and Your Bike to London

By Train

Domestic Rail Services

There are many different rail companies operating services to and from the capital. As a general rule most operators will take bikes free of charge outside rush hour periods (Rush hour periods are 07:00-10:00 and 16:30-19:00 on weekdays). Some rail companies such as Virgin Trains ask that you make a free advance reservation while others such as Anglia Railways charge £3 per bike. Every operator has its own rules which often change so it is best to check with the specific train company at the time of booking.

Eurostar International Services

If you'd like to take your bike on Eurostar, you can fold it up or dismantle it and place it in a bike bag with the saddle, handlebars and wheels removed and carry it on board yourself as part of your luggage allowance, provided the overall size is no bigger than a normal suitcase. Or, subject to availability, you can make an advance reservation for a bike place on the train. To make a reservation call 08705 850 850. Charges are £20 one way and you'll need to quote your Eurostar reference or show your ticket.

By Coach

Some coach companies such as the Oxford Tube accept bicycles at no extra charge subject to space availability, others including National Express do not. Eurolines International services do sometimes carry non-folding bicycles depending on the route but it is imperative to check with the operator at the time of booking your ticket and get written authorization as terms and conditions change.

Flying

Conditions of carriage with all operators dictate that bicycles must be prepared for travel: bicycle pedals must be removed (or fixed inwards), handlebars must be fixed

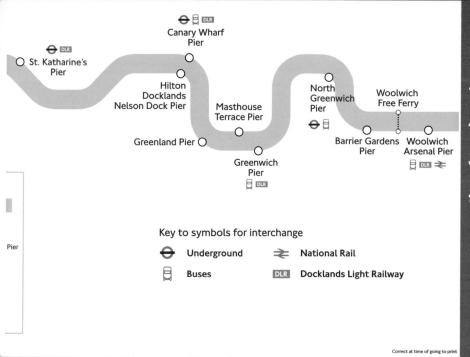

Canary Wharf Pier

St. Katharine's Pier

Hilton Docklands Nelson Dock Pier

Masthouse Terrace Pier

North Greenwich Pier

Woolwich Free Ferry

Greenland Pier

Greenwich Pier

Barrier Gardens Pier

Woolwich Arsenal Pier

Pier

Key to symbols for interchange

Underground	National Rail
Buses	DLR Docklands Light Railway

Correct at time of going to print

---

sideways, the bicycle must be contained in a protective case or bag. You may also wish to deflate the tyres to reduce risk of damage. Wheels may also need to be removed from the frame.

Low Cost Airlines

Easyjet will carry bagged bicycles up to 32kg under sporting goods; the fees each way are £18.50 when pre-booked or £26 if paying at the airport. Anything heavier is charged at £10 per kilo. Ryanair will also carry a bicycle in a protective bag as sports equipment. The weight should not exceed 20kg and the costs each-way are £40 if booked online or £50 if booked at the airport. Ryanair charge £20 excess baggage per kilo - ouch! Other low-cost airlines' prices vary. Please always check with your operator at the time of booking.

Scheduled Airlines

BA and Qantas allow you to take sporting equipment including bicycles within your normal checked baggage allowance. The equipment must be packed to meet the size and weight restrictions (23kg and 190cm x 75cm x 65cm). Swiss will carry a 30kg 162 x 92 x 24 cm item for 70 euro within Europe and 150 euro long haul. United allow for a 23kg bicycle and charge 200USD one-way from the states. Please always check with your operator at the time of booking.

Cross Channel Ferries and Eurotunnel

Eurotunnel charge £16 one-way (or day return) per passenger with a bicycle.

Charges and conditions for taking a bicycle on a Cross Channel Ferry vary by company and route. Bicycles are normally allowed but when you book your ferry ticket you must state that you have a bicycle because even when there is no charge the cycles need a boarding card. The extra per bike normally ranges from £0-20 depending on the route.

Central London

Boarded by Regents Canal in the north and the Thames to the south the elusive 'centre' can best be described as the part of London that the transit system classes as Fare Zone 1. However this zone is in fact two very distinct areas. In the east is the financial district known as The City where gleaming skyscrapers stand above the tight weaving pattern of medieval streets developed organically over of the old walled roman city of Londinium. While in the west around the palaces of Westminster are the grand parks, squares and avenues formally laid out by planners in the 18th century.

Broadly speaking the West-end is a district associated with entertainment, shopping and museums; home to the houses of Parliament, Buckingham Palace and Whitehall. The east-end including The City is traditionally where most of the work is done but surprisingly few people actually live in the financial district, given the density of high-rise buildings in the area, and in the evenings and at weekends the streets have an eerie quietness, a marked contrast with the 24 hour chaotic buzz of the West-end.

The eight rides in this section take in all the major sights using car-free paths and quiet roads whenever possible. Due to the dense urban nature of this region it is impossible to avoid traffic altogether but better cycling provision and the advent of the public cycle hire scheme has meant increasingly safer cycling. Rides 5, 6 and 8 are real sightseeing tours. Ride 1 is a relaxed affair through the mighty parks and Ride 3 is practically car-free following the Regents Canal towpath. Ride 2 links east to west, Ride 4 takes advantage of the tranquil streets at the weekend around The City and Ride 7 follows an ornamental canal from Tower Bridge to the Canary Wharf. All the rides are technically easy, however please be aware that there may be busy roads to cross and the odd area of congested traffic.

A commuter admires The City skyline as he cycles over Waterloo Bridge

Riding a folding bike on one of the many cyclepaths through Hyde Park

At a Glance

Distance 16.7km   **Total Climbing** 108m

Terrain

Smooth surfaced roads and paths half on-road half dedicated cycleway.

Traffic

Certain stretches of road section linking the parks can be busy. Bear this in mind if going with children or shorten the ride to one park if unsure.

How to Get There

St James Park, other nearby stations Victoria, Charing Cross, Waterloo, Paddington and Marylebone are all close to the route. Pay and display street parking in Kensington and Notting Hill and there is a large underground car park off Park Lane on the eastern edge of Hyde Park.

Food and Drink

St James Park Café, Serpentine Bar & Kitchen Numerous eateries along Marylebone high street.

Side Trip

Continue around St James Park down Horse Guard and behind Whitehall and Parliament Square if you want to extend the ride and get a few more sights in.

Links to (other rides) 2, 6, 8, 42.

Bike Hire

Numerous TFL cycle hire points although you will need to switch bikes after 30 minutes to avoid charges

Where to Ride Rating

About...

Pedal through the lungs of the capital and appreciate the changing seasons from blankets of yellow and white daffodils that line The Mall in March to the amber horse chestnut trees dropping their leaves onto wide avenues in October. This gentle ride takes in Hyde Park, Regents Park and St James Park as well as Bond Street, Green Park, Buckingham Palace and London Zoo before looping back through the streets of Mayfair.

Peering through the railings towards the Grade II listed Giraffe house at London Zoo

Although cycling is generally very restricted in the central London parks, the paths where it is permitted are smooth and clearly signed. They often have avenues of trees providing shade from the sun and shelter from drizzle. This ride begins in front of Buckingham Palace the London residence of the Queen, (Aug-Sep, daily 9.45am-3.45pm; £16.50). The route heads north around the gold-topped Queen Victoria Memorial before passing through the grand, iron gates of Green Park. The park has come a long way since its days as a 16th Century plague pit or since the duels and highwayman of the 18th Century, these days it's the greenery that provides the spectacle. The cycleway runs parallel to Constitutional Hill rising to the Wellington monument and the Australian War Memorial before horse traffic lights, yes that's right, whisk you over the giant roundabout into Hyde Park. At 625 acres it is one of the largest parks in central London and is synonymous with the city as a place for concerts, demonstrations or just eating lunch. After crossing the road just inside the park the route heads west down Rotten Row. Watch out for goggle-eyed tourist who stray onto the cycle path. The trail passes the Holocaust Memorial Garden and further along the Princess of Wales Memorial Fountain at the end is the Serpentine Gallery (daily 10.00am-6.00pm; free) hosting contemporary art exhibitions. Over the Serpentine Bridge route turns back along the lake's north bank past moored pedalos and the Serpentine Bar & Kitchen before swinging northwards along a beautiful avenue of mature sycamore trees.

The ride exits the park at Stanhope Place Gate, from here it is a maze of quiet, terraces and squares past Marylebone Station and down narrow, atmospheric Kent Passage into royal Regents Park. The ride follows the outer circle of the park passing the gold dome of London Central Mosque and Winfield House, official home of the American Ambassador to the UK, before reaching London Zoo (daily 10.00am-16.00; £18.50), where you can often glimpse animals through the railings. From here the ride heads south to York Gate and out to smart Marylebone High Street leading to Bond Street, London's premier shopping street for designer fashion boutiques and fine art. At the end of Bond Street is the Royal Academy of Arts (daily 10.00am-6.00pm; £9-£12). There is then a short section along the often busy and congested Piccadilly before passing St James Square, St James Palace and St James Park home to Russian pigeon eating pelicans and the iconic white and green deckchairs facing views of Big Ben and the wheel. Here The Mall leads back to the front gates of Buckingham Palace.

Ride 1 - The Big Three Parks Loop

Ride Log

0.0 Facing away from Buckingham Palace turn left over the road into Green Park. Turn left again up Constitution Hill.

0.8 Cross under the Wellington Monument using dedicated cycle crossing. Enter Hyde Park and cross road before turning immediately left down Rotten Row.

2.3 Turn right along West Carriage Dr, over Serpentine Bridge. Then turn right back along the north bank of the Serpentine.

4.2 Back at Queen Elizabeth Gate turn left, northwards up Broad Walk.

5.5 Exit the park at Stanhope Place Gate beyond Marble Arch and cross the road using the bike crossing. Go up Stanhope Pl and left onto Stanhope Square. At the top of the square turn left along Connaught St and then immediately right up Porchester Pl. Then first right along Kendal St.

6.0 Go straight over the Edgware Rd into George St. Once in Brynstone Square turn left up the square and continue to St Mary's church.

6.5 Dismount and walk around to the right of the church. Get back on and go up Enford St. Cross the busy Marylebone Rd and go up Harwood Ave until you hit junction with Rosemore Rd.

7.2 Turn right along Rosemore Rd over the rail line until very busy Park Rd. Dismount and walk left up Park Rd on the pavement to a set of pedestrian lights. Cross here and walk down Kent Passage exiting onto outer circle of Regents Park.

7.8 Turn left on the outer circle and continue past zoo and southwards. You pass a 60s building on your left and there in a traffic island with a lantern in the middle, turn right and continue along the outer circle.

11.3 When you get to the lights turn left down through York Gate. Left along Marylebone Rd and first right down Marylebone High St.

11.8 Take second left down Beaumont St, continue down Westmoreland St then Welbeck St on left onto Henrietta Pl and immediately right on Vere St over Oxford St and into New Bond St.

12.6 Continue all the way down New Bond St over the cycleway at the end and into Old Bond St ending at Piccadilly.

13.6 Turn left onto Piccadilly and the right down Duke St. Beware of traffic here.

13.8 Turn left into Kings St and around the top of St James Square continue down other side of the square before exiting southwards on the corner with a scooter parking bay. The narrow one-way road takes you onto Pall Mall. Turn right here and then first left down Marlborough Rd.

14.5 At the end of Marlborough Rd turn left along the Mall. Take first right down Whitehall.

15.7 At the end of Whitehall turn right along the bottom edge of the park. At the lights turn right back to Buckingham Palace.

16.7 End of ride.

The Big Three Parks Loop

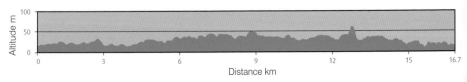

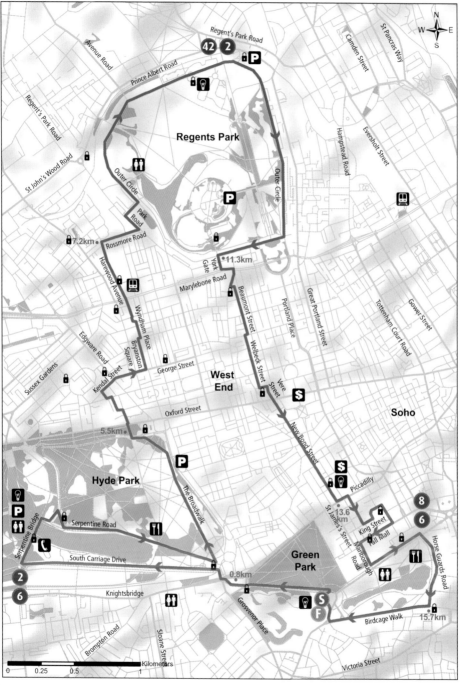

Commuters rushing beneath Brunel's Paddington Station train shed

At a Glance

Distance 16.5km   **Total Climbing** 120m

Terrain

Sealed roads, cycle ways and unsealed canal towpath (bell needed).

Traffic

Generally light, crossing some busy roads.

How to Get There

London Fields Train Station or High Street Kensington tube. Metered street parking around High Street Kensington, Hackney and Islington.

Food and Drink

Lock & Cycle Café near London Fields and Broadway Market for grazing, eateries around Camden Market, The Warrington, Gordon Ramsey's Pub just off Sutherland Avenue or tea at the Royal Garden Hotel Kensington.

Side Trip

Close to Maida Vale is The Warrington, Gordon Ramsey's pub, at 93 Warrington Crescent. They serve hearty seasonal British dishes in a relaxed, elegant restaurant above a Victorian pub.

Links to (other rides) 1, 35, 42, 45.

Bike Hire

Numerous TFL hire points marked. Remember to change every 30 minutes to avoid hire charge.

Where to Ride Rating

About...

The quiet streets above of the Regents Canal chart the course of London's Victorian aspiration, from the old factories and workhouses of Hackney in the east, past the merchant's terraces in Islington and Camden, to the palatial homes of Kensington in the west. Though the smoke of industry has now disappeared the gradually changing architecture, shops and businesses betray the fortunes of those living along the route. You will ride across parks, squares and along canals. Find formal gardens and fight through the crowds of bustling markets, taking in many of the sights and sounds that help understand London's diversity and soul.

Autumn evenings cast long bike shadows over fallen leaves

London Fields, the start of the route, is a small area of common grassland, traditionally used by farmers to graze sheep before market, the space is now home to one of the capital's few 50m lidos while just south of the green is Broadway food market where barrow boys still sell everything from bacon to beans. From here the ride passes along the flat, unassuming Victorian terraces of Dalston and De Beauvoir Square, with its Dutch gables and mullioned windows, before turning northwards to Canonbury where large 18th century houses with even larger gardens are perched on a hill built high above the pollution. Next door is the open space of Highbury Fields surrounded by affluent Georgian and Victorian town houses while across the grass is Freightliners, a small working farm giving inner city children the opportunity to interact with the environment.

Beyond this the ride passes Caledonian Park before reaching the cycle ways through Camden. Here the route joins the Regents Canal towpath passing through the throbbing ethnic stalls of Camden Market. The grungy arts and music scene have made the area a Mecca for spiky haired punks and paled skinned, trench coat wearing Goths. The sizzling food sellers at Camden

Lock are testament to the ever-growing number of tourists flocking to see the bizarre spectacle of people, cloths and fashion synonymous with London. As the towpath meanders beneath the pastel coloured houses of Primrose Hill the hubbub dyes down and the Goths and Punks give way to celebrities and fashonistas with yappy little dogs. The canal cuts through Regents Park and passes the giant aviary at London Zoo before leaving the houseboats and climbing away from the canal towards the mansion houses of St Johns Wood and Maida Vale. This area is known as Little Venice as the canal basin contains so many house boats. The towpath leads to Isambard Brunel's grand Paddington Station. Here the canal ends but the route continues through typical London west end squares and terraces before emerging at Lancaster Gate, Hyde Park riding through the park along West Carriage Drive and over the Serpentine water and along the broad walk to the formal gardens of Kensington Palace.

Ride 2 - Rags to Riches Route

Ride Log

0.0 Turn right out of London Fields Station and right again onto Marlo Terrace. At the end of the road is an entrance to the park. Follow the green cycleway left (south) until the cycle crossroads (100m) and take a right. Continue along cycleway through and out of park and onto Middleton Rd.

1.0 Continue straight over busy Kingsland Rd down Petter Way and through De Beauvoir Square continuing along Northchurch Rd.

2.5 At the end of the road go straight across up Asby Grove then left along Arron Walk and right up Willow Bridge Rd. At the top of the hill is a crossroads, go left along Canonbury Pl. Just after zebra crossing turn right up Compton Rd.

3.5 At the end of the road turn left onto busy St Pauls Rd. After 100m come off road onto pavement and dismount. Cross the road using pedestrian crossing opposite the Little Chicken Theatre. Saddle up and go down narrow Corsica St, then first left onto Calabria Rd.

3.8 At the end is Highbury Fields. Cross the Fields on the cyclepath and on exiting go straight down the road in front of you, Field Way. Cross over the main road into Madras Pl.

4.7 At the end of the road turn right along Westbourne St and then at the end left along Mackenzie Rd.

5.8 At the end turn left down busy York Way then first right along Agar Grove.

6.6 At the end of Agar Grove follow the one way system round to the left on St Pancras Way, keeping to the right hand lane so you can enter separated cycleway, then take first right down Baynes St.

6.8 On your left, just before the end of Baynes St there is a staircase down to the canal. Carry bike down stairs and turn right along towpath. Continue along towpath through Camden Market (you will have to dismount in places). The canal will lead into Regents Park.

9.2 Two hundred metres after an iron bridge there is an exit up the bank, take this onto Charlbert St. At the end turn left onto St Johns Wood Terrace. This road changes names several times but continue along it over all the main roads.

11.6 Then second left after roundabout down Warwick Ave, turn right just before the canal bridge into Bloomfield Terrace then first left over bridge.

12.4 As soon as you reach other side of the bridge there is a canal towpath on the left. Take this towpath down into Paddington Basin. Exit by Paddington Station onto London St. Note there is a lot of development work going on in this area so route may change.

13.2 Once at the back of Paddington Station continue down London St and into Sussex Pl.

13.8 Turn right down Stanhope Terrace and right down Brook St and enter Hyde Park via Lancaster Gate.

14.7 Take the cycleway alongside West Carriage Dr. Just over the Serpentine Bridge and past the gallery there is a cycleway leading right into the park. Take this path until the end then turn left down the Broad Walk.

16.5 At the end of the park you finish in Kensington. Kensington High St and tube station are to your right.

Rags to Riches Route

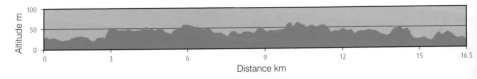

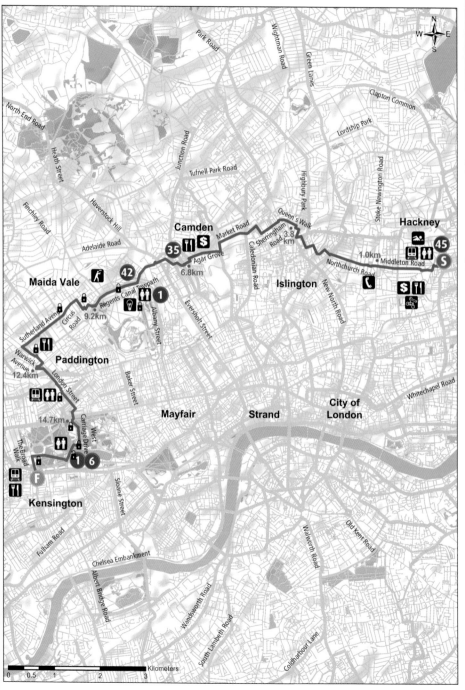

Park Road

Wightman Road

Green Lanes

Clapton Common

North End Road

Lordship Park

Finchley Road

Haverstock Hill

Junction Road

Tufnell Park Road

Stoke Newington Road

Heath Street

Adelaide Road

Camden

Market Road

Queen's Walk

Sherringham Road

3.8 km

Hackney

35

1.0km

45

Middleton Road

S

Maida Vale

42

Agar Grove

6.8km

Caledonian Road

Northchurch Road

Islington

New North Road

Regents Canal Towpath

Circus Road

9.2km

1

Albany Street

Eversholt Street

Highbury Park

Sutherland Avenue

Warwick Avenue

12.4km

London Street

Paddington

Baker Street

Mayfair

Strand

City of London

Whitechapel Road

14.7km

West Carriage Drive

1 6

The Broad Walk

F

Kensington

Sloane Street

Fulham Road

Chelsea Embankment

Walworth Road

Old Kent Road

Albert Bridge Road

Wandsworth Road

South Lambeth Road

Coldharbour Lane

Kilometers

0   0.5   1   2   3

Old dials in the Wapping Project

At a Glance

Distance 9.1km   **Total Climbing** 50m

Terrain

Flat but narrow canal towpath. Very busy with pedestrians especially at weekends, bell essential.

Traffic

Short sections of the route are on quiet back roads with very light traffic.

How to Get There

Wapping Overground Station, Highbury Islington Overground.

Food and Drink

The Wapping Project, The Duke of Cambridge Pub.

Side Trip

Cycle up the Hertford Union Canal and back through Victoria Park to check out the progress on London's Olympic Park

Links to (other rides) 7, 29, 44, 45, 47.

Bike Hire

Kelly's 4 Real Bikes on 303 Commercial Road; Station Cycles at Arch 1-4, Upper Walthamstow; Lock 7 Cycle Café at 129 Pritchard's Road all provide service near the route. There are no shop rental options but TFL cycle hire points are located near Tower Gateway and Angel Stations.

Where to Ride Rating

About...

A practically car free ride from Wapping to Islington. This gentle journey along the popular Regents Canal towpath from its start at the Limehouse Basin to the Islington Tunnel is flat and easy but it can become very congested with pedestrians particularly at the weekend. Sights come thick and fast along the route including houseboats, parks and markets.

This converted Hydraulic Power Station now houses the Wapping Project

Starting at the wacky Wapping Projects gallery space and restaurant the route takes in spectacular views of Canary Warf from the Thames path before cutting inland at the Limehouse Basin, once a port where seagoing ships would transfer their goods to barges to be carried along the regents canal and linking waterways. Since the canals commercial decline the area has been redeveloped into smart residential flats overlooking the water. From here the Regents Canal travels north past several locks. On the east side of the towpath are the recently redeveloped undulating grass mounds and bright goldfish mosaic benches of Mile End Park. On the west bank you'll see some interesting and some mediocre modern architecture as well as more historic buildings including a lock keeper's house.

At Victoria Park the towpath gets much busier particularly at the weekends. Cycling slowly and sensibly here, a bell is essential if you are to avoid ending up in the canal. The route passes pretty houseboats adorned with old bicycles and geraniums and continues along the canal through the park then into more industrial Dalston. Here graffiti covered abandoned warehouses and gasholders tower menacingly over the canal. The area is slowly being gentrified with modern apartment developments but it still has an artistic and run-down feel about it. Past the new east London line rail bridge you can leave the canal for a foody detour at Broadway Market where barrow boys sell everything from apples to Za'atar, a middle eastern spice blend.

The route itself continues to Wenlock Basin and Islington. Here more modern flats and a lovingly restored mill stand on the other side of the lock. The towpath climbs steeply in areas through the locks and it may be necessary to dismount if the path is busy. After another couple of hundred metres there is a sign warning cyclist to exit towpath, this means it's time to leave the canal before it heads underground into the Islington Tunnel. The cycle route however continues down Islington's famous Georgian terraces ending at the Duke of Cambridge organic pub.

Ride Log

0.0 Turn left out of the front gates of the Wapping Project along the cobbled road and over red iron bridge. Once over the bridge a blue sign, 'Thames path' points right down a narrow passageway. Follow the path through King Edward Memorial Park.

0.3 Continue in front of the flats. After 250m the path will then bend steeply to the left around a blind bend (use your bell) before coming out onto Narrow St. You want to continue down Narrow St but you need to go around the one-way so turn left then right onto Horseferry Rd. The road bends right back onto Narrow St. Turn left along Narrow St, over the canal.

1.3 Two hundred metres after the canal there is a small park opposite the Grapes Pub. Go into the park and follow the path around the bandstand and over the bridge. Continue straight then follow the path around keeping the DLR viaduct above you on the right. You go behind the flats until you reach another bridge. Do not go over this bridge but take the sloping path down to the canal towpath.

1.8 Turn right along the towpath and cycle for 10km through changing scenery. Remember to use your bell when coming up behind people or before going under bridges and always give way to walkers and runners. It is etiquette to keep left but not everyone knows this.

A cyclist passing a houseboat on the Regents Canal towpath

8.0 The canal opens up into city Road Basin. There are modern apartments on the other side of the water and you may have to dismount if the path is busy to get up City Road Lock.

8.3 Just beyond the lock there is a sign warning cyclist to exit the towpath. Exit here and turn right along Danbury St for 200m until you reach the Duke of Cambridge Pub on your right.

9.1 End of ride. Reward yourself with something cold or hot, depending on the weather!

Regents Canal East Trail

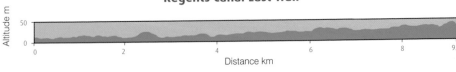

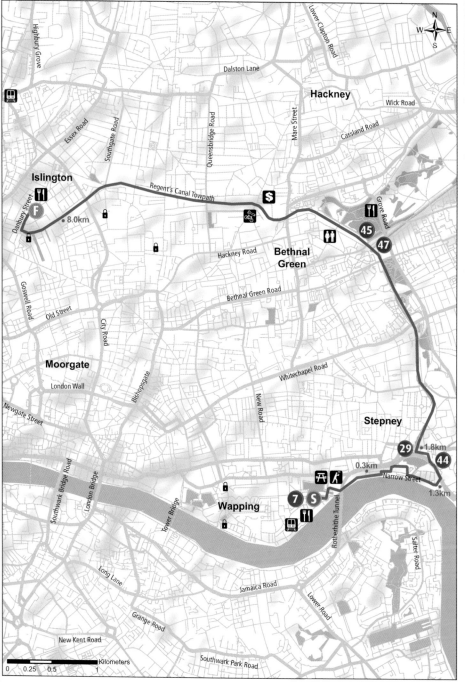

Hackney

Islington

Bethnal Green

Moorgate

Stepney

Wapping

8.0km

1.8km

0.3km

1.3km

The Albion Cafe, shop and bakery on Boundary Street

At a Glance

Distance 9.0km   **Total Climbing** 60m

Terrain

Surfaced roads.

Traffic

Quiet roads at the weekend but busy mid-week.

How to Get There

Liverpool Street Station or Shoreditch Overground.

Food and Drink

Cafés and restaurants on Columbia Road and Brick Lane.

Side Trip

From Brick Lane head south to the Tower of London. The roads are not very cycle friendly but the castle prison, built nearly a thousand years ago, is home to the beefeaters and crown jewels as well as a few ghosts.

Links to (other rides) 5, 6.

Bike Hire

TFL cycle hire points.

Where to Ride Rating

About...

At the weekend the financial district becomes a ghost town of deserted streets. The gleaming skyscrapers tower above closed restaurants, shut up shops and empty roads. However on the city's medieval fringes markets come to life. Columbia Road becomes an orgy of colours as the flower market takes over the street while in Brick Lane and Spitalfields vendors display their colourful wares over market carts or on the pavement in front of bustling crowds. The contrast is a fantastic spectacle.

Comic strip murals are a familiar sight in gritty Shoreditch

Be warned that although the majority of the buildings in the heart of The City are modern glass and concrete architectural statements, the street layout has not changed much since medieval times which means a pattern of narrow weaving one ways and cul-de-sacs can make the route difficult to follow in reverse. The ride begins at Liverpool Street Station, busy in the week with smart commuters, its bold business facade at odds with the jean-wearing weekenders. Just north of the station is Curtain Road a strip of fashionable bars, clothing and design furniture shops. Beyond this is pretty Hoxton Square with its art galleries, cafes and architect studios. Here the route goes east to Columbia Road and the Flower Market (Sundays only) before heading southwards towards Brick Lane passing a gallery of brightly coloured, skilfully stencilled graffitied warehouses along the way.

Brick Lane is busy and crowded but crossing back into The City, past the iconic Foster Gherkin and behind the instantly recognisable industrial steel pipes of the Richard Rodgers Lloyds building, is like entering a different world as you wonder where everyone has gone. Along the way watch out for sites such as Victorian Leadenhall Market and The Monument, erected to commemorate the great fire of 1666. Its high viewing platform will allow you to get your bearings which can be easily lost between the gleaming towers. From here it's up to the Bank of England and the deserted heart of The City before heading west to Sir Christopher Wrens masterpiece, the domed St Paul's Cathedral. At the front steps the ride turns northwards towards the medieval city wall and the Museum of London before heading back to Liverpool Street past Moorgate and Finsbury Circus.

Stencil graffiti and fixed wheel bikes are definitely in

Ride Log

0.0 Turn left out of the station and left again onto Bishopsgate. Take the first left down Primrose St and then right at the end.

0.7 Continue to the corner. In front of you, car traffic is prevented from crossing by pavement and bollards, however you can continue over this into Curtain Rd. At the end of Curtain Rd turn right then left into Hoxton Square. Follow the one-way around the western edge of the square and exit on Mundy St. Cross over Hoxton St into Drysdale St. At the end turn left under the bridge and then right onto Waterson St. At the end, cross over Hackney Rd into Columbia Rd.

2.2 From Columbia Rd turn right down Virginia Rd and left into Swanfield St. Follow cycle route signs down Palissy St into Arnold Circus and around down Camlet St. At the end cross the road into the tunnel under Shoreditch Station. When you pop-out the other side keep going straight on and then turn left down Calvin St. At the end turn right in Grey Eagle St. The road bends to the right and here you need to go left, opposite cycle signs, down narrow Corbet Pl.

3.5 Come out onto Hanbury St, turn left then right down Wilkes St. At the end turn left. Once you get to Brick Ln dismount and turn right. Walk bike down to Fashion St (first right). Cycle to the end of Fashion St and walk bike across pedestrian lights to your right and continue down Whites Row. At the end turn left down Bell Ln. When you get to a chain across the road turn right down New Goulston St.

4.4 Cross over Middlesex St into Gravel Ln.

4.6 At the end of Gravel Ln turn right then left down Stoney Ln. At the end, go straight across by the blue bike sign. Keep following this route across Dukes Pl and into Creechurch Ln.

4.9 Turn right at the end of the lane onto Leadenhall St. Turn left off Leadenhall St just before the Lloyds building onto Lime St. Turn right down Leadenhall Pl and through Leadenhall Market.

5.4 As you come out of the market turn left towards the Monument. At the lights stay right turning back up away from the river onto King William St. At Bank Station take a left down Victoria St. After Mansion House tube get in right-hand lane and turn right up Friday St and then left onto Cannon St.

6.5 At the front of St Paul's dismount and use pedestrian crossing to get onto the Piazza at the front of the Cathedral. Walk through Paternoster Square. This brings you out onto Edward St. Follow the road up and around the Museum of London onto London Wall.

7.7 Turn left up Wood St past the Barbican and right down Fore St. Just past Moorgate Station turn right down Moorgate Pl. Dismount and cross the road and walk bike into Finsbury Circus. Get back on and go around northern edge and exit onto Liverpool St, follow this until you get to station.

9.0 Ride completed.

Sunday in the City Loop

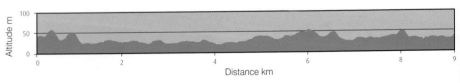

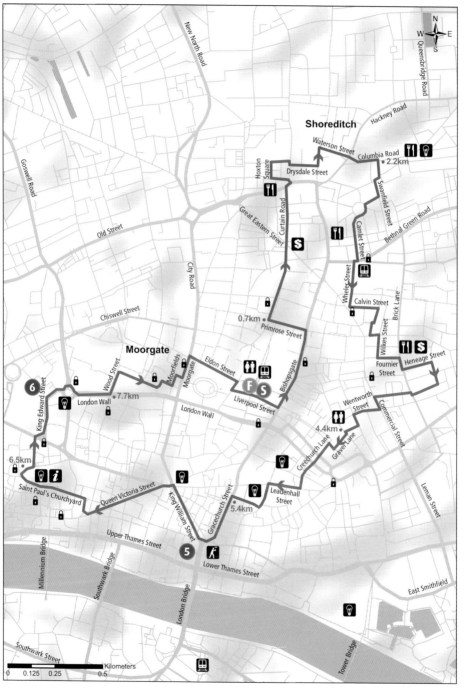

Shoreditch

Moorgate

New North Road

Queensbridge Road

Hackney Road

Waterson Street

Columbia Road

2.2km

Drysdale Street

Hoxton Square

Swanfield Street

Bethnal Green Road

Great Eastern Street

Curtain Road

Camlet Street

Goswell Road

Old Street

City Road

Chiswell Street

Wheler Street

Calvin Street

Brick Lane

Wilkes Street

0.7km

Primrose Street

Fournier Street

Heneage Street

Wood Street

Eldon Street

Moorfields

Moorgate

Bishopsgate

7.7km

London Wall

Liverpool Street

London Wall

Wentworth Street

Commercial Street

4.4km

King Edward Street

6.5km

Saint Paul's Churchyard

Queen Victoria Street

Gracechurch Street

King William Street

Creechurch Lane

Gravel Lane

Leadenhall Street

5.4km

Leman Street

Upper Thames Street

Lower Thames Street

London Bridge

East Smithfield

Millennium Bridge

Southwark Bridge

Tower Bridge

Southwark Street

Kilometers

0   0.125   0.25   0.5

6

5

Waterloo Bridge has fantastic views across the Thames towards The City

At a Glance

Distance 7.9km   **Total Climbing** 46m

Terrain
Surfaced road and surfaced cyclepath, a very short section of cobbles at Clink Street.

Traffic
Mostly quiet back streets but the road along The Embankment can be very busy.

How to Get There
Waterloo Station, Blackfriars, Cannon Street or London Bridge.

Food and Drink
Chain restaurants along the Southbank, Borough Market stalls and Somerset House Café.

Side Trip
On the north side of the Millennium Bridge, leave the river and follow the pedestrian route up to Sir Christopher Wren's masterpiece, the domed St Paul's Cathedral. However you are not allowed to cycle this stretch so leave bike locked-up or wheel them with you.

Links to (other rides) 4, 6, 8, 27, 35.

Bike Hire
TFL cycle hire points

Where to Ride Rating

About...

The mighty Thames: London's most famous and influential geographical feature responsible for the city's very existence. Explore the sights and sounds of 21st century London weaving along the banks of its very creator as it carves a path majestically through one of the busiest and most cosmopolitan metropolises in the world.

A sparklingly clean black cab reflecting the London Eye

Starting by the iconic Westminster Bridge the route takes you behind the Sea Life London Aquarium (Mon-Thur 10am-6pm, Fri-Sun 10am-7pm; adult £16, child £11.75) the largest in Europe, before passing the first great landmark, the London Eye (daily May-Sep 10am-9pm, Oct-Apr 10am-8pm; adult £17.50, child £8.75). From here the route runs behind the bustling South Bank, home to Festival Hall, the Hayward Gallery and the National Film Theatre built for the 1951 Festival of Britain and now an arts hub. The route continues onto the OXO tower, a riverside landmark since the 1930s and now home to some of the UK's most innovative and internationally renowned contemporary designers. On the top floor is the Harvey Nichols Bar and Brasserie with views across to The City.

Further along the route passes Blackfriars Station and the Tate Modern (daily, 10am–6pm; free), Britain's national museum of international modern art. Here the sleek Millennium Bridge tapers off to St Paul's Cathedral. However the ride continues on to the bustling food stalls of Borough Market in the shadow of Southwark Cathedral before crossing at London Bridge to the North Bank and the shimmering glass skyscrapers of The City, London's financial district.

The route follows the Thames Path along the North Bank to the north side of Blackfriars; the station marks the boundary of The City and Westminster. Once in Westminster the path continues along the busy Embankment Road in front of Somerset House a spectacular neo-classical building surrounding a central courtyard filled with dancing fountains in summer and an ice rink in winter. The route continues along The Embankment past Cleopatra's Needle, an original 3,500 year-old Egyptian obelisk and onto Victoria Embankment Gardens that back onto the grand Savoy Hotel. Then under the white, steel struts of Hungerford Bridge and behind Whitehall before Big Ben looms up in front of you, then it's over Westminster Bridge and back to the start of the ride.

Ride Log

0.0 Starting on the south side of Westminster Bridge cycle away from the bridge and take the first left down Belvedere Rd, past the no entry signs (cyclist allowed) towards Jubilee Gardens.

1.3 Continue to follow signs for Cycle Route 4 down Upper Ground. When the road reaches busy Blackfriars Rd follow the odd cycleway down the centre of Blackfriars Rd turning left at the lights and then first left after passing under the railway bridge.

1.9 At the end bear right around the back of the Tate Modern down Holland St.

2.6 Continue across busy Southwark Bridge Rd and at Vinopolis turn left and right down cobbled Clink St. Follow closely signs for Cycle Route 4 taking you right then sharp left and left again the route then goes under London Bridge.

3.3 When the road joins Tooley St turn right and at the end right onto London Bridge. Cross the bridge and take first left down Arthur St at the bottom go straight over Thames St dual carriage way and take the path down to the pedestrian North Bank.

4.0 Go right along the Thames Path with the river on your left.

4.7 After 700m the path leaves the river for a short section, continue to follow the signs for Thames Path back to the river. Continue under Blackfriars Bridge and up the ramp onto the Embankment. Unfortunately here you have to join the busy Embankment Rd.

5.6 Go along the Embankment for 2km until you get to Big Ben and Westminster Bridge.

7.6 Cross over Westminster Bridge back to the start.

7.9 Ride finishes.

The beautiful Christmas ice rink at Somerset House

The Thames City Loop

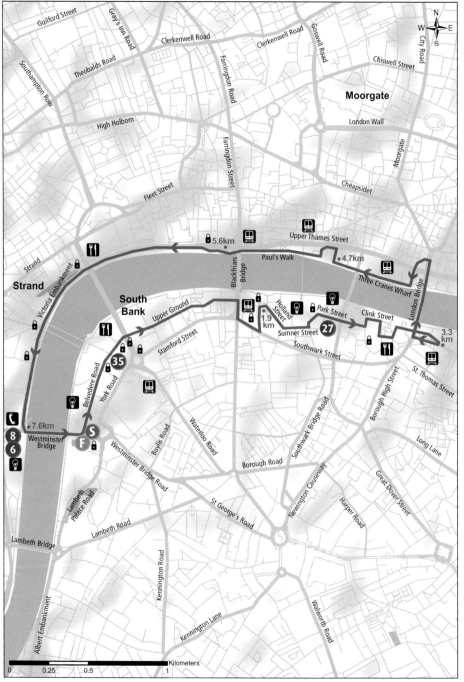

Whizzing through Russell Square towards the British Museum

At a Glance

Distance 13.5km   **Total Climbing** 102m

Terrain
Surfaced roads.

Traffic
Mainly quiet back roads, some busy crossings.

How to Get There
South Kensington tube; car park at Kingston House, 13 Princes Gate.

Food and Drink
Museum and Gallery cafés.

Side Trip
Half way through Regents Park turn south towards Knightsbridge. Amongst the designer boutiques is Harrods, London's most famous department store. Marvel at the food hall displays and at the toy department's games.

Links to (other rides) 1, 2, 4, 5, 8, 35.

Bike Hire
TFL cycle hire points.

Where to Ride Rating

About...

A one-way route starting at what is commonly known as Museum Mile and ending at the British Museum, this ride has more sights than one day could possibly do justice. However if it is raining, you're not in town for long and you feel like a bit of cultural overload then this will fit the bill. Including the National Portrait Gallery, Westminster Abbey, the Imperial War museum, the Tate Modern Gallery and St Paul's Cathedral evenly spaced along the route, there are more than enough dry sights to fill your day.

The iconic entrance hall of the Natural History Museum is dominated by the Diplodocus skeleton

Starting at the Victoria and Albert Museum (daily, 10am–5.45pm; free) - the world's largest museum of decorative arts and design. Next door is the Natural History Museum (daily, 10am–5.45pm; free) famous for its exhibition of dinosaur skeletons, ornate Victorian architecture and most recent addition of the Darwin centre opened September 2009; while just up the road is the Science Museum (daily, 10am–6pm; free) home to a collection of over 300,000 items, including Stephenson's Rocket, the oldest surviving steam locomotive, as well as one of the Apollo spacecraft and model of the lunar Lander.

Exhibition road leads away from the museums, past Imperial College and close to the Royal Albert Hall, to Hyde Park. From here the route cuts through the park down car free Rotten Row, crossing under the Wellington Arch before heading along the edge of Green Park to the front of Buckingham Palace. In front of the Palace, The Mall leads up to Trafalgar Square, Nelsons Column and the National Portrait Gallery (daily, 10am–6pm; free), the first portrait gallery in the world when it opened in 1856 historically housing images of important and famous British people. The collection includes photographs and caricatures as well as paintings, drawings and sculpture.

The ride now turns southwards down Whitehall passing the Houses of Parliament before reaching Westminster Abbey (Mon-Fri 9.30am-3.30pm, Sat 9.30am-2.30pm; adult £15, child £6), the traditional place of coronation and burial site for English monarchs. Then it's over Westminster Bridge to the Imperial War Museum (daily, 10am-6pm; free) its self-proclaimed mission, 'to enable people to have an informed understanding of modern war and its impact on individuals and society'. The next huge gallery along this cultural feast is the Tate Modern (daily, 10am-6pm; free) Britain's national museum of international modern art housed in the former Bankside Power Station converted by architects Herzog and de Meuron and opened to the public in 2000. At this point you have to walk over the Millennium Bridge to Sir Christopher Wren's 17th century magnificent St Paul's Cathedral (Mon-Sat, 8.30pm-4pm; adult £11, child £3.50).

The route then weaves around The City past Smithfield meat market before making its way back into the West End finishing at the British Museum (daily, 10am–5.30pm; free), established in 1753 as a museum of human history and culture. Its millions strong collection is amongst the largest and most comprehensive in the world. Gems include the Egyptian Gallery's Rosetta stone, the Parthenon Marbles and the central reading room.

Ride Log

0.0 Starting outside Science Museum turn left up Exhibition Rd. At the end cross over at the lights into Hyde Park. After 200m turn right down Rotten Row cyclepath.

2.4 At the end, cross over the road under the Wellington Monument using the bike lights. Continue down the edge of Green Park passing in front of Buckingham Palace before continuing up the bike path to the left side of The Mall. At Trafalgar Square go around the roundabout carefully taking the fourth exit down Whitehall.

5.1 At the end of Whitehall turn left at Parliament Square over Westminster Bridge. At the first set of pedestrian lights over the bridge, cross onto the shared use pavement on the other side of the road. Cycling anticlockwise around Park Plaza turning first right down Lambeth Palace Rd.

5.8 Take second left down Royal St becoming Centaur St and at the end turn right down Hercules Rd then first left down Cosser St.

6.5 At the end turn right on the main road and left at the lights down Lambeth Rd then first left down King Edward Walk crossing at bike lights into Morley St and further down crossing Waterloo Rd into Grey St.

7.1 Take the first sharp left into Weber St crossing the busy Cut and Stamford St and at the very end turning right along Upper Rd.

8.4 Now following National Route 4 follow the odd cycleway down the centre of Blackfriars Rd turning left at the lights and the first left after passing under the railway bridge before bearing left around the front of the Tate. Dismount to walk over the Millennium Bridge and up to St Paul's. From the front steps of the Cathedral walk left through Paternoster Square.

10.2 Cross over Negate St then left up Edward St bearing left onto Little Britain. At Smithfield Market turn left then first right through the market. On the other side turn right then first left up St John St followed by first left down St Johns Ln. At the end turn left down Clerkenwell and then right just before the lights down Farringdon Ln. The route crosses busy Farringdon Rd on Ray St before bearing around to the right onto Warner St.

12.0 Cross Pleasant into Phoenix Pl then left down Calthorpe St crossing Grays Inn Rd into Guilford St leading to Russell Square.

13.3 Go around Russell Square to British Museum on Montague Pl.

13.5 End of ride.

Grey Day Museums

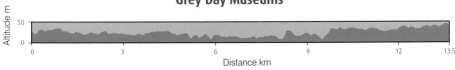

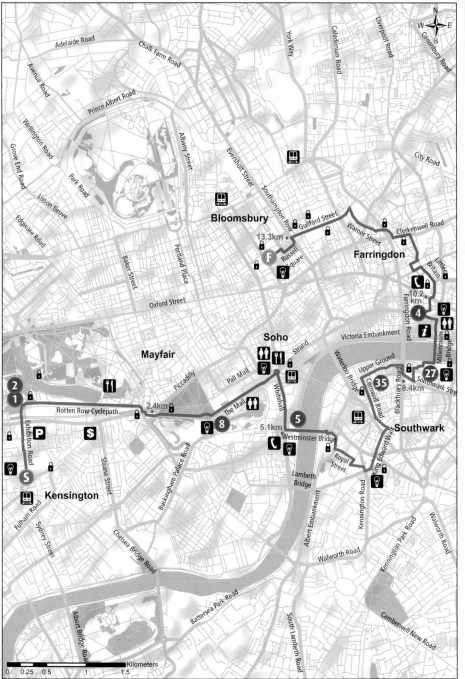

The gleaming tower of Canary Wharf surrounded by other skyscrapers used by the financial services industry

At a Glance

Distance 9.9km **Total Climbing** 43m

Terrain

Surfaced roads and surfaced cyclepaths. A few steps in Rotherhithe when leaving the Thames Path.

Traffic

Mostly dedicated cycleways but light traffic on back road sections.

How to Get There

London Bridge Station, Wapping and Rotherhithe Overground; parking at Canada Water.

Food and Drink

Riverfront restaurants at Canary Wharf, The Grapes Pub Limehouse.

Side Trip

Lock your bikes up at Canary Wharf Pier and take the elevator to Wesferry Road. Wander down West India Avenue to the heart of the Docklands financial district. As well as the offices there is an underground shopping centre and lots of outside restaurants overlooking the water.

Links to (other rides) 3, 8, 29, 44.

Bike Hire

TFL cycle hire points.

Where to Ride Rating

About...

This city loop has it all. From the gothic Tower Bridge along an ornamental canal and the Thames Path to the glass skyscrapers of Canary Wharf. From here a ferry fights the tidal river to Rotherhithe where the once busy Russia docks have since been filled in and replaced with dense woodland and a peaceful ecological park. Spectacular views of Tower Bridge from the Thames Path and a look at the city's warehouse apartments surrounding the design museum turn this ride into a sightseeing gem.

The Thames path around Rotherhithe

Starting at Tower Bridge (daily 10am-6pm; adult £7, child £3) the route goes past the infamous Tower of London (daily 10am-4.30pm; adult £17, child £9.50) before crossing St Katharine's Docks, now a marina surrounded by luxury apartments. The route descends down a cycle version of San Francisco's famous Lombard Street to an ornamental canal with lilies and ducks. The canal passes Spirit Quay and Tobacco Dock, a beautiful warehouse where as the name suggests tobacco was stored. The trail continues through Wapping Wood, planted in 1969 on the site of the Eastern Dock, and onto Shadwell Basin, once one of the most important London docks now surrounded by houses and apartments.

From here the route joins the Thames Path through King Edward Memorial Park weaving along the bank of the river to the Limehouse Basin the start of both Regents Canal and the Limehouse Cut canal. Rejoining the river, just after The Grapes Pub and opposite the park, a modern iron footbridge takes you across Dockland Creek and past the Egyptian styled Four Seasons to a parade of gastro restaurants spilling onto the wide Thames Path in the shadow of the enormous Riverside South building site.

From Canary Wharf Pier a small ferry (Mon-Fri 6.30am-midnight, Sat 9am-midnight, Sun 9am-7pm; £3) can take you and your bike across the Thames to the Hilton Docklands Pier. The trail meanders through Russia Dock Woodland past the Stave Hill Ecological Park, a 5.2 acre mosaic of grassland, woodland scrub and wetland habitat supporting a variety of wildlife, before rejoining the Thames at Bellamy's Wharf. The path continues to Rotherhithe past the Brunel Museum (daily 10am-5pm; Adult £2, child free) and on to the converted warehouses and Design Museum (daily 10am-5.45pm; adult £8.50, child free) at Bermondsey before rejoining Tower Bridge Road near City Hall and the start of the route.

Ride Log

0.0 Starting in front of City Hall cycle around to the back of the building and through Potters Field Park. Turn left into Tooley St and left again into busy Tower Bridge Rd. (If you prefer you can walk with your bike on the pavement across the bridge).

1.0 Once across the bridge continue past the Tower of London and dismount onto the pavement before the lights. Cross over the road at the pedestrian crossing walking away from the tower. Turn right down St Katherine's Way going down towards the river.

1.4 At the end turn left underneath the Thistle Hotel, beware of traffic in the short tunnel. Cross the bridge and continue down road.

1.8 Go straight over mini roundabout and take first left down Redmead Ln and left down pedestrian path to join canal.

3.0 Follow the canal past Tobacco Docks and when canal ends follow path through woods and onto Shadwell Basin.

3.6 Go around the north of the basin. When you rejoin the road on the other side there is a red iron bridge on your right. Turn left and after 10m turn right down a narrow alley signposted Thames Path.

4.3 Continue on the Thames Path through the park and in front of apartments until you join Narrow St. Here you have to dismount or follow one-way around to left, then right and right again rejoining Narrow St eastwards.

5.0 Just past the Grapes Pub and opposite the park the Thames Path is signposted. Cross the footbridge and continue along the embankment until the pier.

5.5 Take the ferry across to Hilton Docklands. Exit the hotel car park right onto Rotherhithe St and then turn left at Acorn Walk onto cycleway through park.

6.0 Follow the path under roads and through woods and turn right at the junction of paths down Beatson Walk following signs for Cycle Route 4 and Thames Path.

7.2 Rejoin the Thames Path keeping the river on your right.

7.8 After a while you pass a pub and have to go up a couple of steps and over a red iron bridge. From here stay on Rotherhithe St past the Mayflower Pub and down an alley before joining the Thames Path (follow signs for Cycle Route 4).

8.3 Follow the path until you get to a building site, the route diverts down Loftie St and right onto Chamber St. However, in time when construction is finished the path is likely to continue along the water front.

8.6 At the end turn left onto George Row and right down Wolseley St, then left up Dockhead. At the end turn right along Jamaica Rd staying on the shared use pavement before turning right down Shad Thames.

8.9 At the end turn left into Maguire St through the bollards and onto Shad Thames.

9.3 Pass under Tower Bridge and you are back at City Hall.

9.9 Ride finishes.

City to Canary Wharf Loop

Altitude m / Distance km

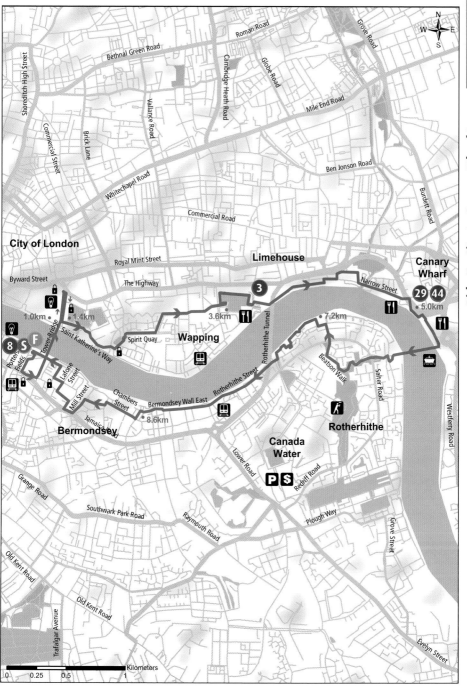

The spiral staircase at City Hall is only open to the public for a few days a year

At a Glance

Distance 10.2km   **Total Climbing** 98m

Terrain

Surfaced roads.

Traffic

Most of the route is along quiet backstreets, however there are some busier sections both with car and pedestrian traffic. There is a longish set of steps away from the Mall you need to be aware of.

How to Get There

St James Park tube, Victoria Station; parking at Arlington House along Piccadilly or metered street parking around St James Square.

Food and Drink

Chain restaurants along Southbank, Chinese restaurants in Soho, cafes around Covent Garden, street stalls at Borough Market.

Side Trip

From Piccadilly you can venture up busy Regents Street to Oxford Street, London's famous shopping street with mighty department stores and flagship boutiques. However watch out, the area is as busy with people as it is with traffic.

Links to (other rides) 1, 5, 6, 7, 27, 35.

Bike Hire

TFL cycle hire points.

Where to Ride Rating

About...

A frantic one way journey through the heart of London taking in many of the city's most famed attractions including Buckingham Palace, St James Park, Horse Guards, Leicester Square, Trafalgar Square, the London Eye, Borough Market, Tower Bridge and the Tower of London. Feel the pulse of the city as you cruise beneath the bright lights of Piccadilly Circus, draw in the sweet smells of China Town and get caught up in the shopper chaos of Covent Garden.

Green Park's stripped deckchairs face Big Ben on a breezy spring day

Starting outside Buckingham Palace (Aug-Sep, daily 9.45am-3.45pm; £16.50) the ride passes around the southern edge of sedate St James Park before turning left up Horse Guards passing government buildings including the Cabinet War Rooms (daily 9.30am - 6pm; adult £12.65, child free) and 10 Downing Street. Drink in the calm of the deckchairs, regal cavalry and greenery as over The Mall a set of steps take you up to Regent Street where the chaos begins. Regent Street rises to the bright neon and video billboards of Piccadilly Circus and the Eros sculpture where crowds gather. It is said that if you stand here long enough you will eventually bump into everyone you know! The traffic can be quite intense but cycle confidently and obey traffic rules and drivers are relatively accommodating.

Going eastwards now the route passes the Trocadero and west end theatres before reaching Leicester Square. North of the square is pedestrianised Soho, London's China Town. The bustling street's restaurants and oriental supermarkets along with the noise, smells and crowds add to a unique far east atmosphere. It may be necessary to walk through the crowds in places. The route then weaves through quiet alleys before emerging at bustling Covent Garden Market, home to street entertainers, shops, bars and restaurants as well as The Royal Opera House and London Transport Museum (daily 10am-6pm; adult £10, child free).

Returning westwards the ride goes through Trafalgar Square, past Nelsons Column and down Whitehall to the Houses of Parliament and Big Ben before crossing the river on Westminster Bridge. Traffic on the approach and bridge is heavy. Stay in the bus lane and cycle confidently at least a metre from the curb. Here the route turns eastwards again passing the London Eye (daily May-Sep 10am-9pm, Oct-Apr 10am-8pm; adult £17.50, child £8.75) the South Bank Centre, the OXO Tower and the Tate Modern (daily 10am-6pm; free). The South Bank itself is too busy to cycle but the road behind is a welcome break from people and traffic.

Next stop is thriving Borough Market, London's gourmet food market atmospherically located under noisy Victorian railway arches in the shadow of the Shard of Glass, London's newest skyscraper towering above London Bridge Station. On the waterfront is moored HMS Belfast (daily Mar-Oct 10am-6pm, Nov-Feb 10am-5pm; adult £10.70, child free) overlooked by City Hall, home of the Mayor of London. The route then crosses the river at iconic Tower Bridge (daily 10am-6pm; adult £7, child £3) ending at the Tower of London (daily 10am-4.30pm; adult £17, child £9.50) originally built by William the Conqueror in 1078, it is now a World Heritage site, home to the instantly recognisable Beefeaters.

Ride Log

0.0 Facing away from Buckingham Palace front gate turn to your right down Spur Rd and at the end left down Birdcage Walk.

0.8 At the edge of the park turn left up Horse Guards. At the end opposite you over the Mall and slightly to the left is a set of steps climbing to Waterloo Pl. At the end of Waterloo Pl use the pedestrian crossing on your left to cross over onto Regents St.

1.9 At Piccadilly Circus go right down Coventry St. At the end before Leicester Square turn left then second right onto pedestrianised Gerard St through China Town. At the end dismount and walk down the no entry to the right and then left down short Newport St.

2.7 At the main road turn left then first right to continue down Newport St. Continue over busy Long Acre into Garrick St then after only 50m look out for Floral St Alley. Take this to the end crossing St. James St. It may be heaving with pedestrians so be prepared to dismount. At the end turn right down Bow St and then second right down Tavistock St.

3.5 At the end of Tavistock St turn right up Southampton and left along Henrietta. At the end turn left then first right down Chandos which turns into William. Turn left at the end of William down to Trafalgar Square. At the lights you need to go straight on, down Whitehall.

5.0 When you reach Parliament Square turn left over Westminster Bridge. At the first set of pedestrian lights over the bridge come off road onto the pavement following signs for Cycle Route 4 left. Pass London Eye and continue along Route 4 to busy Blackfriars

Rd. Here the route turns right into a short section of cycleway running down the middle of the road, follow this turning left at the lights and then left again immediately under the railway. Go around the back of Tate Modern following Route 4 signs turning left at Vinopolis under the arch and then right away from the pedestrian thoroughfare.

8.1 Then it's first left and left again past Southwark Cathedral and through a tunnel under London Bridge Rd.

8.8 Continue along this road until it joins with Tooley St and continue left along Tooley St. Just past Potters Fields Park on your left you need to turn left up Elizabeth St and then left again onto Tower Bridge Rd.

9.9 Once over the river find a bike stand.

10.2 The Tower of London is on your left. End of ride

The iconic red phone box in Parliament Square is the stage for many a photo

Sunny Day Sights Route

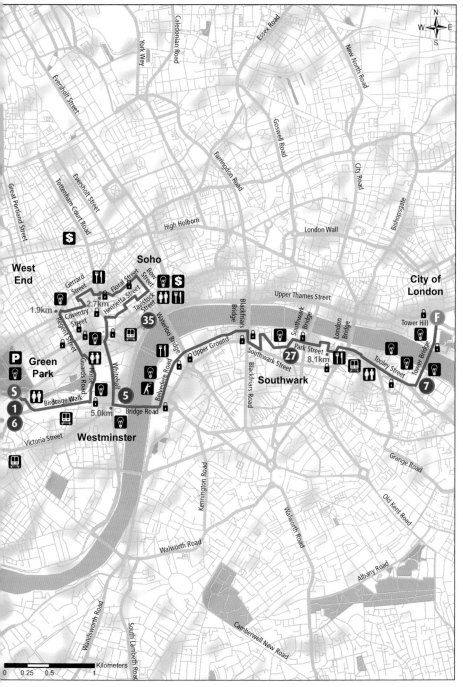

West End

Soho

Green Park

1.9km

2.7km

35

City of London

Tower Hill

F

27

8.1km

Southwark

7

5

5.0km

Westminster

Victoria Street

S

1

6

You can pick up a TFL hire bike 24 hours a day, all year round...

TIM BERKEL
IRONMAN CHAMPION
Photo by Ben Wolstencroft

South West London

Along with the Thames Path and the area's vast green spaces, the principal attractions of this affluent corner of London are the numerous royal palaces and opulent mansions that dot the river banks. There are friendly riverside pubs perfectly situated for that iconic relaxing view of rowers gliding past on the waterway, while slightly further out are extensive countryside trails along lanes and bridleways teaming with wildlife.

Clapham, Battersea, Wandsworth and Fulham are the closest of the SW districts to central London. The area was largely still fields until the 18th century, at this time the city expanded rapidly westwards and Victorian developers carpeted the gentle hills with row upon row of terraced houses leaving only the odd treasured park or common in their wake. Today Battersea Park and Brockwell Park have matured into green oases between the stretching suburban streets.

Further west are the districts of Kew, Richmond, Twickenham and Kingston. Kingston was where the Saxon kings were crowned and the area's pleasant riverside local ensured that it continued to bask in the glow of royal patronage for the centuries to follow. The Palace at Hampton Court, an example Tudor and baroque splendour, is still a Royal Palace but open to the public while Richmond deer park, once a hunting ground, is now a popular open space.

Just beyond the suburbs to the south are the North Downs. These chalky hills are still true countryside. As well as arable land the area is popular with equestrians and the bridleways provide some fantastic challenging mountain bike trails through the protected wild ancient forests of Epson Common.

Rides 9 and 10 are mountain bike trails around The Downs, whereas Rides 12 through to 16 and 19 explore the palaces and parks in the west. The remaining rides will have you touring the commons and parks in the more central parts of the SW postcode.

A scorching summer day in the wilderness of Epsom Common

Cycleway alongside Christchurch Road

At a Glance

Distance 19.3km **Total Climbing** 163m

Terrain

MTB hilly.

Traffic

Almost all off-road or on country lanes. Short sections on busier roads with fast traffic.

How to Get There

Epsom Station, 35 minutes from London Waterloo, parking at the station.

Food and Drink

The Cock Inn Headley, Amato Inn on Chalk Lane, The Cricketers Inn next to Epsom Common.

Side Trip

The route links nicely into Ride 10 'Horton Country Park' if you fancy punishing yourself further.

Links to (other rides) 10.

Bike Hire

None nearby.

Where to Ride Rating

About...

Racehorses, steep hills, narrow bridleways and ancient forests are the principle sights along this challenging mountain bike ride just outside the city. The reward for climbing the North Downs to Epsom Racecourse is the view towards London in the distance, while in the fields and valleys beyond there are pretty villages, country pubs and impressive equestrian centres.

An Epsom Common wooden trail marker

Starting at Epsom station the route weaves through suburban streets before climbing Chalk Lane to the striking Epsom Racecourse on the top of the North Downs. The imposing white steel and glass grandstand has long distance views to the city skyscrapers. The racecourse holds around 15 meets between April and October. Outside these months the windy hilltop can seem very exposed and desolate and is best avoided after prolonged periods of heavy rain as the paths into the valley can become extremely muddy. The route crosses over the racetrack before a bone-shaking chalky path descends steeply to the bottom of the valley.

Here the ride joins a narrow lane that climbs back out of the valley to the village of Tadworth. The lane and track are popular with riders, particularly those on racehorses, so be aware that you should slow down or stop at the side of the path as the horses can become a bit twitchy. From Tadworth a narrow bridleway falls away through fields and hedgerows towards the M25 orbital. The bridleway continues under the motorway and on to the pretty village of Headley. The village has a pub, church and traditional local stores selling a range of homemade and local produce including colourful boiled sweets in rows of large jars.

From here it's a smooth, gently undulating tarmac road. You'll need to look out for a hidden path on the right near Tyrell's Wood, this bridleway leads onto Stane Street, an ancient Roman road lined with horethorn and holly woodland. The route passes the outskirts of Ashtead before plunging into the forest at Ashtead Park. The route then disappears into the wilds of Epsom Common and its ancient oak forests. A maze of tracks brings you back out to Epsom and it's a short ride back to the station.

The rolling fields of Walton Downs; popular with horse riders

Ride Log

0.0 Turn left out of the station and right at the traffic lights. At the next set of lights continue straight on entering the one-way system and out straight ahead onto the B290, Ashley Rd.

0.5 Almost immediately to the right there is an entrance into Rosebury Park. Turn into the park and follow Madans Walk across Avenue Rd until you come out onto Chalk Ln.

1.2 Turn left up Chalk Ln and follow the road to the top. At the top, keep right and then turn left over the road and into the racecourse by Rubbing House.

2.8 A track called Walton Rd crosses the course away from the grandstand and drops off steeply down a chalky path.

3.8 At the valley bottom the path meets the small Ebbisham Ln. It's then another steep climb to the village of Tadworth. Ignore the left hand turn but at the top of the hill turn right, then left into the sign-posted bridleway.

6.2 Go down the bridleway under the motorway, after 1km you reach Headly.

8.0 Turn right along the road and please beware of fast traffic. Continue through the village.

10.1 Just after Headly Court there are tracks leading off the road on both sides marked bridleway. Take the track to the right down Pebble Ln (Stane St) and back over the motorway.

10.7 After 600m there is a crossroads in the track. Take the left turn signposted Ashsted.

11.4 After 700m the track brings you out onto Crampshore Ln and after a further 400m a footpath

breaks between the houses to the right, take this onto Chalk Ln.

12.6 At the end of Chalk Ln turn left then first right in Rookery Hill. After 300m, opposite the entrance to the London Freemans School, there is a path to the left into Ashtead Park.

14.1 At the end of the path is the busy A24. Turn right and then first left into Craddocks Ave.

14.3 Here there is a large Corporation of London sign marked Ashsted Nature Reserve. Take the bridleway to the right. Dismount and cross the rail line with care. Many paths crisscross the bridleway but continue straight on in a north-westerly direction through a short meadow and into ancient woodland.

16.3 After 1.5km there is a clear crossroad of tracks at Woodcock Corner. Here there is a wooden post marked Woodcock on the back and Epsom Common on the front. Turn right following the blue arrows.

16.7 Shortly after you pass a pond the paths divide again. There is a red marker bashed into a tree and a wooden barrier. Here you need to go left around the wooden barrier.

17.0 This path brings you out onto busy Christchurch Rd. Turn right along the road for about 1.5km until you are back in Epsom.

18.8 Close to the bottom of the hill you pass under a railway bridge. Take the first left after the bridge back to the station.

19.3 Once back at the station lock up your bike and go for celebratory drink!

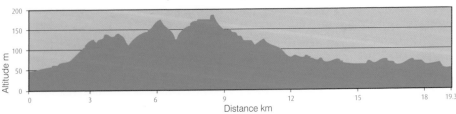

Epsom Countryside Loop

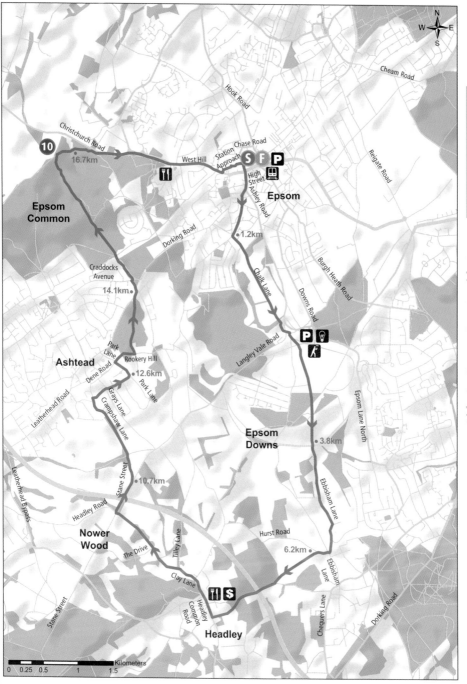

An enchanting bridleway descends towards Claygate Common

At a Glance

Distance 12.4km   **Total Climbing** 59m

Terrain

MTB on off-road tracks and paths.

Traffic

Mostly off-road but short sections on country roads with fast traffic.

How to Get There

Chessington South Station, free parking on the residential streets around the station.

Food and Drink

The Star near Princes Coverts; The Cricketers Inn, Epsom Common.

Links to (other rides) 9.

Bike Hire

None nearby.

Where to Ride Rating

About...

A gentle ride on mostly off-road tracks through Horton Country Park linking Epsom Common, Chessington and Claygate. Plenty of woodland paths and a small chance of getting lost in Epsom Forest make this an exciting adventure. You will probably need to lift your bike over gates at some point during the ride.

Autumn leaves collect near Chessington train station

Starting at Chessington South Station, this ride is not far from the entrance to Chessington World of Adventures (daily, May-Sep; adult £24, child £17), a popular London theme park with rollercoaster rides and a small zoo. From here suburban roads lead to a farm track where, at the end, a bridleway crosses over the A3. On the other side the ride goes down and into a wonderful woodland track with overhanging trees resembling an enchanted forest from a fairytale. Then it's on to the woodland and open countryside of Claygate Common before crossing back over the A3 and into the woodlands of Prince's Coverts.

The Prince's Coverts are owned and looked after by the Crown Estates, but are open to the public. They are a working, managed forest where traditional coppicing is still undertaken to improve habitats for flora and fauna, so be aware that there may be logging in this area. The rules on cycling here are not clear so you may be asked to walk through this area, also the gates are often locked so don't be surprised if you have to climb over some. The main trees are Oak and Western Hemlocks, a fir used for building. Continuing on, the route crosses into Epsom Common, a local nature reserve and Site of Special Scientific Interest with more than 400 species of trees and plants including a healthy population of Roe deer. A compass may be useful to find your way through the maze of tracks before you reach the main road.

From here the route enters the 400-acre Horton Country Park. The park lies on a very thick layer of London Clay, unlike the nearby chalk lands of Epsom and Walton Downs. There area is home to ancient woodland, in spring a carpet of bluebells cover the ground beneath the trees. Wildlife includes Green Woodpeckers and the common has one of the largest roosts of Jackdaws in the London area. The well maintained gravel paths through the park emerge back at Chessington. Here a series of quiet roads lead you back to the station.

Ride Log

0.0 Turn right out of Chessington South Station and cycle over the railway bridge down Garrison Ln. At the end of the lane go over the busy road into Barwell Ln. Follow the track through the farm and around to the left. After 130m there is a right turn onto a bridge over the A3.

1.6 Once over the bridge continue straight on down the bridleway. After 800m just inside Claygate Common there is a crossroads of paths, turn left here.

2.5 When the path meets Holyrod Rd turn right and at the end left onto Coverts Rd and down another track leading back over the A3.

2.9 Continue straight on Southwards through the woods. At busy Fair Oak Ln, cross straight over into Princes Coverts. Public are allowed in this area but there is an unclear cycling policy in the Coverts so you might be asked to dismount. If this happens continue to walk up the stoney track.

4.0 At Jessops Well. You'll see a group of houses in the forest and there may be locked metal gates that you will have to lift your bike over. Once over these continue straight on for several kilometres to Kingston Rd. Turn right, then immediately left down a farm track continuing onto bridleway.

6.0 After 200m there is a smaller path to the left, take this and continue straight on in a north-easterly direction ignoring paths to the left and right.

8.2 After you pass the pond look out for a path bearing left. This will take you up to Christ Church Rd. Turn right then, at the large roundabout, turn left up Horton Ln.

8.9 At the next roundabout continue straight on. After 30m turn left down a track, past a farm, before emerging into a field. Stay to the right of field turning left as the path crosses another track. Continue straight on over another track and past a farm on the right.

9.9 Continue straight on for 1km. When you reach the clearing stay left as the paths divide and then bear right at the next junction. After 100m metres turn left into a field and continue along the path at the edge of the field before emerging onto a track that joins Green Ln / Church Ln. Turn right along Church Ln and left when you reach the Church.

11.8 Continue down Garrison Ln until you reach Chessington South Station.

12.4 Turn right into the station.

Horton Country Park Loop

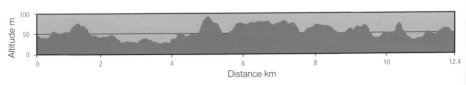

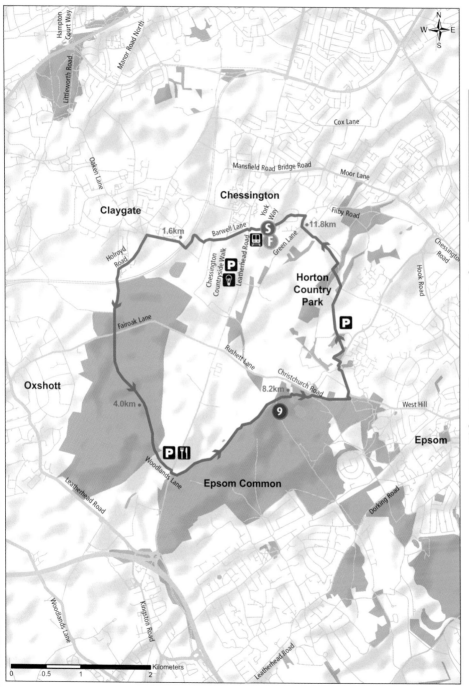

Hampton Court Way

Littleworth Road

Manor Road North

Cox Lane

Oaken Lane

Mansfield Road Bridge Road

Moor Lane

Chessington

Claygate

1.6km

Barwell Lane

York Way

11.8km

Filby Road

Chessington Road

Holroyd Road

Chessington Countryside Walk

Leatherhead Road

Green Lane

Horton Country Park

Hook Road

Fairoak Lane

Rushett Lane

Christchurch Road

P

Oxshott

4.0km

8.2km

9

West Hill

Epsom

Woodlands Lane

Epsom Common

Leatherhead Road

Dorking Road

Woodlands Lane

Kingston Road

Kilometers

0   0.5   1   2

Leatherhead Road

The inviting azure blue water of Brockwell Lido is one of two outdoor pools along the route

At a Glance

Distance 15.6km   **Total Climbing** 64m

Terrain

Surfaced roads and paths. An easy ride, with a mixture of quiet roads and park tracks. Largely flat but with a couple of steep sections. Beware of muddy tracks after rain.

Traffic

Road sections are low traffic with speed bumps and 20mph zones. Dismount to cross busy roads at pedestrian lights or on short sections of pedestrian path.

How to Get There

Herne Hill Station.

Food and Drink

Cafés in Brockwell Park, Tooting Common and Clapham Common. The Hope pub by Wandsworth Common and the Windmill by Clapham Common.

Links to (other rides) 26.

Bike Hire

Go Pedal on Battersea Rise near Wandsworth Common.

Where to Ride Rating

About...

A quick journey around and through South West London's famous Commons and Parks; Clapham Common, Wandsworth Common, Tooting Common and Brockwell Park as well as the streets of terraced houses in between. Take in the changing seasons along the dedicated cycle ways and around undulating back streets. In summer make the most of the parks lidos and in December pick-up a Christmas tree at Northcote Road market.

A bike bell is very useful along shared footpaths

The ride starts in the pleasant Herne Hill area, inside the sloping grounds of Brockwell Park. The park was formally a private estate of Brockwell Hall, first opened to the public in 1892 which now houses a Grade II listed café at the top of the hill. The route heads around the edge of the park passing the newly restored, olympic sized, Brockwell Lido, a popular deep blue oasis on hot summer days. After the children's play area the route leaves the park and crosses Tulse Hill Estate, you emerge on the other side to quiet Victorian terraces leading you to Clapham Common.

The Common is a 220 acre triangular area of grassland bordering Clapham, Battersea and Balham. Crossing grassland past Long Pond the path joins Windmill Drive. Opposite Eagle Pond and further down on the right, Mount Pond, are two of the lakes predominantly used for angling as they contain a variety of species including Carp, Roach, Tench and Bream. From here the route continues out of the common and through more Victorian terraces. At the bottom of the valley is Montholme Road leading to Northcote Road and if you fancy a detour you'll find fresh fruit and vegetables, flowers, delis and a market (Mon-Sat). There are also a number of craft

stalls selling clothes, pashminas, cushions and throws, baskets, handbags, pictures, ceramics and furniture.

The next Common is Wandsworth Common where the route crosses the railway. To the south of the Common is Bellevue Road with pretty knick-knack shops, cafes and restaurants overlooking the grass. The route continues southwards along quiet Victorian terraces before entering Tooting Common, home to another giant 1930's lido with pretty painted changing room doors, Tooting Bec Lido. After a beautiful avenue of Chestnut trees the path leaves the park cutting through Streatham before returning to Brockwell Park. From here it climbs to the top of the hill with fantastic views of the city before cruising back down the other side of the park to the end of the route.

Ride Log

0.0 Turn left out of Herne Hill Station and cross the busy road via the pedestrian lights and enter Brockwell Park on the other side. Once in the park take the shared footpath to the right along the edge of the park past a miniature railway and then the lido.

0.8 Before the path exits the park take a sharp left hand turn onto another shared footpath. As you pass the playground you will see an exit to the park on your right. Follow the path across Tulse Hill Rd and up through Tulse Hill Estate.

1.6 Once through the estate turn right down Leander Rd bearing left into Josephine Ave.

2.2 At the end of the road cross busy Brixton Hill into Lambert Rd. At the end follow cycleway signs down Mandrell Rd then take a left and right at the end into Crescent Ln.

3.7 Where Crescent Ln crosses Abbeville Rd ignore the no entry signs and carry on (cyclists are ok on this official cycle route) up to Clapham Common. Carefully cross the busy road into Clapham Common.

4.3 Turn left through the common along one of the shared paths until you reach Windmill Dr.

5.0 Turn right down Windmill Dr crossing The Avenue using the lights and continuing on the path opposite until you reach the edge of the park.

5.5 Turn left along Westside through the bollards and then right down Thurleigh Rd and up the other side to Wandsworth Common.

6.7 Turn right along Bolingbroke Grove then left into the common on the cyclepath.

7.0 Dismount to cross the railway line and then take the cyclepath diagonally to the left crossing busy Trinity Rd at the lights and continuing down the path to Lyford Rd.

7.7 Turn left down Lyford Rd. At the end follow the cycleway to the left bringing you into Sandgate Ln then cross straight over the roundabout into Beechcroft Rd.

9.2 Cross busy Upper Tooting Rd into Brudenell Rd.

10.4 At the roundabout at the end take the third exit into Furzedown Rd and at the mini roundabout turn left into the cycleway through Tooting Common going straight across Tooting Bec Rd and Bedford Hill Rd.

12.4 At the northern edge of the common turn right along Emmanuel Rd then first right then left down Telford Ave.

13.7 At the end dismount and cross busy Brixton Hill using the pedestrian crossing then enter Wavertree Rd on the opposite side.

14.0 Take first left, Daysbrook Rd. A quick right at the end of the road, then left takes you into Roupell Rd.

14.5 Cross the main road and at the end go down Upper Tulse Hill, over the main road and then turn left opposite the church on your way down the hill.

15.3 On the left there is an entrance into Brockwell Park. Go through and head up the hill.

15.6 From the top head down the other side back to the park entrance.

South West Parks

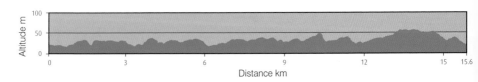

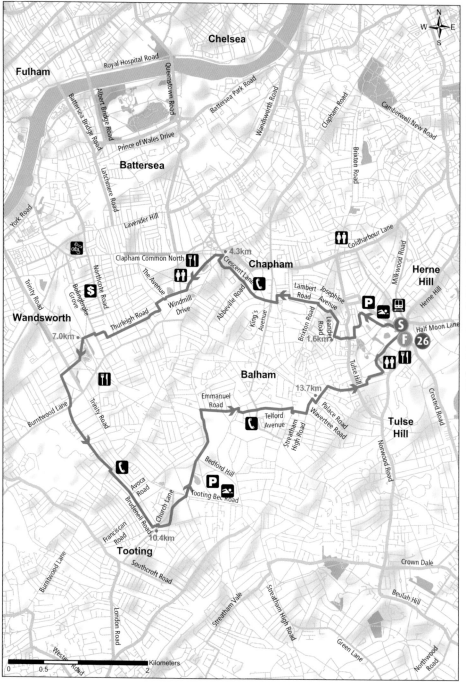

Chelsea

Fulham

Royal Hospital Road

Battersea Park Road

Wandsworth Road

Clapham Road

Camberwell New Road

Queenstown Road

Albert Bridge Road

Battersea Bridge Road

Prince of Wales Drive

Latchmere Road

Brixton Road

Battersea

York Road

Lavender Hill

Trinity Road

Northcote Road

The Avenue

Clapham Common North

4.3km

Crescent Lane

Chapham

Coldharbour Lane

Milkwood Road

Herne Hill

Half Moon Lane

Bolingbroke Grove

Windmill Drive

Abbeville Road

King's Avenue

Lambert Road

Josephine Avenue

Brixton Road

Leander Road

Herne Hill

S

F

26

Thurleigh Road

Wandsworth

7.0km

Tulse Hill

13.7km

Balham

Emmanuel Road

Telford Avenue

Wavertree Road

Palace Road

Tulse Hill

Croxted Road

Burntwood Lane

Trinity Road

Streatham High Road

Norwood Road

Bedford Hill

Avoca Road

Church Lane

Tooting Bec Road

Franciscan Road

Brudenell Road

10.4km

Tooting

Southcroft Road

Streatham Vale

Streatham High Road

Crown Dale

Beulah Hill

Burntwood Lane

London Road

Green Lane

Northwood Road

0   0.5   2   Kilometers

The ornate palace gates of Hampton Court

At a Glance

Distance 5.3km **Total Climbing** 31m

Terrain

Flat, smooth, un-surfaced path and dedicated cycle lane. There is a busy road at start of route.

Traffic

Segregated at start and then car free for the rest of the route.

How to Get There

Kingston-Upon-Thames railway station, services from Waterloo; parking in the John Lewis car park.

Food and Drink

Cafés and restaurants at Kingston waterfront at the start of the route and a café at Hampton Court Palace at the end. There are no eating or drinking places along the route.

Side Trip

Lock your bikes up and take a trip into the palace. Get lost in the maze and marvel at the enormous kitchen.

Links to (other rides) 18, 19.

Bike Hire

Thameside Cycles in Kingston.

Where to Ride Rating

About...

From the handsome Kingston Bridge, along the gravel Barge Walk towpath, you can take in the sights and sounds of the Thames before reaching magnificent Hampton Court Palace. Away from any roads and traffic free the path is flat, pretty and peaceful with interesting sights at both ends of the short route. It is the perfect ride for children and those getting back into cycling.

Early morning rowers on the Thames

The village of Kingston-Upon-Thames was built at the first upstream crossing point of the river from London Bridge and a bridge still exists at the same site now. First recorded occupation of Kingston was by the Romans and later it became the market town where Saxon kings were crowned. Today central Kingston is a busy retail centre with a small number of commercial offices and civic buildings.

The route takes you along Barge Walk. As the name suggests there are many houseboats and transient visitors moored-up along the banks often sharing the water with proud swans grooming themselves or nursing signets. On this side of the riverbank there are no restaurants or cafés to distract you - only the distant hint of hustle and bustle on the opposite bank. As the path continues you'll encounter many other cyclists and walkers and on the river there are often training rowers; the ride is a great antidote to bustling city life. In late April the blossoms are gorgeous, the houses attractive, the riverside nooks and crannies varied - giving a feeling that they remain part of another era.

As you reach the end of the towpath, you'll come across the stunning regal golden gates protecting Hampton Court Palace's Privy Gardens. Hampton Court Palace (daily, Oct-Mar 10am-4.30pm, Apr-Sep 10am-6pm; adult £14, child £7) was originally built in 1514 for Cardinal Wolsey, a favourite advisor of King Henry VIII. In 1529, as Wolsey fell from favour, the palace was passed to the King. In the century that followed, William III commissioned a large rebuilding and expansion project intended to rival Versailles. Work halted in 1694, leaving the palace in two distinct contrasting architectural styles, domestic Tudor and baroque. While the palace's styles are an accident of fate, a unity exists due to the use of pink bricks and an, albeit vague, symmetrical balancing of successive low wings. Today, the palace is open to the public, and is a major tourist attraction. It is cared for by an independent charity, Historic Royal Palaces, which receives no funding from the government or the Crown.

Ride Log

0.0 From Kingston Station follow the cycle path to the right then cross over the lights at the bike crossing into the pedestrian area (Wood St).

0.5 Take the first right and continue along the cycle track on the left side of the main road travelling up and over Kingston Bridge.

0.8 As soon as you are over the bridge there is a left turn by a Richmond-upon-Thames sign. This takes you into Barge Walk. Continue for 4.7km until the track reaches Hampton Bridge.

5.3 Here turn right until you reach the entrance to Hampton Court Palace.

A rusty bike parked outside Kingston Station

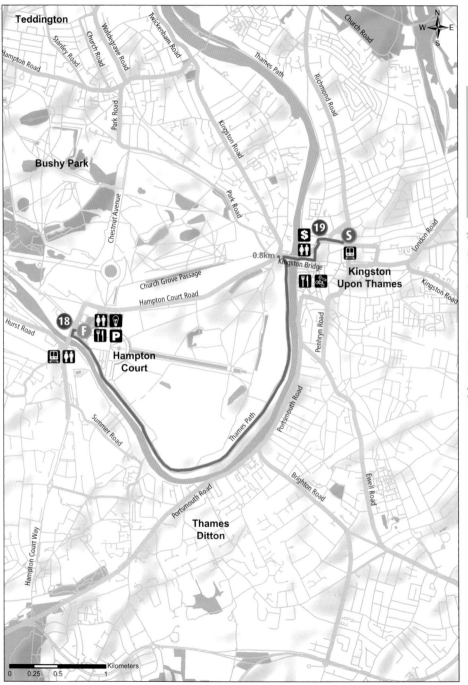

Teddington

Bushy Park

Kingston
Upon Thames

0.8km

Kingston Bridge

Hampton
Court

Thames
Ditton

Cycling along the yellow gravel trail as it weaves around the edge of the park

At a Glance

Distance 11.8km   **Total Climbing** 67m

Terrain
Smooth off-road path.

Traffic
Traffic free.

How to Get There
Richmond train station; six car parks within Richmond Park located at Sheen Gate, Roehampton Gate, Pembroke Lodge (always very busy), Isabella Plantation and Kingston Gate.

Food and Drink
Pembroke Lodge Cafeteria.

Side Trip
Visit the village of Richmond to the north of the park for riverside restaurants and cafes.

Links to (other rides) 17, 19.

Bike Hire
April through September, cycle hire is available daily in the car park near Roehampton Gate. Out of season hire is by arrangement with the hire company. Cost is £8 for 1 hour, £10 for 2 hours, £13 for 3 hours, £17 for 4 hours. ID required as deposit.

Where to Ride Rating

About...

Richmond Park covers over 2000 acres, almost three times as large as New York City's Central Park. It is Britain's largest urban walled park, and the largest of the Royal Parks in London. The area is famous for its red and fallow deer, which number over 600. The ride follows the parks well maintained Tamsin Cycle Trail around the park dropping southwards along the western perimeter before returning up along the eastern edge to complete the loop.

A proud stag watches as cyclists wheel by

Starting at Richmond Gate, in the north, the yellow gravel trail leads to King Henry VIII's Mound, the highest point within the park. From here there is a protected view of St Paul's Cathedral as well as views towards the London Eye, NatWest Tower and 'the Gherkin', over 16km to the east; a telescope is installed on the mound for a better viewing experience. From here the path passes Pembroke Lodge, originally the home of first Earl Russell now the only cafeteria in the park. The Grade II listed Georgian mansion stands in its own garden with views to the west over the Thames Valley. The path continues southwards and downwards through ancient oak forests before emerging on the park's open slopes. The grassland is mostly managed by grazing herds of red and fallow deer roaming freely within much of the park. A cull takes place each November to ensure numbers can be sustained.

At the southern edge of the park the path passes around the Isabella Plantation, an important and attractive woodland garden containing numerous woods and copses, some created with donations from members of the public. Established after World War II from an existing woodland, it is organically run, resulting in a rich flora and fauna and is a major visitor attraction in its own right. From here the route follows the eastern edge of the park to Robin Hood

Gate before heading northwards and upwards through Broomfield Hill Wood and up to Roehampton Gate. Here there is a coffee stop, car park and cycle hire. The route crosses the road heading westwards climbing along Teck Plantation back to Richmond Gate.

Richmond Park is a Site of Special Scientific Interest, a National Nature Reserve and a Special Area of Conservation for the Stag beetle as well as being an important refuge for other wildlife, including woodpeckers, squirrels, rabbits, insects; not to mention numerous ancient trees, and varieties of fungi. There is pedestrian access to the park 24 hours a day except when a deer cull is taking place. This means it is not uncommon to find cyclists, walkers and runners using the park at all times of the day and night. During the deer cull the majority of the gates are locked and warning signs are displayed forbidding access to the park. The park has designated bridleways and cyclepaths. These are shown on maps and notice boards displayed near the main entrances, along with other regulations that govern use of the park. The law limits cycling to: main roads; the Tamsin Trail and other hard (i.e. concrete or cement) surfaces. Cycling along the park's mud paths is forbidden. Speed cyclists must observe the 32kph limit and recreational cyclists must not ride away from the designated cyclepaths.

Ride Log

0.0 Enter the park through Richmond Gate and follow the yellow gravel cycle path right. The route heads downhill past Pembroke Lodge.

2.5 Here you will reach Ham Cross Gate. Turn right on the road towards the gate then left after 300m back onto the yellow cycle path and continue for another 1.3km.

3.6 At the bottom of the hill the route crosses over Kings Grove in front of Kingston Gate before climbing slightly past Ladderstile Gate and onto Robin Hill Gate.

6.4 From Robin Hood Gate the path climbs gently northwards crossing the road and car park at Roehampton Gate.

8.3 From here the route climbs again gently for 3km back to Richmond Gate.

11.8 At Richmond Gate you have completed the loop.

A well earned rest on one of the many great picnic spots around the park

Richmond Park Loop

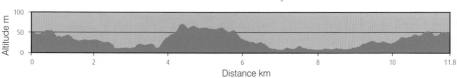

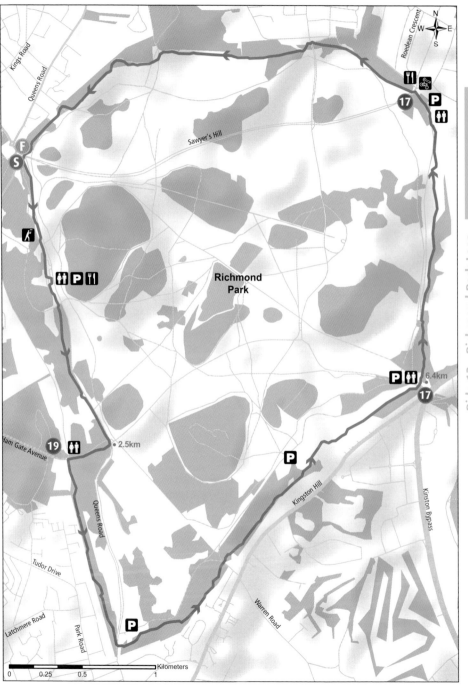

Richmond Park

Sawyer's Hill

Kings Road
Queens Road
Roedean Crescent

17

6.4km

17

19

Ham Gate Avenue

2.5km

Queens Road

Kingston Hill

Kinston Bypass

Tudor Drive

Latchmere Road

Park Road

Warren Road

N
W E
S

0   0.25   0.5   1   Kilometers

A sweet smelling bread stall just outside Kew Gardens Station

At a Glance

Distance 11.9km   **Total Climbing** 32m

Terrain

Surfaced roads and paths through parks.

Traffic

Mostly light but busy crossings around Kew Bridge and Richmond Bridge.

How to Get There

Kew Bridge Station also Kew Gardens and Richmond stations; car park at NCP The Quadrant in Richmond or Kew Gardens car park near the Brentford Gate.

Food and Drink

Cafés and restaurants around Kew Station and in The Royal Botanic Gardens, Kew itself. There are also restaurants along Richmond waterfront and The London Apprentice pub in Isleworth.

Side Trip

Have a look at the other rides that link into this one for detours. Make sure you visit the Royal Botanic Gardens.

Links to (other rides) 16, 39, 40, 41.

Bike Hire

WiZZBiKE 113-114 High Street, Brentford,

Where to Ride Rating

About...

A flat route on predominantly quiet roads through Syon Park, past Isleworth, Twickenham riverside over Richmond Bridge and Richmond Green and up through suburban north Sheen to Kew Gardens Station before passing Kew Garden Pier entrance and re-crossing the river at Kew Bridge. Sights along the route include the splendid Botanical Gardens at Kew and the Duke of Northumberland house in Syon Park.

One of many plant shops and florists just outside the botanical gardens

South West

From Kew Bridge Station the route heads west past the Kew Bridge Steam Museum, through the Haversfield Estate and along suburban roads to Brentford, crossing the River Brent before entering Syon Park, the 200-acre grounds of Syon House (Mar-Oct Wed, Thu, Sun, 11am-5pm; £9 adult, £4 child). The house belongs to the Duke of Northumberland and is now his family's London residence. The park borders the Thames looking across the river to Kew Gardens' 'near bank' which is a tidal meadow flooded twice a day. The Great Conservatory in the gardens, designed by Charles Fowler in 1828, was the first conservatory to be built from metal and glass on a large scale. On the other side of the park is the pretty suburb of Isleworth with Georgian and Victorian houses facing the river.

The route passes Richmond Lock, passing under Twickenham Bridge then reaching the stone arched Richmond Bridge, the oldest surviving bridge spanning the Thames. Once in Richmond the route take you to Richmond Green, surrounded by large affluent houses. A footbridge over the busy Twickenham Road brings you into the Edwardian suburbs of North Sheen before reaching Kew Garden Station where old fashioned shops and cafes surround outside market stalls on the forecourt of the fine station house. This is the closest point on the route to the main entrance and visitor centre of The Royal Botanic Gardens, Kew (daily 9.30am-dusk; adult £13, child Free). The grounds cover an extensive 121 hectares of gardens and botanical glasshouses.

Kew is responsible for the world's largest collection of living plants and the organisation employs more than 650 scientists and other staff. The living collections include more than 30,000 different kinds of plants, while the herbarium, which is the largest in the world, has over seven million preserved plant specimens. Iconic structures include the lofty Chinese Pagoda built in 1761, the Palm House built by architect Decimus Burton and iron-maker Richard Turner in 1848 and a new Treetop Walkway opened in 2008. The impressive walkway is 18 metres high and 200 metres long and takes visitors into the tree canopy of a woodland glade. From here the route continues north past the garden Kew Pier entrance before crossing Kew Bridge back to Kew Bridge Station.

Ride Log

0.0 Turn right out of the station down Kew Bridge Rd, then first right down Dragon Ln. After 500m turn left along Clayponds which becomes Netley Rd. Cross straight over busy Ealing Rd into Braemer Rd.

1.5 Once you reach the end of Braemer it's a quick left then right in Latewood Rd leading in to St Pauls. Then it's left and right again into Lion Way. At the top of Lion Way you'll see the busy high street. Turn right into the high street crossing over the River Brent. Continue on along the main road and take the second left (about 150m). The road leads into Syon Park.

3.0 Continue all the way through the park exiting left onto Church St. Over a little river the road bends around to the right. After 120m you reach a mini roundabout, turn left onto North St.

4.8 At the end turn left onto South St. Follow the main road for 250m until you cross a little river. Take the first left immediately after the river down Railshead Rd. This leads onto the shared riverside Isleworth Promenade. The Promenade in turn becomes Ranelagh Dr. Continue under Twickenham Bridge along Ducks Walk until you reach Richmond Bridge.

6.7 Join Richmond Rd and cross Richmond Bridge. Dismount and walk on the pavement if you feel more comfortable.

7.0 Once over the bridge take the first left at the roundabout down Hill St. At the lights as the main road bears right continue straight on down Kings St and into Richmond Green.

7.4 Stay to the left of the Green before turning right along the top of the Green. After traversing the top edge, look for a path leading away from the corner between two red pillars. Take this over the railway line and into the car park. In the car park turn right passing all the way through until you see a footbridge. Exit the car park and use the footbridge to cross the main road turning right along the cycleway on the other side.

8.2 Continue along the cycleway for 300m then turn left along Kew Foot Rd before the cycleway reaches a big roundabout.

8.6 After 350m turn right along Jocelyn Rd. Follow to the end and cross at the lights and go down Selwyn Ave. Take the first left at the road fork continuing down Selwyn Ave. At the end a quick right then left into St Pauls St and then turn left into Stanmore Gardens.

10.5 After 900m the road bears right ending at Sandycombe Rd. Turn left here.

10.8 After passing some shops there is a traffic island. Turn right immediately after the island up Leyborne Park. Cross over the busy Mortlake Rd into Forest Rd. At the end turn left down Bushwood Rd which will bring you to Kew Bridge. Cross the bridge on the shared pavement. On the other side opposite you is Kew Bridge Station.

11.9 Cross over using the lights and you've reached the end of the ride.

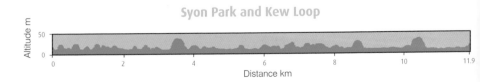

Syon Park and Kew Loop

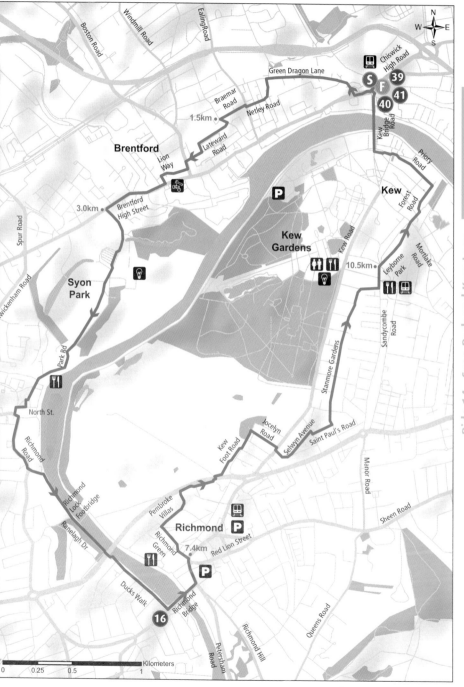

Windmill Road
Boston Road
Ealing Road
Green Dragon Lane

Chiswick High Road
S **F** **39**
40 **41**

Braemar Road
Netley Road
1.5km
Lateward Road

Brentford
Lion Way

3.0km
Brentford High Street

Kew Bridge Road
Priory Road

Kew
Forest Road

P

Kew Gardens

Kew Road

Mortlake Road

Spur Road

10.5km
Leyborne Park

Sandycombe Road

Syon Park

Twickenham Road

Park Rd

Stanmore Gardens

North St.

Jocelyn Road

Kew Foot Road
Selwyn Avenue
Saint Paul's Road

Richmond Road

Richmond Lock Footbridge

Manor Road

Ranelagh Dr

Pembroke Villas

Richmond Green

Richmond
P

7.4km
Red Lion Street

Sheen Road

P

Ducks Walk

Richmond Bridge

16

Queens Road

Petersham Road
Richmond Hill

Kilometers
0   0.25   0.5   1

Ride 14 - Syon Park and Kew Loop

Fine Georgian houses line the Hammersmith Waterfront

At a Glance

Distance 28.6km   **Total Climbing** 60m

Terrain

Sealed and unsealed paths, sealed roads.

Traffic

Over half the route is traffic free or on quiet back roads. Some short busy crossings.

How to Get There

Earlsfield Station, trains from Waterloo or Wandsworth Town; parking in Wandsworth town centre.

Food and Drink

The River Café - Fulham, Blue Anchor pub - Hammersmith, food stalls at Bennett's Courtyard Market.

Side Trip

Close to the Thames Path in Barnes is the WWT London Wetland Centre, a site of Special Scientific Interest. The centre, opened in 2000, is home to many birds that cannot be found anywhere else in London.

Links to (other rides) 17, 20, 41.

Bike Hire

Go Pedal on Battersea Rise.

Where to Ride Rating

About...

A long, largely car-free ride weaving in and out of Wandsworth, one of inner London's largest boroughs, taking in the River Wandle Trail, Bennett's Courtyard market, Wimbledon Common, Putney Heath, the Barnes Thames Path, Hammersmith Bridge and Fulham. The route gently undulates between large open spaces, narrow woodland paths and less attractive but interesting abandoned industry along the River Wandle.

Starting at Earlsfield Station the ride soon joins the river Wandle Trail, heading south through a narrow stretch of woodland bordering industrial parks and old factories. The path emerges into the Wandle Meadow and from here a series of suburban streets lead to a large retail development. A dedicated cyclepath follows the river rejoining the trail at Bennett's Courtyard Market with food stalls and arts and crafts shops including a pottery studio next to an old waterwheel. The path continues along the Wandle to Morden Hall Park and Deen City Farm where children can assist in farm activities as well as visiting the animals. On the other side of the park the route leaves the greenery and follows suburban streets through Merton crossing the railway line on a footbridge before climbing up steep Thornton Hill emerging onto Wimbledon Common.

The Common is over twice the size of Hampstead Heath, the 1140 acres include golf courses, woods, horse rides, lakes and ravines. The route follows two miles of bridleway, past the Wimbledon windmill, across the common to Putney Heath. Here a car free dirt road joins Putney Heath with Barnes Common and the Thames Path. The Thames Path can be a particularly busy section with cyclists and walkers at weekends, keep to the left and use your bell when coming up behind people. After a couple

of kilometres, with views across the river towards Fulham, the route passes the Harrods Depository, a fine building that has been converted into luxury flats, before crossing the river at Hammersmith Bridge, an ornate suspension bridge.

Once over the river quiet roads weave past the famous Riverside Television Studios, The River Café one of London's best Italian restaurants, and Craven Cottage, the historic Fulham Palace football ground. A short stretch through the beautiful Bishops Park leads you to Putney Bridge. On the other side the route rejoins the Thames Path, heading south, through Wandsworth Park and across the River Wandle. The creek has seen better days, a sunken boat lies in the mud beneath the pipes of the old Ram Brewery. London Pride Beer was brewed here until 2006 and the forlorn building now stands empty. Beyond this are new riverfront apartments and an industrial estate. Here the ride crosses into Wandsworth, an old town maze of suburban terraces as it climbs back to the start of the Wandle Trail, past Southfields playing fields and back to Earlsfield Station.

Ride Log

0.0 Turn left out of Earlsfield Station along Garrett Ln then first right along Summerley St. One hundred metres along as the road bears left there is a pedestrian path to the right which crosses a bridge and joins the Wandle Trail. Turn left onto the trail following the river southwards.

1.6 Cross Plough Ln at the lights and rejoin the Wandle Trail. Turn right onto North Rd then first left at mini roundabout along East Rd followed by second right onto Allsaints Rd. First left onto Hanover Rd which, after a little kink becomes Laburnham Rd.

3.6 Just before the end of Laburnham Rd follow the cycleway signs left and then left again into Merton High St. At the first set of pedestrian lights turn right off the road onto the pavement and over the blue footbridge around to the right of the supermarket. After 150m cross at the bike lights and rejoin the Wandle Trail opposite.

5.2 One hundred metres after crossing the tram line take the right hand fork in the path up to Morden Rd. Cross at the lights and cycle along shared pavement to roundabout. Turn

Ride Log

right up Kenley Rd, left around circle gardens and continue along Kenley Rd.

6.6 At the end turn right along Mostyn Rd then after 200m turn right down Church Path. At the end of the path turn left along Watery Ln continuing along cycle path at the end into Manor Rd.

7.4 At the end turn right onto Cannon Hill L crossing busy Kingston Rd into Chatsworth Ave. At the end take the cyclepath right and at the end of the path left onto Merton Hall.

8.5 At the end take the footbridge over the railway into Elm Grove leading to busy Warpole Rd. Turn right then left up Thornton Hill. At the end cross over Ridgway to the left to continue up Lauriston Rd. At the end take the public footpath straight on across Wimbledon Common crossing Cannizaro Rd and continuing to an island of houses.

10.2 There is a path to the right parallel with West Pl towards the Windmill. Continue straight on northwards at the Windmill and pass under Roehampton Ln into Putney Heath Woodland. At the path fork go right into Portsmouth Gardens and then left into Telegraph Rd.

13.5 Coming out onto a mini roundabout go straight on down Putney Park Ln path. Keep going straight on for 1.6km. The path emerges at the busy Richmond Rd. Cross over down Gipsy Ln then right along Queens Ride.

15.3 Cross over roundabout continuing along Queens Ride to the mini roundabout. Turn left along Lower Richmond Rd then immediately right after a height restriction sign onto a dirt path along the edge of the field.

16.2 Across the field the path turns right through woodland towards the Thames Path. At the Thames Path turn left.

18.5 Go right over Hammersmith Bridge and then immediately right down steps at the end of the bridge.

18.8 Once back on the Thames Path, walk bikes around to left joining Queen Caroline St then turn right down Crisp Rd. At the end follow bike signs left then right towards Putney Bridge.

21.1 Just past the football ground take entrance to Bishops Park on the right and follow cycleway through park emerging at Putney Bridge. Cross the bridge.

22.6 Just past the church turn onto the pedestrian square. This takes you in front of Putney Wharf onto the South Bank Thames Path before going inland left onto Deodar Rd. At the end, walk through the modern development into Wandsworth Park. Once through the park the path again leaves the river front, into Point Pleasant Rd.

24.0 After 80m there is an arch under a new development on the left. Go through this onto Osiers Rd, as the road curves right there is an industrial estate to the left. Go through to the end where a cycleway crosses the Wandle River into Smugglers Way.

25.0 At the end, go straight over at the bike lights onto a brick road. As soon as you pass under the railway line there is a bike path to the left into Alma Rd. At the top of the road cross using the lights into Melody Rd (a little to the left). At the end turn right onto Cicada Rd, then left again back onto Melody Rd. At the end turn right down Farthing Ln.

26.7 Fifty metres before Garret Ln take a right into Vermont Rd then fourth left down Borrodaile Rd, at the end a cyclepath crosses to Garret L. Cross using bike lights and go down the 'No Entry' Mapleton Rd via the shared use pavement.

27.2 Over the bridge on the left is an entrance to the park. Follow the cycleway along the Wandle Trail, 250m after crossing Kimber Rd the cycleway forks. Follow signs to Earlsfield Station left over pedestrian bridge bringing you out on St Johns Dr. At the end turn right onto Garrett Ln until you reach the station.

Wandle Trail Loop

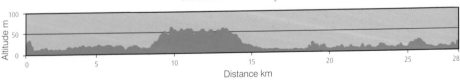

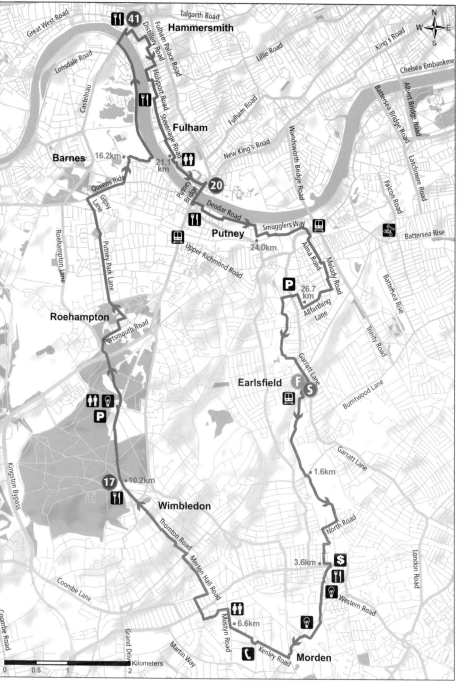

Talgarth Road

Hammersmith

Great West Road

Lonsdale Road

Fulham Palace Road

Distillery Road

Holyport Road

Stevenage Road

Lillie Road

King's Road

Chelsea Embankme

Castelnau

Barnes 16.2km

Queens Ride

Gipsy Lane

Roehampton Lane

Putney Park Lane

21.1 km

Fulham

Fulham Road

New King's Road

Putney Bridge

20

Deodar Road

Wandsworth Bridge Road

Battersea Bridge Road

Albert Bridge Road

Latchmere Road

Falcon Road

Smugglers Way

24.0km

Battersea Rise

Putney

Upper Richmond Road

Alma Road

Melody Road

Battersea Rise

Roehampton

Portsmouth Road

26.7 km

Allfarthing Lane

Garratt Lane

Trinity Road

P

Earlsfield

F
S

Burntwood Lane

Kingston Bypass

P

Garratt Lane

17 10.2km

1.6km

Wimbledon

Thornton Road

Merton Hall Road

North Road

London Road

3.6km

S

Coombe Lane

Western Road

6.6km

Mostyn Road

Kenley Road

Morden

Coombe Road

Grand Drive

Martin Way

Kilometers

0   0.5   1   2

Ham foot ferry sign on the north bank

At a Glance

Distance 9.8km   **Total Climbing** 11m

Terrain
Off-road smooth, unsurfaced paths.

Traffic
Traffic free path, small section on back streets.

How to Get There
Richmond Station; car park at NCP The Quadrant in Richmond.

Food and Drink
Richmond riverside restaurants, Ham House café.

Side Trip
Just off the Thames Path on the Twickenham side of the river is Marble Hill House, the last surviving of many elegant mansions and gardens that bordered the Thames between Richmond and Hampton Court in the 18th century.

Links to (other rides) 14, 19.

Bike Hire
None locally.

Where to Ride Rating

About...

Green, flat and almost completely car free this short ride skirts the banks of the Thames, taking in Richmond, Ham House, Teddington Locks, Ham riverside lands, a foot ferry with detours to Orleans House Gallery and the Twickenham riverside walk.

A long cycle path leads towards the back gates of Ham House

Starting on Grade 1 listed, 18th century stone arched Richmond Bridge, the oldest surviving Thames bridge in London, this historic ride passes the shops and boutiques of Richmond's Hill Street before turning off down the cobbled Water Lane, passing the Water Lane Pub and joining the Richmond riverside. You have to walk your bike for a short section of pedestrian path as it passes in front of smart eateries and moored rowing boats back towards Richmond Bridge. On the other side of the bridge arch you are allowed to cycle again as the path weaves along the river bank through native trees before emerging into the tall grasses and floodplain of Petersham Meadows. Continuing along the south bank of the upper tidal Thames the route passes through Ham Nature Reserve, past the Thames Young Mariners, where colourful boats skim across the lake, and into Ham riverside lands. Beyond the grassland are Teddington Locks. Built in 1856 the complex of three locks and a weir mark the end of the tidal Thames.

Opposite the locks the trail blazes inland through alleyways and suburban roads before emerging at Ham Common open ground. From here the route branches northwards along a wide car-free, tree lined avenue

leading to the back gate of Ham House, claimed by its present owners, the National Trust, to be "unique in Europe as the most complete survival of 17th century fashion and power". Built in 1610 for Sir Thomas Vavasour, Knight Marshal to James I, the house is said to be haunted by the Duchess of Lauderdale and her dog. The path leads around the eastern edge of the gardens to the front of the house and the public entrance. From here a short path leading away from the front of the house crosses an area of open grassland before rejoining the Thames Path at the foot ferry pier. From here you can either go back to Richmond along the path you came or take the public foot ferry to the north bank of the river, You will have to hail the ferry operator who waits on the other side (10am-dusk; £1 adult, 50p children). On the north bank the route continues northwards back to Richmond Bridge.

Ride Log

0.0 Starting on Richmond Bridge head east towards Richmond. At the mini roundabout turn left down Hill St and second left down Water Ln. At the end dismount and walk bike left along bank under Richmond Bridge.

0.6 On the other side ride along Thames Path to Petersham Meadows. Continue along the bank of the river for 5km to Teddington Lock.

5.2 At the lock turn left away from the river. The path emerges on Riverside Dr.

5.5 Cross over the road and continue along path in front crossing Hardwicke Rd and ending at Broughton Ave. Turn right then left up Lock Rd leading into Ham Common.

6.4 Ride along Ham Common for 100m and you will see a straight track leading off to the left. Take this track, crossing Sandy Ln and eventually reaching the back gate of Ham House.

7.2 The track goes around to the right here and then left around the tall garden wall. At the end of the wall the entrance to Ham House is on the left, should you wish to visit. Continue straight on across the field and into the trees until you join the river.

7.7 At the river you will see steps to a small platform by the water and a sign for the foot ferry. Flag the ferry master on the other side who will collect you. (adults £1, children 50p).

7.9 On the other side turn right along the riverbank trail.

9.8 Return to Richmond Bridge.

Looking down from Richmond Bridge towards colourful rowing boats

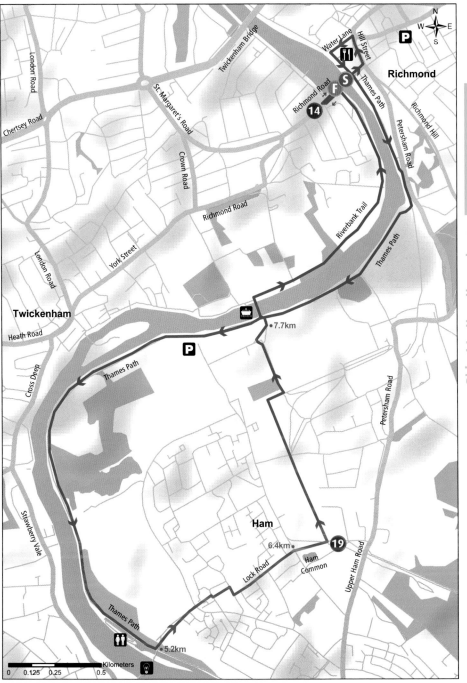

The island of houses in Wimbledon Common, close to The Fox and Grapes pub

At a Glance

Distance 10.6km   **Total Climbing** 32m

Terrain
Mostly off-road on smooth unsurfaced paths, other sections on surfaced roads.

Traffic
Mostly traffic free, some sections of quiet back roads through Alton Estate and there is a busy crossing at Roehampton. You can walk along the pavement for this section if you want.

How to Get There
Wimbledon Train Stations; car parking at the windmill on Wimbledon Common.

Food and Drink
Fox and Grapes on Wimbledon Common, cafés in Wimbledon Village.

Side Trip
Visit Wimbledon Village and the All England Club on Church Road. The ground is home of the Wimbledon Tennis Championships. There is a Lawn Tennis Museum which offers tours of the courts (adult £10, child £5.50).

Links to (other rides) 13, 15.

Bike Hire
Smith Bros on Church Rd, Wimbledon Village, service only

Where to Ride Rating

About...

Wimbledon Common lies in the leafy suburbs of South West London. Affluent Wimbledon Village shares the top of the hill with the 1140 acres of open grass and ancient woodland. The ride takes in several of the gravel bridleways that criss-cross the common, leading to Putney Heath and Richmond Park. Highlights include the Wimbledon Windmill, Richmond Park's deer as well as wooded paths and open spaces that this huge wild area has to offer.

Cycling away from the modernist Alton Estate

The ride starts at the Fox and Grapes pub, one of only a few buildings that create an island of old houses surrounded by common; however only a short distance across grassland are the affluent boutiques and delicatessens of Wimbledon Village.

From the pub a wide cyclepath heads due north to the Wimbledon Windmill, built in 1816 by Charles March. The working sails are now Grade II listed as it is the only example in Britain of a hollow post mill, with the drive to the grinding stones passing directly through the centre of the main post. The windmill is now a museum, detailing its own history, as well as the history of windmills in general (Fri-Sun; 2pm-5pm; £1 adult, 50p children). From here the wide path continues northwards through scrub woodland of twisted dwarf oaks before crossing through a subway under the busy Kingston Road.

On the other side the path emerges in Putney Heath narrowing along a horse ride through the trees before joining the road at Roehampton. Many would argue that the pretty 18th century village was blighted by the construction of the vast modernist Alton Estate. However the 1958 development has been acclaimed for its mix of low and high-rise concrete architecture 'consisting of subtle Scandinavian-influenced vernacular and buildings inspired by the work of French architect Le Corbusier'. Make of it what you will...

On the other side of the estate the route enters Richmond Park through Roehampton Gate. A wide surfaced road, popular with Sunday drivers, cuts through the park as it scales Sawyers Hill. The ride leaves the traffic at the crossroads returning southwards through the centre of the park passing herds of deer grazing under the trees. Along here you'll pass White Lodge, home to the royal Ballet School, before entering Spankers Wood. The shady trees are a great place for a picnic. Once through the woods the ride leaves the park at Robin Hood Gate crossing the busy main road before re-entering Wimbledon Common. Now get your legs into gear for the uphill along off-road tracks back to the Fox and Grapes Pub.

Ride Log

0.0 Left out of Fox and Grapes and then left after 50m on footpath parallel with West Pl.

1.3 At the windmill cross the road and continue straight on along cycle track bearing left down Windmill Rd. At the end the road passes through a subway under Roehampton Ln.

2.2 On the other side continue straight on ignoring turns left and right. At the pond, bear down the left path bringing you out onto Medfield St.

3.0 Turn left to the end and then right along busy Roehampton Ln (Walk and use pedestrian crossing if you feel more comfortable).

3.3 At the lights turn left. The road bears right into Danebury Ave. Keep going through 'No Entry' to the end.

4.6 At the end turn left on Priory Ln, then left into Richmond Park.

4.8 At mini roundabout just inside park go straight on up Sawyers Hill.

5.5 After 700m turn left at mini roundabout.

7.0 After 1.5km when the road comes to a T-junction turn left. After 800m you will reach Robin Hood Gate. At the mini roundabout go straight on down 'No Entry' and exit park.

8.0 Cross very busy Kingston Bypass using bike lights and enter Wimbledon Common on the other side. A dirt track joins Beverley Ln.

8.9 The dirt lane turns left onto Robin Hood Rd and after 1.2km becomes Sunset Rd.

10.6 Back at the Fox and Grapes.

The vast open spaces of Richmond Park

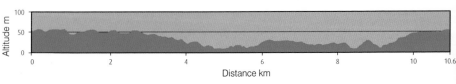

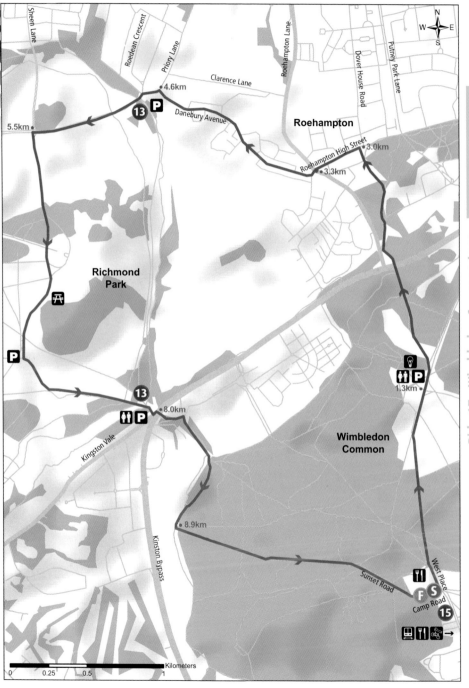

Roehampton

Richmond Park

Wimbledon Common

Sheen Lane

Roedean Crescent

Priory Lane

Clarence Lane

Roehampton Lane

Dover House Road

Putney Park Lane

4.6km

5.5km

Danebury Avenue

Roehampton High Street

3.0km

3.3km

1.3km

8.0km

Kingston Vale

8.9km

Kinston Bypass

Sunset Road

West Place

Camp Road

0   0.25   0.5   Kilometers   1

Commuting through Bushy Park

At a Glance

Distance 8km   **Total Climbing** 18m

Terrain
Surfaced roads, unsurfaced smooth riverside path.

Traffic
Light traffic on quiet back roads, one busier crossing into Bushy Park. No traffic on Thames Path and park sections.

How to Get There
Hampton Court train station. Parking available at Hampton Court Green.

Food and Drink
Cafés around Hampton Court Station and in Hampton.

Side Trip
Instead of taking the ferry why not continue the 32kms to Windsor. This is a full day trip along the Thames Path taking you past houseboats and villas, famous islands and willow lined meadows as well as pretty lock cottages, attractive steeples and ancient waterside inns. You will need to get the train back from Windsor.

Links to (other rides) 12, 19.

Bike Hire
Hampton Court Cycles near the station or Birdie Bikes on Wensleydale Rd in Hampton. Neither rent bikes but both do service.

Where to Ride Rating

About...

A leisurely loop taking in a short section of the Thames Path before crossing the river by ferry to the old village of Hampton. Here quiet residential streets lead to Bushy Hill Park where a cycle track heads back through the meadows to Hampton Court Palace. River sights include houseboats, rowers and barges, while in Bushy Park there are deer, squirrels and beetles. A fun, flat ride for all the family with pretty sights along the way.

A proud stag is un-phased by people and cyclists

South West

Starting at Hampton Court train station the route quickly joins the Thames Path westwards along national Cycle Route 4 which actually ends in Fishguard Wales. Don't worry, you leave the path after about a kilometre at Hurst open space by the foot ferry sign (daily, 10am-6pm or dusk if earlier; adult £1, child 50p). You may have to wave at the driver as his boat is more often moored on the other side. Once off the jetty on the north side a path rejoins the road at pretty Hampton. The small domed building with pillars you see is Garrick's Temple, it was built by the 18th century actor-manager David Garrick in 1756 to celebrate the genius of William Shakespeare. The temple is open to the public on Sundays between April and October. From Hampton the high street weaves up away from the river. The route diverts along quiet affluent residential streets to Bushy Park.

The history of the park is inextricably linked to neighbouring Hampton Court Palace, yet it has always had its own distinct rural character. Red and Fallow Deer still roam freely throughout the park, just as they did when Henry VIII used to hunt here. There are currently about 320 deer and their grazing is essential to maintain the high wildlife value of the park's grasslands. The route passes down Chestnut Avenue, conceived by Sir Christopher Wren as a formal approach to Hampton Court Palace in the reign of William III and Mary II. The road is flanked on both sides by a single row of horse chestnuts and four rows of limes. It marks the park's zenith in terms of royal ambitions and sophistication and its centrepiece is the famous Arethusa 'Diana' Fountain.

Past the fountain the avenue joins busy Hampton Court Road and on the other side is Hampton Court Palace (daily, Oct-Mar 10am-4.30pm, Apr-Sep 10am-6pm; adult £14, child £7), originally built for Cardinal Wolsey, a favourite of King Henry VIII, circa 1514; in 1529. As Wolsey fell from favour, the palace was passed to the King, who enlarged it the following century. William III's massive rebuilding and expansion project, intended to rival Versailles, was begun. Work halted in 1694, leaving the palace in two distinct contrasting architectural styles, domestic Tudor and baroque. The palace houses many works of art and furnishings from the Royal Collection. Finally past the palace the route crosses the Thames again at Hampton Court Bridge to take you back to the station.

Ride Log

0.0 Turn right out of Hampton Court Station and then left onto Bridge Rd leading onto the River Bank Rd. On the right a set of steps take you to the Thames Path.

The Hampton Ferry pier on the north bank of the Thames

1.7 Just over 1.5km along you pass an island on the right and a car park on the left. Just after the island a path leads away from the main Thames trail across the grass to the river bank and the foot ferry departure point. Flag the ferry operator on the other side if necessary.

1.9 Once over the river join the road again and turn right up the High St.

2.2 Take the third left up Ormond Ave and then the first right onto Ormond Cres. Follow the road round until it reaches Ormond Dr and turn right onto Ormond Dr.

3.4 At the end turn right onto busy Uxbridge Rd and then left at the end onto the High St.

3.8 After 250m there is an entrance to Bushy Park on the right. Once in the park follow the avenue bearing right when it joins another cyclepath.

4.3 Continue along here, the road widens slightly then passes a car park before reaching Chestnut Ave.

5.9 Turn right along the avenue. After just under 1km pass around the fountain back onto the avenue until it reaches Hampton Court Rd.

7.2 Turn right along the road following it as it bears left to a roundabout.

7.8 Go straight on passing the front entrance of the palace then cross over the bridge.

8.0 Once you're over the river the station is on your left.

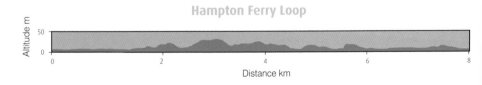

Hampton Ferry Loop

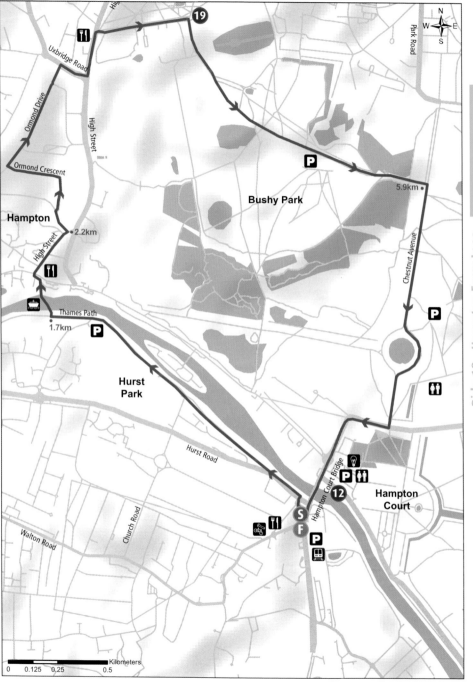

Uxbridge Road

Ormond Drive

High Street

Ormond Crescent

Hampton

High Street

2.2km

Thames Path

1.7km

Hurst Park

Hurst Road

Church Road

Walton Road

Bushy Park

Chestnut Avenue

Park Road

5.9km

Hampton Court Bridge

Hampton Court

N
W E
S

19

12

S
F

Kilometers
0   0.125   0.25   0.5

Neatly stacked competitive rowing boats sit on a trailer by the riverbank

At a Glance

Distance 12.6km   **Total Climbing** 24m

Terrain

Surfaced roads and unsurfaced but smooth riverside path.

Traffic

Light traffic on residential roads. Busier on short section of Teddington High Street, however after the lock the ride is predominantly path or segregated cycleway.

How to Get There

Kingston-Upon-Thames railway station. The next closest two are Hampton Wick and Teddington stations. Multistorey car park at Kingston John Lewis or try for limited spaces in Bushy Park.

Food and Drink

Riverside restaurants in Kingston or The Anglers pub looking over Teddington Lock.

Side Trip

Join Ride 13 and do the Richmond Park Loop. It's an extra 12km with some steep ascents but it is car free and a beautiful ride.

Links to (other rides) 12, 13, 16, 18.

Bike Hire

Bicycle Warehouse 214 Kingston Road or Evans Cycles 48 Richmond Road. Both do service but no rental.

Where to Ride Rating

About...

This circular ride from Kingston-Upon-Thames passes through royal Bushy Park to Teddington Locks using the foot bridge to cross the Thames before continuing on the south side inland to Ham Common. You'll then skirt the edge of Richmond Park beyond before returning to the Thames Path leading down to Kingston. Much of this flat ride is along quiet roads or car free paths with interesting, changing scenery typical of this affluent western London suburb.

Teddington footbridge

South West

Starting at Kingston railway station the route briefly takes in some of the town's shopping areas before crossing the river on Kingston Bridge. On the other side, the road turns northwards through Hampton Wick and into Bushy Park, the second largest of the London Royal Parks, at 445 hectares. The history of the park is inextricably linked to neighbouring Hampton Court Palace but it attracts its own visitors with its fishing and model boating ponds, horse rides and formal plantations of trees and other plants. The park is also a conservation area, home to the herds of both Red and Fallow Deer roaming just as they did when Henry VIII used to hunt here. There are currently about 320 deer and their grazing is essential to maintain the high wildlife value of the park's grasslands.

Once through the park the route weaves around the quiet suburban streets of Teddington before joining the busy high street leading up to the Teddington Locks. Built in 1811 with its weir across the river, this was the first and the biggest of five locks built at the time by the City of London Corporation. It also marks the end of the tidal Thames. The route crosses the two footbridges that pass over the locks. They were built between 1887 and 1889, funded by donations from local residents

and businesses replacing the ferry that gave its name to Ferry Road at Teddington. The western bridge consists of a suspension bridge crossing the weir stream and linking the island to Teddington. The eastern bridge is an iron girder construction crossing the lock and linking the island to Ham on the Surrey bank. From here the route heads away from the river to Ham Common and on to the edge of Richmond Park before turning southwards along quiet wooded lanes to rejoin the Thames Path. Taking the Thames Path southwards the route arrives back at Kingston town centre and the station.

Pleasure boats and houseboats moored on the banks of the Thames

Ride Log

0.0 From Kingston Station follow the cycle path to the right then over the lights at the bike crossing and into the pedestrian area (Wood St). Take the first right and continue along the cycle track on the left side of the main road up and over Kingston Bridge.

0.8 Over the bridge go straight on at the roundabout into Hampton Court Rd, then take the first right into Church Grove.

1.5 After 450m there is an entrance to the park on the left. Go through along the cycle way crossing over Chestnut Ave and continuing westwards for 2km.

4.4 Here the main path bears sharply to the left but you should carry straight on. The path ends at Hampton Rd. Cross over into Kings Rd, then first right down Connaught Rd.

5.5 At the end turn left, then right into Stanley Rd. Take the second left of Stanley Rd into Sutherland Grove bearing right when you reach the T-junction.

6.3 At the end turn right onto Church Rd and then left onto the High street. Cross over the roundabout and continue straight on through Teddington.

7.4 At the lights after the graveyard continue straight on towards the bridge. And then cross over the lock.

7.7 Once over the bridge continue on the path straight on, away from the river.

8.0 The path emerges on Riverside Dr. Cross over the road and continue along path in front crossing Hardwick Rd and ending at Broughton Ave.

8.2 At Broughton Ave turn right then left up Lock Rd leading into Ham Common. Continue on the road around the common crossing over busy Upper Ham Rd into Ham Gate Ave.

9.1 Cycle on the shared use path alongside the road. Take the first right (after about 900m) down Church Rd.

10.4 Bear left on the bend down Latchmere Ln. Continue going straight on over Tudor Dr until Latchmere Ln joins Latchmere Rd.

11.3 Turn right along Latchmere Rd crossing busy Richmond Rd into Bank Ln.

11.9 At the end cross the park to join the Thames Path left (southwards) back to Kingston.

12.6 Turn right back onto the road just before the railway line. At the main road follow the cycleway signs left to get back to the station.

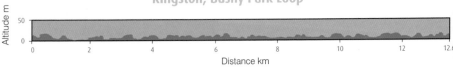

Kingston, Bushy Park Loop

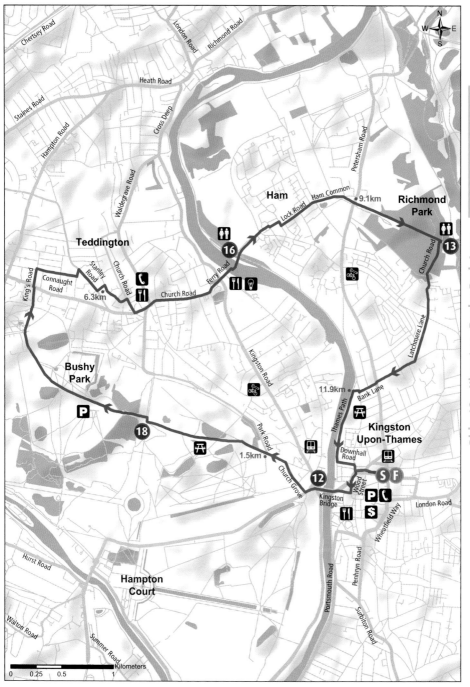

Chersey Road
London Road
Richmond Road
Heath Road
Staines Road
Cross Deep
Hampton Road
Waldegrave Road

Ham

Lock Road
Ham Common
9.1km
Petersham Road

Richmond Park

Teddington

King's Road
Connaught Road
Stanley Road
Church Road
Church Road
6.3km
Ferry Road
Church Road
16
13
Church Road
Latchmere Lane

Bushy Park

Kingston Road
11.9km
Bank Lane
18

Thames Path
Kingston Upon-Thames
Park Road
1.5km
Church Grove
Downhall Road
12
Kingston Bridge
Wood Street
S F
P
S
Wheatfield Way
London Road
Portsmouth Road
Penrhyn Road
Surbiton Road

Hampton Court

Hurst Road
Walton Road
Summer Road

Kilometers
0   0.25   0.5   1

Battersea Thames riverbanks at low tide; houseboats modern flats and an ancient church

At a Glance

Distance 13.9km   **Total Climbing** 29m

Terrain

Surfaced roads.

Traffic

Mostly light traffic however busier section along the embankment. Cycle along shared use pavement on this section.

How to Get There

Battersea Park Station, trains from Victoria, alternatively Putney Bridge tube station on district line or Putney Station trains from Waterloo or Imperial Wharf Overground; parking in Battersea Park.

Food and Drink

La Gondola Al Parco - Battersea Park Café, cafés in Battersea Square and on Putney river front.

Side Trip

On the north east bank of the Albert Bridge are the Chelsea Physic Gardens. This 'secret walled garden' is a centre of education, beauty and relaxation. Founded in 1673 by the Worshipful Society of Apothecaries, it continues to research the properties, origins and conservation of over 5000 plant species (Apr-Oct, Wed-Fri and Sun 12pm-6pm; adult £8, child £5)

Links to (other rides) 15, 42.

Bike Hire

Putney Cycles on Putney Bridge Road, Phoenix Cycles on Battersea Bridge Road. Both offer service no hire.

Where to Ride Rating

About...

From the surreal Peace Pagoda at Battersea Park to Chelsea's Imperial Warf riverside development, the route passes through a multitude of different scenery, from the typical Victorian Fulham terraces around the famous Hurlingam Club to the rowing boats at Putney and the runners in Wandsworth Park. The ride then heads west along roads close to the north side of the Thames before returning back along the south bank, mostly along the Thames Path through Wandsworth and Battersea.

Putney Bridge

Starting at Battersea Park Station in the shadow of the iconic chimneys of the Power Station the route skirts around the outside of beautifully kept and extensive Battersea Park, passing the magnificent Peace Pagoda looking across the Thames to Chelsea. The route crosses the pink Albert Bridge and continues past the barges and houseboats moored off Chelsea embankment before going past the regeneration area of Chelsea's Imperial Wharf, once an area of industry now an on going building site of apartments and design related businesses overlooking the Thames.

The route leaves the river weaving through the neat Victorian terraces around Fulham passing around the famous Hurlingham Club, a grand private members sports and social club with quintessentially English traditions and heritage, and on to Putney Bridge tube station.

From here the route crosses back to the south side of the river over Putney Bridge, instantly recognisable by its lanterns as the starting point of the annual Oxford versus Cambridge boat race. The route swings back eastwards in front of the new restaurants and cafes next to Putney Wharf tower before crossing Wandsworth Park beneath a parade of mature London Plane trees

popular with joggers. On the other side the modern flats of Prospect Quay back onto an industrial park of storage units and small factories near the mouth of the River Wandle where it meets the Thames. Here the ride crosses the Wandle River behind the old Young's Brewery. The narrow creek has seen better days, an upturned ship lies in the mud beneath disused pipes. The path becomes Smugglers Way and more new apartments, shops and DIY centres passing the Ship Inn, a good pub with plenty of outdoor seating making the most of the sunsets and river views.

The route continues to Battersea High Street and the pretty Battersea town square where cafes and restaurants spill out onto the cobbles beneath the trees. The path rejoins the river path by Battersea Church where old houseboats lie at juxtaposition with iconic glass apartments of the Rodgers Montevetro building. From here enjoy the waterfront ride back to Battersea Park.

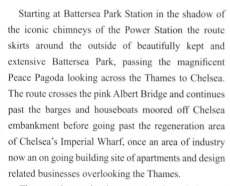

Ride Log

0.0 Starting at Battersea Park Station, cross the roundabout and enter the park. Head northwards along East Carriage Dr turning left at the end into The Parade.

1.7 On exiting the park turn right and over the Albert Bridge. Once over the bridge turn left onto the shared use pavement and continue for 1km until the main road leaves the embankment.

3.0 At this point turn left down Lots Rd.

3.4 At the end of the road turn left. The road goes down under Imperial Wharf Station and through a barrier and over a roundabout.

4.0 Continue over two further roundabouts then keep your eyes peeled for a right turn into Glenrosa St (third right after roundabout).

4.5 At the end of Glenrosa St turn left down Stephendale Rd. Continue across busy Wandsworth Bridge Rd into Hugon Rd.

5.3 At the end turn right then left into Sulivan Rd and at the end turn right into Broomhouse Ln.

6.3 At the end turn left down Hurlingham Rd and then first left after the park down Napier Rd.

6.9 At the end of Napier turn right down Ranelagh Gardens. Go past the tube station and then turn right up Fulham High St. Here you get to busy Putney Bridge.

7.3 Cross the bridge and just after the church there is a left into a pedestrian precinct. Take this and follow the Thames Path round into Deodar Rd and through a new development into Wandsworth Park.

8.9 On the other side of the park continue along the path to Prospect Quay where the path leaves the Thames down Point Pleasant. After 100m turn left under an arch in a modern white building. This brings you onto Osiers Rd. Then it's first left into Enterprise Way industrial park. At the end a pedestrian footbridge takes you over the River Wandle and into Smugglers Way.

9.7 Rejoin the Thames Path at the new apartments and continue along until it leaves the river again behind the Ship Inn.

10.3 Cross over Wandsworth Bridge Rd using the pedestrian lights and re-join the Thames Path. The path leaves the river at Bridges St and passes behind a Heliport and onto Lombard Rd.

11.6 Turn left onto Lombard Rd and take the second right down Gwynee Rd and first left down Battersea High St.

12.6 Cross over busy Westbridge Rd into Battersea Church Rd turning left at the church to rejoin the Thames. Continue along the waterfront back to Battersea Park.

13.6 At the park turn right down Albert Bridge Rd to the entrance. Cycle through the park back to the station.

13.9 Arriving back at the station completes the loop.

Battersea to Fulham Loop

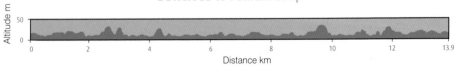

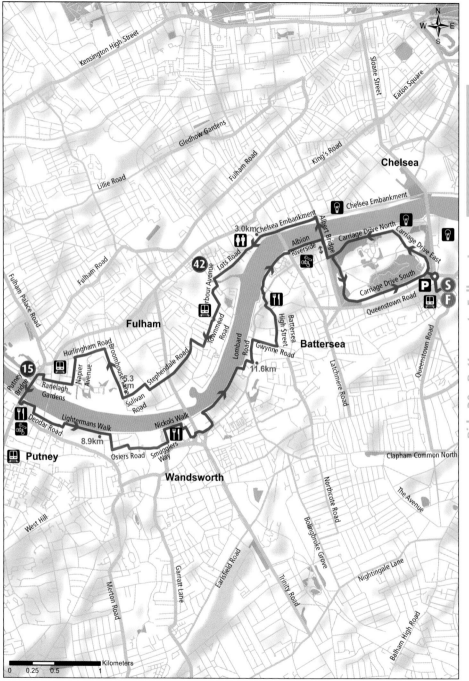

Chelsea

Chelsea Embankment

3.0km Chelsea Embankment

Albion
Riverside

Albert Bridge

Carriage Drive North

Carriage Drive East

42

rbour Avenue

Lots Road

Townmead
Road

Carriage Drive South

Queenstown Road

Fulham

Fulham Road

Lillie Road

Gledhow Gardens

Kensington High Street

Sloane Street

Eaton Square

King's Road

Fulham Road

Fulham Road

Hurlingham Road

Napier
Avenue

Broomhouse Lane

5.3
km

Stephendale Road

Sulivan
Road

Lombard
Road

Battersea
High Street

Gwynne Road

Battersea

11.6km

Latchmere Road

Queenstown Road

15

Putney
Bridge

Ranelagh
Gardens

Fulham Palace Road

Lightermans Walk

Deodar Road

Nickols Walk

8.9km

Osiers Road

Smugglers
Way

Putney

Wandsworth

Clapham Common North

West Hill

Merton Road

Garratt Lane

Earlsfield Road

Trinity Road

Northcote Road

Bolingbroke Grove

Nightingale Lane

The Avenue

Belham High Road

Kilometers

0   0.25   0.5   1

South East London

This underrated corner of the capital is poorly served by public transport but is easily accessible by bike. Familiar sights on the tourist trail are the Southbank, Shakespeare's Globe and the Tate Modern while east of Tower Bridge beyond the warehouses and disused dockyards of Rotherhithe lies Greenwich. Here the river widens as it reaches for the sea. Inland southeast London seems to continue forever, a patchwork of Victorian terraces rolling over gravel ridges to the North Downs.

Aside from the bustling Southbank, it is Greenwich's maritime associations that draw the crowds. The Cutty Sark and the Old Naval College are well worthy of their attention, however the region has even more to offer off the beaten track. Travelling east, along the Thames Path, past the white canopy of the O2 and the sleek reflective domes of the Thames flood barrier are the old artillery barracks at Woolwich and beyond lie the Thames salt marshes. Inland, the exposed grassy expanse of Blackheath provides a great spot for kite flying with views from the royal observatory back towards the city. Just west a trail follows the Ravensbourne River inland towards the heights of Crystal Palace. At the foot of the hill is pretty Dulwich Village, a collection of affluent 18th century mansions still surrounded by parks and open ground. North of Dulwich are the ethnic districts of Camberwell and Peckham where open shops and colourful food markets sell fruit and veg from all over the world. South of Dulwich lie the suburbs of Beckenham, Bromley and Biggin Hill, here suburban streets give way to farm lanes and quiet bridleways.

The nine rides in this chapter range from challenging mountain bike tracks in the countryside to sedate riverside paths. Rides 23 and 27 have sights galore and Rides 22 and 24 get away from it all. What might first appear mundane is in fact full of surprises and delight.

Southern entrance to the Greenwich foot tunnel

The path from Beckenham Place through the park towards Ravensbourne

At a Glance

Distance 34.9km   **Total Climbing** 138m

Terrain

Quiet suburban roads, parkland roads and surfaced paths, with occasional sections through gravel paths.

Traffic

Light traffic on residential streets and traffic free cyclepaths.

How to Get There

Kent House Station, regular trains from Victoria. Other stations on the circuit include New Beckenham, Ravensbourne, Bickley, Petts Wood and Eden Park. Parking on suburban streets. There is also car park at Beckenham Place Golf Club.

Food and Drink

Lots of places enroute to enjoy a good picnic. One of the better pubs is the Bickley Gastro Pub, Southborough Road.

Side Trip

Crystal Palace Park is just west of Kent House Station. The park contains the foundations of the original Crystal Palace, a cast iron and glass building originally erected in Hyde Park for the 1851 Great Exhibition but later moved to the park before burning down in 1936.

Links to (other rides) 24, 25.

Bike Hire

SE20 Cycles, 160 Maple Road near Kent House Station; Bigfoot Bikes 50 Hayes Street.

Where to Ride Rating

About...

Bromley is the largest of London's 33 boroughs, on the fringes of Greater London. It's classic suburbia, with pleasant parks, broad streets and low-density housing all making for a relaxed ride with little traffic. Mingle among the checked-trouser golfers in Beckenham Place Park or watch the patient locals fishing in Norwood Country Park. At nearly 35km, this is one of the longer rides, but as a near figure of eight, it neatly cuts into two loops if you want to do it over a weekend.

Starting at Kent House Station the route passes through Cator Park to New Beckenham and on to Beckenham Place Park. The Georgian mansion was built in 1773 by John Cator and is surrounded by more than 200 acres of open space including ancient woodland, grass/meadow areas and a public golf course. The route follows the capital Green Chain ring to Ravensbourne then through suburban Shortlands to the green recreational space of Norman Park. Beyond this, Jubilee Country Park leads to Petts Wood. The small area of trees is managed by the National Trust and has oak, birch, rowan, alder, ash, hornbeam and sweet chestnut amongst its species of native trees. On the other side the route goes through Orpington's 20th century Metro land suburbs before crossing Holwood Park on a pretty bridleway where you may encounter equestrians. There is then a short but adventurous section through Poulters Wood where a maze of forest tracks crisscross the upper Ravensbourne stream. On the other side is a short section of busier road to the suburb of Hayes and on to Langley Park sports centre and golf course.

The next big area of green is South Norwood Country Park bisected by the Croydon Tram. During the blitz much of the rubble around Croydon was piled in the park to form what is now the large hill with views on a clear day across to the Docklands, Shirley Hills, and Crystal Palace.

Ride Log

0.0 Leave Kent House Station along Station Approach, and right on to Kings Hall Rd.

0.3 Turn left along cyclepath into Cator Park (blue sign Beckenham Rd tram stop). In the park take the left-hand shared use path.

0.8 Turn right on to Lennard Rd, blue signpost Beckenham/Bromley.

1.1 At Beckenham Station dismount and continue under the railway line. Once through the station turn left up Coper's Cope Rd.

1.9 Cross the main road into Greycot Rd then right into Braeside.

2.7 At the end cross over busy Southend Rd bearing left into Beckenham Place Park.

2.9 At the columned clubhouse, turn left through the car park, and then immediately right, signposted Green Chain Walk. At junction of tracks bear right following yellow arrows. At the next junction of paths bear left following Green Chain Walk to Ravensbourne Station.

5.7 After passing through fields, exit park turning right onto Crab Tree Hill Rd then bear left onto Downs Hill. Turn right onto Downsbridge Rd. At the end cross the busy Bromley Rd into Scott's Ln.

7.1 Take the fourth left down Shortlands Grove. At the end turn right into Shortlands Rd and then first left into Den Rd. This becomes South Hill Rd. At the end turn right onto Westmoreland Rd and immediately left into Broad Oaks Way.

9.1 At the end turn left into Barnhill Ave then at the end of this right on Cornford Cl. The road bends to the left and after 100m there is a break in the wall on the right allowing you to squeeze your bike through to Bourne Vale.

9.8 Turn left onto Mead Way and then cross over the mini roundabout into Norman Park.

11.0 Once through the park turn left onto busy Bromley Common Rd then right into Walpole Rd. At the end continue straight on through the recreation ground. Keep right of the football pitch and turn left before the row of houses.

12.3 Turn right into Southlands Rd, cross over mini

Ride Log

roundabout then take the second left up Georges Rd then after 200m left into Hawthorn Rd.

13.6 At the mini roundabout turn right then immediately left into Thornet Wood Rd. Continue to the end and then go along the cyclepath through Jubilee Country Park. Follow signs Petts Wood / Orpington.

14.9 Exit park left into Crestview Dr. Continue along Queensway past Petts Wood Station. Pass over roundabout and take first right down Jersey Dr. At the end cross over the road into a cyclepath through Petts Wood.

17.4 Exit into Ormand Ave, turn left into Crofton Rd, then right after the church into Oakwood Rd. At the end turn right down Lovibonds Ave.

18.8 At the end turn right then left into Hilda Vale Rd. At the end cross the main road into a bridleway signposted London Cycle Network.

20.1 At the end turn right along busy Westerham Rd then immediately left into Rolinson Way. Bear right down Swires Shaw. Pass through the black gate and take forest track to the right (northwards). Just before third wooden footbridge turn right and follow stream. Turn left across stream on wooden footbridge then immediately right. Turn left before wider footbridge.

22.0 The path meets Commonside Rd. Turn right, then left along busy Croydon Rd then first right down Five Elms Rd. At the end bear right along busy Baston Rd.

23.6 After 1km turn left into West Common Rd and then right into Ridgeway and right again into The Knoll.

24.3 At the end go straight over the crossroads following Husseywell Cres left just after the park, then take second right down Stuart Ave. At the end turn left into Chatham Ave and at the end of Chatham turn left again into Mounthurst Rd.

25.0 At the end of Mounthurst turn left then right along Pickhurst Ln then left again down Pickhurst Rise.

27.5 At the end turn right into Red Lodge Rd where pavement becomes shared use path. Go left at roundabout into Hawksbrook Ln.

29.4 Once through the sports ground cross into Upper Elmer's End Rd using shared use pavement under railway bridge. Then turn left into Monks Way and right into Eden Way. Turn right into Lodge Gardens then left along busier Elmers End Rd and left again down Altyre Way.

31.2 Left into Orchard Way and after 600m right into Orchard Grove. At the end turn left then right into Woodmere Ave.

33.1 Take fifth right up Gladeside and at the end cross over the busy road into South Norwood Country Park. Cross the tramline and continue straight on before bearing right through the golf course.

33.8 Exit left on Busy Elmers End Rd then turn right along Beck Ln. At the end of Beck Ln turn left and then right back to Kent House Station.

34.9 This completes the loop.

Bromley, Beckenham Loop

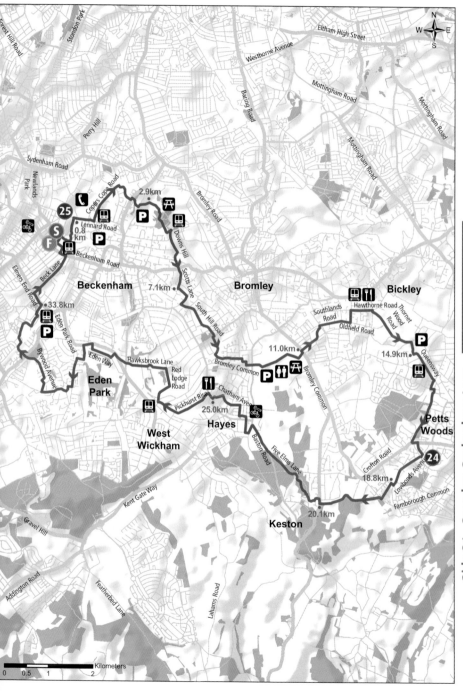

Ride 21 - Bromley, Beckenham Loop

Sustrans trail through the Salt Marshes

At a Glance

Distance 18.4km   **Total Climbing** 22m

Terrain

Flat coastal path. Mostly surfaced but the final 3km are dusty gravel.

Traffic

Almost all traffic free cyclepath however there is a short 1.5km section on mediumly busy roads through Erith.

How to Get There

Starting in the west the closest station is Woolwich Arsenal Station. In the east is Slade Green Station. A train runs between the two to make the loop. Street parking around Slade Green. Two hours free parking at Morrison's in Thamesmead. Parking by the Waterfront Leisure centre in Woolwich.

Food and Drink

The first McDonalds in the UK opened in Woolwich in 1974, sadly the area's cuisine has not evolved since. There are a few run down pubs along the route, however there are some great spots for picnics and supermarkets where you can stock up on goodies.

Side Trip

Continue 5km on from Slade Green to the enormous Bluewater retail park for a shopping fix.

Links to (other rides) 23, 28, 44, 50.

Bike Hire

The closest cycle hire shop is Greenwich Cycle Hire at 95 Old Woolwich Road. For service only try Harry Perry Cycles, Unit 6, 88-104 Powis Street.

Where to Ride Rating

About...

A flat traffic free ride along the lower reaches of the Thames as it leaves London towards the sea. As the river gets wider industry is left behind and weather beaten barren scrub seems to go on for miles punctuated by the odd passing container ship. Towards the end of the ride the Dartford crossing looms on the horizon marking the edge of London's orbital motorway and the sea beyond.

Colourful fishing ropes on the quay

Starting at the Woolwich Ferry, and the lesser-known Woolwich foot tunnel, the route joins the Thames Path passing the defunct Woolwich Dockyard and the Royal Arsenal, dating back to 1471. The town still retains an army base at the Royal Artillery Barracks on the hill but the Royal Arsenal scaled back operations and finally closed in 1994. The area carried out armaments manufacture, ammunition proofing and explosives research and the Royal Artillery Museum, Firepower (Wed-Sun, 10.30am-5pm; adult £5, child £2.50), was set up to preserve Royal Artillery's history. The museum has large collections of historic and modern weapons, home to interesting exhibitions on the area's illustrious history. Fittingly the Woolwich Barracks are due to host the shooting events during the London 2012 Olympics. As part of the regeneration of the area there are new apartments, a Thames Clipper service to central London, a reinvigorated Woolwich market and an interesting sculpture of iron figures by Peter Burke.

Beyond the Arsenal the houses of Thamesmead begin to disappear behind the scrub. The Crossness Engines Museum, built as a sewage pumping station in 1865 is not yet open, but visits to the beautiful Grade 1 Listed building can be arranged through www.crossness.org.uk. From here the route passes an industrial area where aggregate for building is transferred along overhanging lattice iron bridges to huge vessels berthed on jetties precariously reaching into the estuary.

Further along the trail are the space-age looking incinerators of Crossness where dried sewage is burned to make electricity. On the opposite bank you can just see Creekmouth and the graceful wind turbines used to power the giant Ford motorcar plant at Dagenham. The Thames Path leaves the river through Erith before rejoining a new Sustrans trail, past Erith Yacht Club through wild salt marshes in the shadow of the Dartford crossing before winding up the River Darent to Slade Green Station and trains back to Woolwich.

Ride 22 - Docks to Salt Marshes Trail

Ride Log

0.0 From the Woolwich Ferry turn left along the Thames Path keeping the river on your left. Continue along the Thames Path for 10km.

10.0 When the path leaves the Thames turn left along West St and then at the roundabout straight on along Erith High St.

11.6 As the road goes up a hill turn left down Wharf Side towards Morrison's supermarket. Go straight on at the roundabout and at the end of the road go left rejoining the Thames Path.

11.9 After a few hundred metres the path leaves the river again. Continue to follow signs for national 'Cycle Route 1' left along shared cycleway next to Manor Rd.

12.6 After 700m turn left past Erith Yacht Club onto the Sustrans trail. Continue along the trail as it bears right away from the Thames up the River Darent.

15.9 One kilometre after the flood barrier take the right turn past pretty Hobury Farm surrounded by a moat. Join Moat Ln and continue straight on to the station.

18.4 Slade Station is the end of the route. You can catch a train from here back to Woolwich.

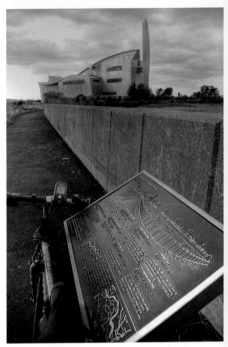

The modern Crossness incinerator burning sewage to make electricity

Docks to Salt Marshes Trail

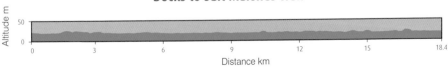

Altitude m

Distance km

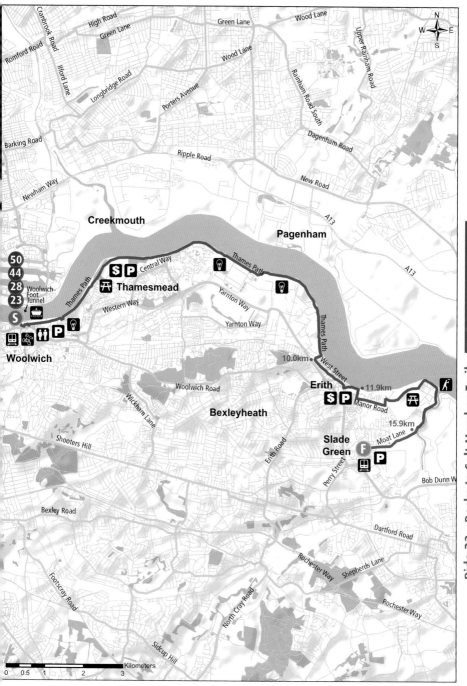

Peter Burke Assembly sculpture at Woolwich Arsenal

At a Glance

Distance 8.2km   **Total Climbing** 33m

Terrain

Surfaced paths and surfaced roads.

Traffic

Mostly traffic free. Sections on quiet residential streets in Greenwich. Be aware of some HGVs accessing the industry on the Greenwich peninsular.

How to Get There

Trains to Greenwich Station and boats to Greenwich Pier. If doing the route in reverse trains to Woolwich Arsenal Station and boats to Woolwich Pier.

Food and Drink

Many restaurants in Greenwich and food stalls in Greenwich market. Chain restaurants inside the O2 Arena.

Side Trip

Visit Greenwich Park and the Observatory for views back towards the skyscrapers of Canary Wharf.

Links to (other rides) 22, 25, 29, 44, 50.

Bike Hire

Greenwich Cycle Hire at 95 Old Woolwich Road.

Where to Ride Rating

About...

Taking in some of London's most iconic buildings this ride starts at Maritime Greenwich before passing through quiet Victorian terraces then emerging into industrial North Greenwich dominated by the O2 Arena. Across the peninsular the route joins the Thames Path with views back towards the Docklands. Ahead you'll see the sleek silver domes of the Thames Barrier and the odd sight of a laden Woolwich car ferry crossing the wide river.

The sleek silver domes of the Thames flood barrier

Starting in the centre of Unesco World Heritage Greenwich the route leaves the indoor market for the waterfront. Here the Tea Clipper Cutty Sark (due to re-open after refurbishment in 2011) lies in a dry lock next to Sir Christopher Wren's Old Royal Navel College now part of the University of Greenwich. Highlights include the Painted Hall and Chapel which are open to the public to marvel at. From here the ride goes along Victorian back streets emerging on a nasty busy stretch of congested motorway leading to the Blackwall tunnel. Fear not, there is a segregated cycleway but the loud cars and acrid smells of nearby factories are not pleasant.

At this point there are two choices. The longer route passes around the North Greenwich peninsular on the Thames Path passing in front of the giant white canvas of Millennium Dome built to celebrate Greenwich position on the Meridian for the year 2000. The Dome was later turned into The O2, an entertainment complex of cinemas, restaurants and at its centre a large arena used for music concerts and sports amongst other things. The shorter route takes you on a footbridge across the motorway and alongside the Greenwich Millennium Village, a regeneration project

of colourful eco built apartments and an ecology park. Here it rejoins the Thames Path and the other route.

The ride passes futuristic Greenwich Yacht Club and Christies Wharf where aggregate passes on conveyors overhead into large ships. Ahead is the Thames Barrier. Between each of the shimmering beaten metal structures is plate that can be swung round preventing London from flooding during spring tides. There is a visitors centre (daily 10am-4pm; adult £2, child £1) on site which explains the engineering and function. The Thames Path ends here so the route heads inland along roads before returning to the riverbank near the Woolwich car ferry.

Ride Log

0.0 Facing away from the Greenwich Foot Tunnel entrance turn left (river on your left) onto the shared use path through the old Royal Naval College. At the end exit through the car park right onto Park Row.

0.6 Take the first left down Old Woolwich. At the end turn left down Lassell St and at the end right. This road bears into Pelton Rd.

The blue tiles of North Greenwich tube station

1.2 Take the third left down Christchurch Way. At the end turn right along Mauritius Rd and left along Blackwall Ln then second left along Tunnel Ave. There should be a segregated cyclepath but be careful of lorries as they often park on it.

2.7 At the end continue up on cycleway to the motorway.

2.8 For route one (shorter version) cross the footbridge and turn left on Boord St crossing onto cycleway straight ahead at the end rejoining Thames Path. For route two (longer version) turn left and join Thames Path all the way around the peninsular.

3.2 The two routes rejoin at the Thames Path just south of the QEII pier. From here continue along Thames Path to Thames Barrier.

5.4 Just past the barrier follow the cycleway away from the river and turn left onto Woolwich Rd.

6.5 At the big roundabout turn left down Ruston Rd and left again at the end to rejoin the Thames Path.

7.1 Continue along Thames Path to the Woolwich Ferry.

8.2 The ferry is the end of the route. To return to Greenwich you can take a riverboat from the Woolwich Pier or easier is a train from Woolwich Arsenal Station. Alternatively, cycle back along Rides 44 or 50.

Greenwich to Woolwich Trail

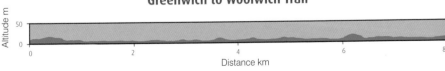

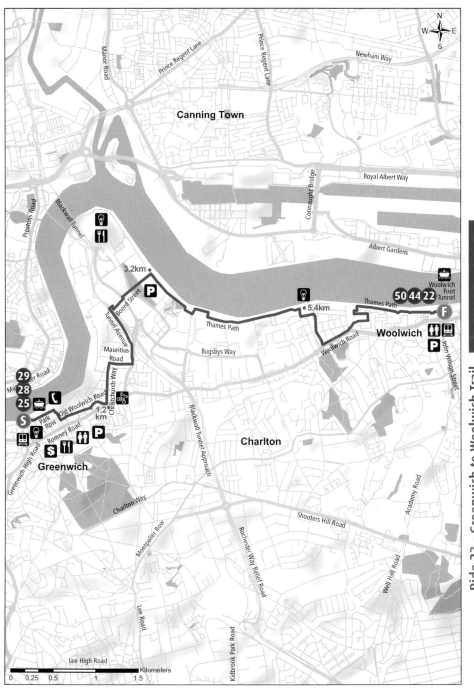

Ride 23 - Greenwich to Woolwich Trail

Biggin Hill Loop

Houses near the church in the pretty village of Cudham

At a Glance

Distance 32km **Total Climbing** 304m

Terrain
Rough MTB tracks and bridleways. Short sections on surfaced country lanes and residential roads. Mountian bike essential.

Traffic
Mostly car free with short sections of quiet country lanes. However be aware of horses on bridleways and of fast moving cars on roads.

How to Get There
Orpington Station trains from Victoria, Charing Cross and Cannon Street; pay car park at Orpington Station, free parking along the residential streets along the start of the route.

Food and Drink
Blacksmith's Arms in Cudham or the White Bear in Fickleshole are both charming old style country pubs with beer gardens adorned with geraniums.

Side Trip
Ride 21 will link this ride with other routes in the guide.

Links to (other rides) 21.

Bike Hire
No cycle hire but for service try Cycles UK Orpington, 247 High Street.

Where to Ride Rating

About...

One of the most challenging rides in the guide. This is a hilly mountain bike trail up and down the often muddy trails of the North Downs. The summits have views of the surrounding rich verdant fields and countryside beyond while in the dips are forests, streams and abundant wildlife including deer, pheasants and squirrels. The circular route takes in pretty villages and quiet, rural farm tracks, bridleways and lanes. But don't get too relaxed, the steep climbs and descents need skill and stamina and the right sort of bike.

A typical forest bridleway

Starting at Orpington Station the route snakes around suburban roads joining the busy A21 at the Green Shire Lane. A shared use path goes alongside the busy road to the easily missed Snag Lane bridleway that gently climbs through woods and across open fields to Snag Farm. Here the route drops away before climbing out of one valley then another.

Close to the bottom of the second valley the route climbs steeply southwards to Mace Farm before rising again more gently across the field to the pretty village of Cudham with its old Church of St. Peter and St. Paul with original parish registers going back to 1653. The route passes the village pub, the Blacksmith's Arms, before dropping away steeply down Newbarn Lane. The lane then climbs relentlessly to Hawley's Corner before climbing again more gently now along beautiful Chestnut Avenue, lined with its namesake trees, to Little Betsoms Farm. At 245m this is the highest point on the ride. From here it is a cruisey undulating route along the top of the North Downs with far reaching views across the Surrey and Sussex countryside.

The ride turns off along Approach Road past Beaver Water World (daily, 10am-5pm; adult £4, child £3), home to Canadian beavers, deer, owls, parrots and a reptile house, and down through a corner of Tatsfield. From here a bridleway turns off Lusted Hall Lane climbing again gently before falling very steeply into a valley.

The climb out the other side is as steep again reaching Beddlestead Road and on to Beddlestead House. Here the ride joins another bridleway where the path again falls off very steeply, climbing on the other side up to Chelsham Court Farm. From here a gentle country lane winds to the village of Fickleshole with a pretty pub, the White Bear. Beyond here a long section of off-road biking goes down Highams Hill and back up the other side to Jackass Lane and on to Keston. Here at the busy A233 a cyclepath goes across the back of suburban streets through Ninehams Wood before a series of suburban roads wind back up to Orpington Station.

Ride Log

0.0 Turn right out of the station down the Approach Rd. At the bottom turn left then first right down Tubbenden Ln. Fourth left down Southcroft Rd then right down Roseberry Gardens. Then right down Lemington Ave, at the end left down Borkwood Way and first right down Harley Gardens. At the end left again and then third left onto Haywood Rise leading to Crescent Way.

2.3 On the main road turn right and then right again down Shire Ln. Continue along path popping out at the roundabout, turn left along main road using shared cycleway pavement. Continue straight over next roundabout and after 200m on the right is a concealed entrance to Snag Ln bridleway, continue for 3km.

5.5 Pass farm and turn left continuing on bridleway down hill into woods, up other side and down again. At the bottom take path right (southwards) past Mace Farm.

7.5 Five hundred metres after the farm take footpath on the left through playing fields to Cudham. Join the road left and then take first right down Barn Ln. Continue down and up for several kilometres to Hawley's Corner junction. Go straight across down Chestnut Ave track.

12.7 The lane becomes a road before joining Clarks Ln. The traffic goes surprisingly fast here so be careful as you turn right. Continue along the busy road for 1km before turning right down Approach Rd signposted Tatsfield. After another kilometre the route turns left down Lusted Hall Ln.

16.4 On the bend as you go up the hill there is a bridleway leading off across the fields. Down and then up the other side the path emerges on a small lane, turn right. At the crossroads go straight on to Fickleshole.

22.0 As the road bears right through the village go straight on at the junction. Shortly afterwards there is a cycleway sign left. Take this along a disused road before it rejoins the lane. At the T-junction continue straight on into the farm. Past the farm the bridleway goes through fields then into a wood. The track bears left and reaches a road. Cross over road onto Highams Hill cyclepath. Ignore paths left and right and continue straight on emerging at Blackness Ln.

26.0 Here turn left and left again onto Jackass Ln. At the first junction bear right onto Fox Ln and at the roundabout right onto Heathfield Rd. After 400m turn left onto Fishponds Rd that runs along side a green.

28.4 At the end turn left and using the pavement go along busy Westerham Rd. After 200m there is a path on the left between the edge of Holwood Park and back gardens.

30.0 At the end of this turn right then left up Hilda Vale Rd. At the end of Hilda Vale turn right then left up Lovibonds. At roundabout turn right onto Crofton then left into Rusland. At the end turn right then left down Pound Court Dr bringing you out onto busy Croft Rd. Turn right and use the pavement to cycle back to the station.

32.0 This completes the loop.

Biggin Hill Loop

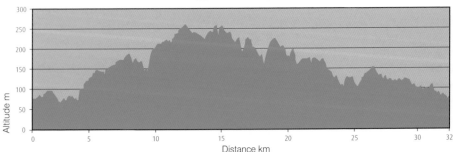

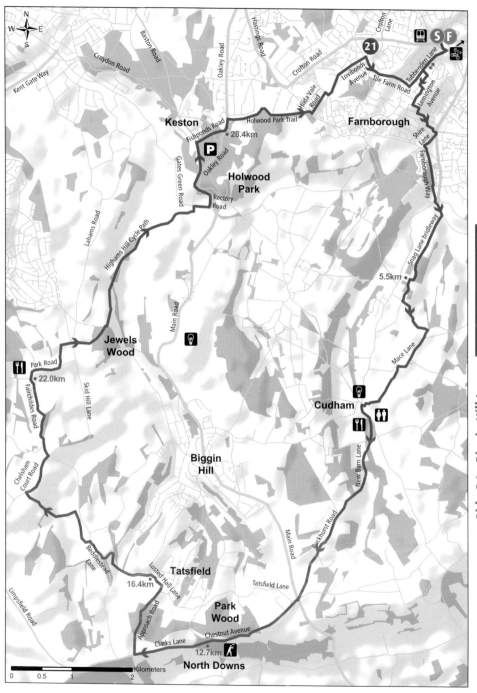

Fresh fish at Lewisham market

At a Glance

Distance 14.5km **Total Climbing** 29m

Terrain
Suburban surfaced roads and surfaced riverside trail. Short section of gravel path.

Traffic
Mostly car free though some sections on quiet residential roads and route crosses some busier high streets.

How to Get There
Crystal Palace Overground Station. If doing route in reverse Greenwich Train Station. Parking in Crystal Palace Park.

Food and Drink
Many restaurants in Greenwich, also try the indoor food stalls at Greenwich market.

Side Trip
Visit Greenwich Park and the Royal Observatory for views northwards towards the Canary Wharf skyscrapers.

Links to (other rides) 21, 23, 27, 28, 29.

Bike Hire
For hire try Greenwich Cycle Hire at 95 Old Woolwich Road; for service only try Compton Cycles, 25 Catford Hill.

Where to Ride Rating

About...

Starting at the top of Crystal Palace and finishing on the banks of the Thames this largely downhill ride courses along the route of the River Ravensbourne northwards through nature reserves, playing fields and handsome backstreets to its mouth at Deptford Creek. This green, road bike route has plenty of interesting sights as it weaves quietly through regenerating east London.

Parked bikes near Deptford DLR

South East

The ride starts at the site of the Crystal Palace, once an impressive cast-iron and glass building, now just the foundations remain. Originally erected in Hyde Park to house the Great Exhibition of 1851, the building was moved to a new park giving the name to the area. Sadly the structure burnt down in 1936. The park, gardens and foundations remain along with headless statues and giant sphinx. The route crosses down through the park past the Crystal Palace National Sports Centre where an athletics stadium, a 50 metre swimming pool and other sports facilities were developed for Sport England. Once out of the park the route crosses Penge and New Beckenham suburbs before joining the course of the River Ravensbourne through playing fields and an industrial estate. On the other side is Riverview Walk, a pretty, new cycleway running alongside the babbling brook.

From here the ride turns greener as it heads northwards through Ladywell Fields nature reserve. The route continues along the river as it passes through Catford. Catford derives its name from the place where cattle crossed the River Ravensbourne in Saxon times but now the area has been scared with brutal 60's architecture and heavy traffic. However, the route

passes away from this towards Lewisham, the seat of the borough with extensive shopping.

Beyond Lewisham the ride continues along the path of the Dockland Light Railway. The extension was recently built following the course of the river through Brookmill Park. Here a new bend in the river was constructed to give more natural banks creating a better habitat for flora and fauna. The river emerges at Deptford Creek where in 1580 Queen Elizabeth I knighted Francis Drake on board the Golden Hind upon his return of circumnavigating the globe. The Golden Hind remained moored in the creek until it broke up.

Further along the Thames Path is Greenwich and the route ends at the world famous Cutty Sark clipper ship. Built in 1869, she served as a merchant vessel (the last clipper to be built for that purpose), and then as a training ship until being put on public display in 1954. Preserved in dry dock, the ship was badly damaged in a fire in 2007 while undergoing extensive restoration. The ship will be reopened in Spring 2011.

Ride Log

0.0 Starting at the top of Crystal Palace Park weave down through the park eastwards at the bottom exit onto High St. Pass under the railway and take fourth left, just before church, up St Johns Rd, then second right along Queen Adelaide Rd.

3.0 At crossroads turn left onto Penge Ln under railway and right onto Parish Ln. Take fourth left up Tennyson Rd and at the end turn right onto Lennard Rd.

4.4 Cross over mini roundabout and when you see Cator Park on right be ready to turn left onto cyclepath by blue cycle signs.

5.0 Towards the end of the cyclepath turn right into industrial estate. Beware of lorries. Turn right after a kilometre, following blue cycle sign to Lower Sydenham Station. Turn left at station down path emerging on Fambridge Cl. Turn right and cross Stanton Way into Riverview Walk.

6.0 The trail continues to Catford coming out at a retail park; continue left through the car park and then pass under Catford Rd in tunnel emerging on Adenmore Rd. Continue to end of road. Towards the end before the car park, turn left under railway line and over river. Bear right along the river.

8.3 The path crosses back over the river and under the railway following the bank to another elaborate cycle bridge of another railway. Turn left here back over the river and continue along the path to the right of the

playing fields. The path ends at Ladywell Rd.

9.9 Turn left over railway then first right along Algernon Rd. As the road forks continue right along Algernon and then first right along Marsala. At the end of Marsala St turn right, under railway, along Elmira St. At the end turn right then left onto Thurston Rd.

11.4 At end of cycle contra flow turn right through cycle tunnel under railway marked Cycle Route 21.

11.7 Cycle straight on to the river and turn left. When you reach Elverson Rd DLR ride along footway and follow route 21 signs straight on. Cross the end over Elverson Rd into Brookmill Park.

12.0 Stay on left bank of river and bear left through park. At the end bear right crossing over the river to arrive at Deptford Bridge DLR. Cross over main road at cycle lights and turn left along green cycleway. At junction follow cycleway around to the right and continue. At the end of the cycleway at the roundabout turn right down Creekside.

12.6 Just before the main road, turn right down Copperas St. At the end use bike lights to cross and turn right along shared use pavement next to Creek Rd.

14.2 Once over bridge turn left down Norway Rd and at the end turn right then first left to bring you to the Thames Path. Go along Thames Path to Cutty Sark and the end of the ride.

14.5 You have reached your destination.

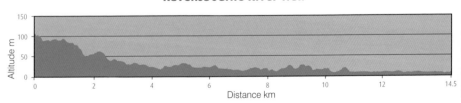

Ravensbourne River Trail

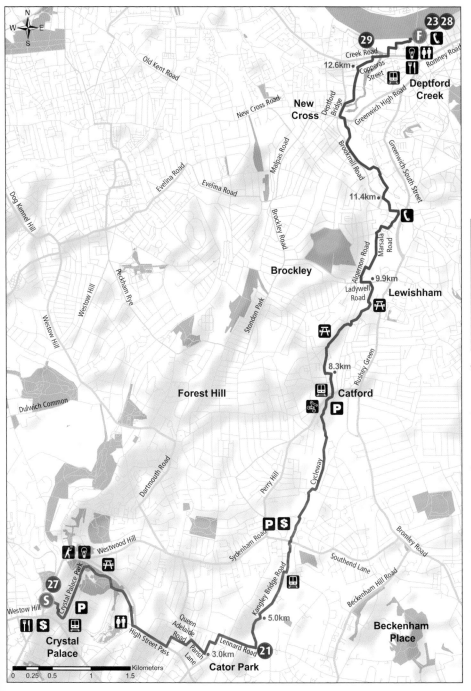

Ride 25 - Ravensbourne River Trail

View from the fine Georgian houses that line Camberwell Grove on Cycle Route 23

At a Glance

Distance 11.4km   **Total Climbing** 64m

Terrain
Surfaced roads and surfaced paths through parks.

Traffic
Light traffic on residential roads. Some car free sections through parks.

How to Get There
Denmark Hill Station or Peckham Rye Station; Pay and Display car park at Peckham Multiplex Cinema opposite Peckham Rye Station and parking in Dulwich Park.

Food and Drink
Petitou Café Peckham, The Cambria Pub, Cambria Road near Loughbourgh Junction, The Sun & Doves, Camberwell are amongst many of the excellent places to stop-off near this route.

Side Trip
On a Saturday you can visit Northcross Road Market just off the buzzing Lordship Lane. The market has bric-a-brac and fine food stalls. Try the Blue Mountain Café opposite for a full roast coffee.

Links to (other rides) 11, 27.

Bike Hire
London Recumbents in Rangers Yard, Dulwich Park rent unusual recumbent bikes or if you just need service try Wilsons Cycles, 32 Peckham High Street or Balfes Bikes at 50 East Dulwich Road.

Where to Ride Rating

About...

South London's varied parks and open spaces contrast with each other as much as the area's small residential districts. From colourful African street markets in Peckham to the Baroque and renaissance portraits in the Dulwich Picture Gallery; to the bohemian lido at laid back Brockwell Park to the grand Georgian terraces and crescent on Camberwell Grove, the ride could be described as real London in a microcosm. See how the affluent live cheek by jowl with the arty while the newest arrivals neighbour the traditional establishment.

Reflections on the children's paddling pool in Ruskin Park

This top London ride starts at Grade II listed Denmark Hill Station before climbing up through the traditional grand Georgian London Terraces of Camberwell Grove. The route turns into leafy Grove Park past large Victorian villas before gently going down to the Bellenden Road area of Peckham. This arty district of cafes and bookshops leads into Choumert Market, a vibrant orgy of brightly coloured exotic vegetables and gruesome butchers fizzing with a buzz of gospel and colourful dress.

From here quiet Victorian back roads lead to the open areas of Peckham Rye. The route passes through the park area in the centre of the common, home to beautiful flowers and ponds. You'll then travel along more suburban roads to Dulwich Park. Through the park is affluent Dulwich Village with its Georgian mansions, neatly kept lawns and picket fences. The traditional post office, village shops, cafes and red phone box really do have a village feel and it's hard to believe you're in London. The area is home to The Dulwich Picture Gallery (Tue-Sun, 11am-5pm; adult £5, child free) housing one of the world's most important collections of European old master paintings of the 1600s and 1700s.

The route turns down towards Herne Hill passing beneath fine iron railway bridges before entering Brockwell Park. At the top of the grassy hill is an old Palladian mansion now a park café. There are views across all of London and at the bottom of the hill still within the park is a beautiful 1930's Lido. Outdoor swimming is still possible in the summer. The route continues down through a more run down area on the edge of Brixton towards Loughborough Junction passing a new city Academy designed by eminent architect Zaha Hadid. At Loughborough Junction the route turns up into Ruskin Park, past tennis courts and Kings College Hospital coming out back at Denmark Hill.

South East

Ride Log

0.0 Turn left out of Denmark Hill Station and left up Champion Park. Just after the road bends to the right turn left down an alley next to the George Canning pub. You will need to dismount as the alley gets narrower.

0.4 On the other side turn right up Camberwell Grove. Take the first left down Grove Park and then first right. The road bends around to the left and goes down hill.

1.4 At the end dismount and walk your bike straight ahead on the pavement to avoid one-way then turn right up Bellenden Rd. Take the first left down Choumert Rd.

1.8 At the no entry signs turn right along Alpha Rd. At the end turn right then second left into Anstey Rd. Take the second right down Amott and then first left down Gowlett Rd. At the end cross off busy East Dulwich Rd bearing right into Oakhurst Grove.

2.8 Take the second left along Oakhurst in Kelmore Grove bringing you into The Gardens. Continue straight on, and at the end turn left crossing the road into Peckham Rye Common.

3.3 Turn southwards into the inner park and continue southwards on the other side until you join Colyton Rd. Go right here.

4.1 At the end cross over busier Forest Hill Rd into Dunstans Rd. Continue to the end.

5.3 At the end turn left on Lordship Ln then immediately right on Court Ln. The entrance to the park is on the left after 150m.

5.8 Pass through the park and turn right on College Rd. Go left (second exit) on the roundabout onto Burbage Rd and then left onto Turney Rd.

7.7 At the end turn sharp right onto Rosendale Rd. At the end of Rosendale cross over busy Norwood Rd into Brockwell Park.

8.2 Turn right on the path around the edge of the park and exit in front of the Lido.

8.9 Turn left along Dulwich Rd and then right down Shakespeare Rd.

10.5 At the end turn right along Coldharbour Ln. Go straight on at both sets of lights but take second right up Cambria Rd. Pass under the railway line and take first left down Northway Rd leading into Ruskin Park.

11.2 Continue through the park and on the other side cross over busy Denmark Hill at the lights and go up Champion Park. The station is on your left.

11.4 Back at Denmark Hill you have completed the loop.

South East Parks Loop

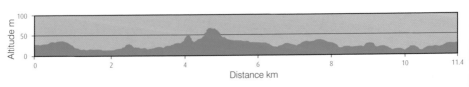

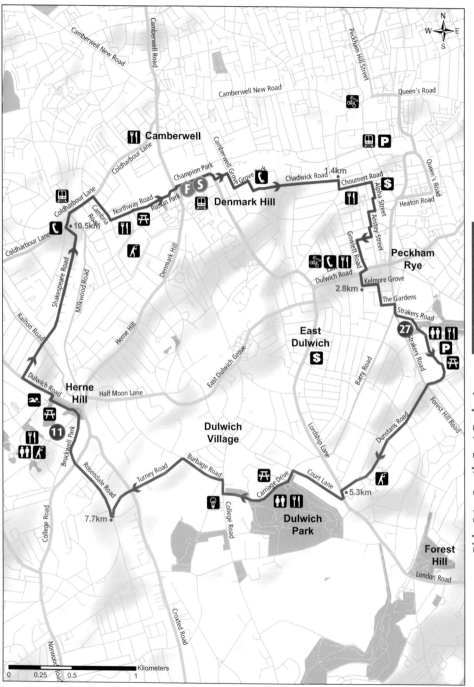

Torn posters in the depths of Elephant and Castle tube station

At a Glance

Distance 15.4km   **Total Climbing** 93m

Terrain

Surfaced roads and surfaced paths.

Traffic

Most of the route is along quiet suburban roads designated as cycle routes. There are some busy crossings and some sections on dedicated car free cycleways through parkland.

How to Get There

Blackfriars Station Southbank exit (opening mid-2011) or London Bridge Station; parking at the northern end of the route is limited but there are car parks in both Burgess and Dulwich parks.

Food and Drink

Leon behind the Tate Modern on the southbank sells wholesome seasonal fast food or try Petitou Café off Bellenden Road in Peckham. Dulwich Park has a popular café and there

are plenty of great bars and cafés around Crystal Palace.

Side Trip

Try to link in Ride 26 for a tour around some of the nicest areas in South East London.

Links to (other rides) 5, 6, 8, 25, 26.

Bike Hire

TFL cycle hire scheme points are located around the Tate modern at the northern end of the route but there are no docking points beyond Zone 1 so renting this way may be expensive; for service try Wilson's Cycles, 32 Peckham High Street or Balfes Bikes at 50 East Dulwich Road.

Where to Ride Rating

About...

The borough of Southwark stretches like a pointed finger from the Southbank of the urban heart of London through to the rolling hills, fields and woods of Dulwich and Crystal Palace deep in the capital's leafy suburbs. It is perhaps this contrast combined with extensive regeneration in the last decade with the avant-garde development of galleries, housing, transport hubs, markets and skyscrapers that make a ride through this area so interesting.

Franks summer rooftop café at the Hannah Barry Gallery in Peckham

The Tate Modern, at the start of the route, highlights the borough's change from declining industry and factories to culture and residential. The ride follows the Thames, passing the southern entrance to Blackfriars Station, before weaving through bustling Borough Market in the shadow of Dickensian Victorian railway arches. Towering above is the sleek shard of glass, at 310m it's London's tallest skyscraper.

Here the route leaves the river passing through historic Trinity Square before reaching Elephant and Castle where menacing concrete housing estates await demolition in the area's bid for regeneration. The wares and food stalls of East Street Market are a welcome flash of colour on the way to Burgess Park. Here the large expanse of open ground was created in the 1970s by clearing terraced streets. The park continues to feel a little unfinished with some of the old disused roads still cutting through the grassland. The greenway follows the path of the filled in Surrey Canal, beneath fine iron bridges, to Peckham Square.

On one side is the iconic, modern, Peckham Library resembling a giant cobalt blue tetris block crowned with a bright orange scallop row. From here the ride weaves up the start of Bellenden Road, beyond which is a bohemian area of cafés and bookshops, but the route turns eastwards towards the hubbub of Peckham Rye. The lively high street is buzzing with open fronted halal butchers and African grocers with Yams and chillies, punctuated with nail salons and gospel churches. The ride continues southwards towards Nunhead. Known for its Grand Victorian cemetery, one of the finest of the magnificent seven, where serene stone angels gaze towards heaven through the sea of deep green ivy.

The route continues to climb gently through the open spaces of Peckham Rye Common and Dulwich Park reaching tranquil Dulwich Village and the Dulwich Picture Gallery. Further south the ride passes grand Dulwich College school. Behind the white picket fences and neat lawns are cricket pavilions and playing fields. From here climb steeply through Sydenham Woods ending at the top of Crystal Palace Park with views across suburbia to the countryside beyond.

Ride Log

0.0 From the front of the Tate facing towards the Millennium Bridge go right (eastwards). Take the first right away from the river down Cap Alley.

0.5 At the end turn left onto Park St. At Vinopolis turn right and then second right up Redcross Way crossing straight over busy Southwark St. Turn left at the next wide street - Union St.

1.2 Cross straight over Borough High St into Newcomen St then first right up Tennis St. Cross straight over busy Long Ln into a pedestrian square leading through to Tabard St.

1.7 At Tabard St turn left then right onto Pilgrimage St. Cross busy Great Dover St into Globe St. At the end turn right then left into Trinity Square. Continue along Brockhurst St through the back of the square crossing Harper Rd into Bath Terrace. At the end turn left then right. Cross the New Kent Rd at lights and join the segregated cycleway going left on the other side.

2.9 Take the first road right, Rodney Pl, bearing left at the end. After 100m turn right at traffic island onto cyclepath exiting left onto Brandon St.

3.3 Continuing going straight. After 1km when the road reaches Burgess Park turn right at the lights and then left onto cycleway into park.

4.6 At the crossroads of paths turn left and follow path under the subway and along the straight route of the old canal on the other side. Cross Trafalgar Ave. Back into park and follow the path as is bears right

towards Peckham. Continue up the old canal route till it emerges at Peckham Square.

6.8 Through the square turn right onto Peckham High St. then left after Burger King up Bellenden Rd.

7.3 At the mini roundabout turn left then right up Elm Grove. At the end turn right onto Rye Ln and then left, just after the railway line, down Bournemouth Rd. At the end go left and then bear right at the traffic island along Consort Rd. Go left down Brayards then right, just before the rail line, up Gordon Rd. At the end bear right onto Nunhead Ln then left up Linden Grove.

9.3 Take first right down Forester and follow blue bike signs into Peckham Rye Common.

9.8 Go straight on through common keeping inner-park on your left. At the far edge of inner-park bear left up path and cross Peckham Rye Rd at the bike lights into Friern Rd and continue to the end.

11.6 Turn left on Lordship Ln then first right down Court Ln. After 200m take entry to Dulwich Park on your left. Cross through park westwards emerging in front of the Picture Gallery. Turn left on College Rd. Continue over busy road past college and through car toll. After the station the road climbs steeply. Continue upwards to a big roundabout at the top.

15.2 Here turn right and after 600m turn left into Crystal Palace Park.

15.4 Enter the park and enjoy the view.

Southwark Sights Route

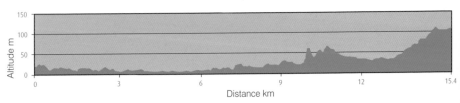

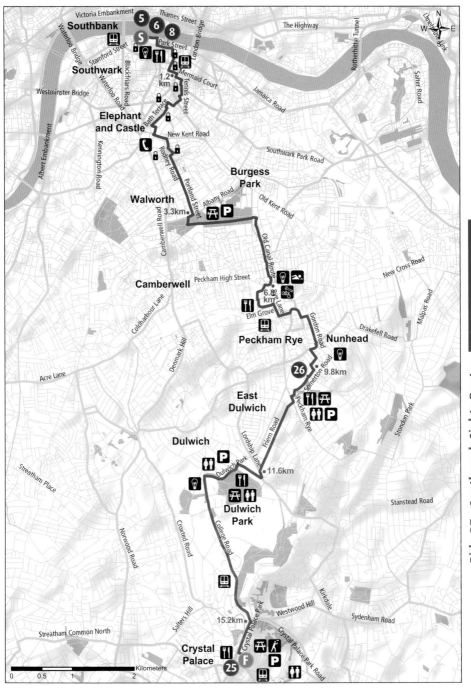

Ride 27 - Southwark Sights Route

Bikes against the railings of Greenwich Park

At a Glance

Distance 11.7km   **Total Climbing** 60m

Terrain
Surfaced roads and surfaced paths.

Traffic
Most of the route is on quiet suburban roads. There are a few car free sections through Blackheath, Kidbrooke and through the Royal Arsenal.

How to Get There
Greenwich Train Station services from London Bridge; Greenwich Pier for riverboats from central London; parking at the Royal Observatory, Greenwich Park.

Food and Drink
Zero degrees Micro Brewery in Blackheath, restaurants and market in Greenwich.

Side Trip
The rolling hills just east of the Royal Observatory are a great place for a picnic. Lock up your bike and relax in the grass.

Links to (other rides) 22, 23, 25, 29, 44, 50.

Bike Hire
Greenwich Cycle Hire at 95 Old Woolwich Road.

Where to Ride Rating

About...

From one of the most beautiful views of the city to one of her most terrifying and a reminder of how London's affluent areas are, so often, only a stone's throw from the most deprived. Nowhere is this clearer than the stark contrast of pretty Blackheath Village neighbouring the decaying concrete sprawl of the Ferrier estate. From the beauty of the painted ceiling in Greenwich to the damp dripping subway beneath the Kidbrooke A2, this ride is bound to confuse your emotions and divide opinions.

This olive seller is one of many food stalls in Greenwich covered market

South East

Starting at Maritime Greenwich between the Tea Clipper Cutty Sark (due to re-open after refurbishment in 2011) and the old Royal Naval College now part of the University of Greenwich and home to the magnificent Painted Hall, the route heads southwards passing the Georgian terraces of World Heritage listed Greenwich. The narrow, lantern lit alleys are home to bakers, cafes and markets. On the left is the Maritime Museum (daily 10am-5pm; free), the largest museum of its kind in the world, and on the right Greenwich antique market. Ahead the ride climbs up along a tree-lined avenue through Greenwich Park.

At the top is the Royal Observatory (daily 10am-5pm; free) built on the Greenwich Meridian Time (GMT) line. The buildings include a museum of astronomical and navigational tools and the view across the meandering Thames to the Docklands skyscrapers is one of the most splendid in London. At the edge of the park the route crosses into the windswept expanse of Blackheath Common, the start point for the London Marathon, where a path gently slops down to All Saints Church. Behind are the pretty Georgian terraces of Blackheath Village. The route continues along the high street, past shops and restaurants before turning down

past the palatial mansions of Blackheath Park then crossing into the contrasting gloomy concrete towers and urban decay of the Ferrier Estate.

The 1970s social housing lies next to the busy A2. From here a series of subways and cyclepaths lead to the suburban 1920s and 1930s houses of the Kidbrooke Park Estate. On the other side the ride crosses busy Shooters Hill Road to Baker Road, following the edge of Woolwich Common all the way to the Royal Artillery Barracks. Beyond is Woolwich town centre, the market and Royal Arsenal. The area which carried out armaments manufacture, ammunition proofing and explosives research and the Royal Artillery Museum, Firepower (Wed-Sun, 10.30am-5pm; adult £5, child £2.50), was set up to preserve Royal Artillery's history. After the museum the route joins the Thames Path, following the river for a short section westwards to the Woolwich Ferry.

Ride Log

0.0 Starting next to the Greenwich Tunnel facing away from the river go on the right side of the Cutty Sark ship. Join the road at the end and continue straight on. At the lights bear right and at the next set of lights, left.

0.4 Turn left up Stockwell St then left again along Nevada St before turning right into Greenwich Park. Follow the wide avenue straight on up to the top of the hill and go right at the roundabout.

View from the Royal Observatory towards Blackheath

1.8 At the end cross over the A2 at the bike lights and continue on the path which joins Duke Humphery Rd.

2.1 Turn left off the path towards the church. Go around to the left of the church and at the end turn left then sharp right down Montpelier Row. Continue going straight on past the station.

2.9 At the mini roundabout at the top of the hill bear left down Lee Park then left again through white gates onto Blackheath Park.

3.5 Take the second right down Brooklands Park and then second left along the second of two Castlebridge roads.

4.0 After 100m turn right onto a path leading onto Moorhead Way. Turn left on Moorhead way following the road round.

4.8 Just after Kidbrooke Station take the subway left under the A2. On the other side go left and left again at the junction back under the A2 road again. On the other side turn right along the path.

5.4 When it comes out turn left on Kidbrooke Way then right down Rochester Way. Take the footbridge over the A2 on your right.

5.6 On the other side cross over into Dursley Rd and continue to the end.

6.6 At the end turn right along Holburne Rd then left into Corelli Rd.

7.2 At the end go right along busy Shooters Hill then first left down Baker Rd. Cross straight over HaHa Ln into Repository Rd.

9.3 At the lights turn right onto Artillery Pl. Cross straight over busy road into Wellington St. At the end go straight on (bicycles and buses only).

10.5 At the end use the bike lights to cross into The Royal Arsenal and pass through down to the Thames.

10.9 Turn left on the Thames Path and follow back to Woolwich Ferry.

11.7 The ferry is the end of the route. You can return on the train from Woolwich Station or cycle back along Rides 23 or 50.

Blackheath to Woolwich

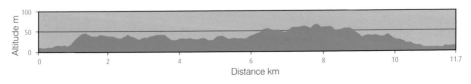

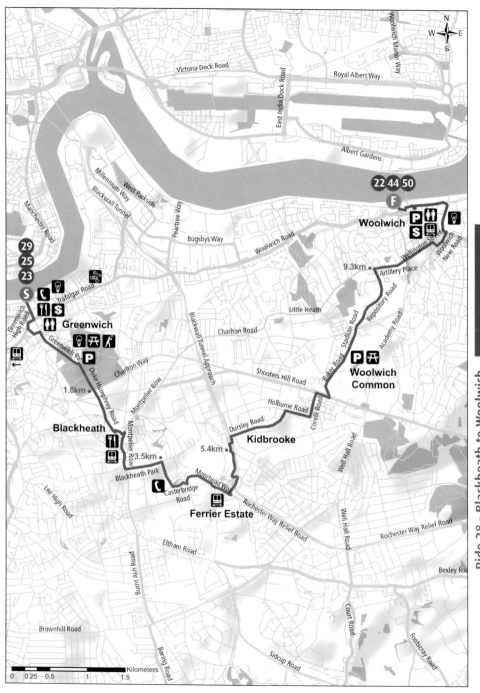

N
W — E
S

Victoria Dock Road

Woolwich Manor Way

Royal Albert Way

East India Dock Road

Albert Gardens

Millennium Way
West Parkside
Blackwall Tunnel

22 44 50
F

Peartree Way

Bugsbys Way

Woolwich Road

Woolwich
P
S

9.3km

Artillery Place

Wellington Street
Woolwich New Road

Manchester Road

29
25
23
S

Trafalgar Road

Little Heath

Repository Road

Academy Road

Greenwich

Greenwich High Road

Greenwich Park
P

Charlton Road

Blackwall Tunnel Approach

Charlton Way

Stadium Road
Baker Road

P

Woolwich Common

1.8km

Duke Humphrey Road

Montpelier Row

Shooters Hill Road

Holburne Road

Corelli Road

Dursley Road

Blackheath

Montpelier Row

3.5km

Blackheath Park

5.4km

Kidbrooke

Well Hall Road

Lee High Road

Casterbridge Road

Moorhead Way

Ferrier Estate

Rochester Way Relief Road

Well Hall Road

Rochester Way Relief Road

Brownhill Road

Eltham Road

Burnt Ash Road

Baring Road

Sidcup Road

Court Road

Bexley Roa

Footscray Road

Kilometers
0   0.25   0.5   1   1.5

You have to walk your bike through the Greenwich foot tunnel

At a Glance

Distance 15.4km   **Total Climbing** 49m

Terrain

Surfaced roads and surfaced riverside path. There are some short sections of cobbles.

Traffic

Predominantly light traffic on quiet roads and car free sections along the Thames Path, however there are two areas where heavier traffic should be expected. The congested Rotherhithe Tunnel where the ride uses the pavement and Westferry Road on the Isle of Dogs, which is a moderately busy road.

How to Get There

Shadwell Overground Station or Wapping and Rotherhithe Overground stations; parking at Surrey Quays shopping centre near Canada Water and underground parking at Canary Wharf.

Food and Drink

Riverside restaurants at Canary Wharf, The Grapes on Narrow Street near Limehouse. There are many other pubs and cafés along the route.

Side Trip

Southwark Park, just south of the southern entrance to the Rotherhithe Tunnel is a good spot for a picnic.

Links to (other rides) 3, 7, 23, 25, 28, 44, 50.

Bike Hire

TFL London cycle scheme bikes are available nearby at Tower Gateway. Alternatively for service try Robinsons Cycles, 172 Jamaica Road

Where to Ride Rating

About...

The Thames Tunnel was the first tunnel to have successfully been constructed underneath a navigable river. Construction took Isambard Kingdom Brunel 43 years and the tunnel eventually opened in 1843. Two further tunnels across the river were built using the protective shield technology developed by Brunel's father. This ride follows the banks of the Thames taking in all three; Rotherhithe, Greenwich Foot Tunnel and passing both sides of the Thames Tunnel now used by the overground railway.

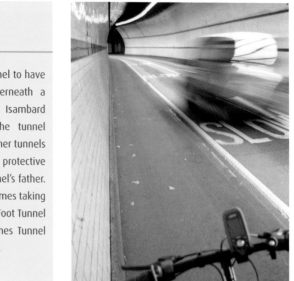

Cycle along the pavement of the busy Rotherhithe Tunnel

South East

Starting at Limehouse, close to the northern entrance of the Thames Tunnel at Wapping, the route passes around the Limehouse Basin. The basin opened in 1820 as the Regent's Canal Dock, an important connection between the Thames and the canal system, where cargoes could be transferred from larger ships to the shallow-draught canal boats. This mix of vessels can still be seen in the basin; canal narrow boats rubbing shoulders with sea-going yachts. However the warehouses and workshops have long gone, replaced with luxury apartments overlooking the marina. From here the route joins the Thames Path to Westferry Circus in the shadow of the docklands skyscrapers. Travelling southwards, past an odd sculpture of blinking traffic lights, the ride takes West Ferry Road to the end of the Isle of Dogs.

At Island Gardens the Greenwich Foot Tunnel burrows beneath the river to Greenwich emerging by the Cutty Sark. The entrance shafts at both ends lie beneath glazed domes, with lifts and spiral staircases allowing pedestrians to reach the sloping, tile-lined tunnel at the bottom. Cycling is not allowed in the tunnel so you will need to push your bike. Once back in the open air the Thames Path heads westwards along the southern bank of the river to Greenland Dock. Created in 1699, it is the oldest of London's riverside docks. The majority of the other docks in the Rotherhithe peninsular were filled in the 1960s and 70s when the shipping industry changed to standardised containers. The ride passes through the old Russia Dock now a woodland and ecological park. From the small rise of Stave Hill it is possible to have a panoramic view of the whole area. The route rejoins the river path near Bellamys Wharf. Around the pretty converted warehouses of Rotherhithe is the Brunel Museum (daily, 10am-5pm) situated near the southern entrance to the Thames Tunnel.

The ride continues to the Rotherhithe Tunnel, originally designed to serve only foot and horse-drawn traffic passing between the docks on either side of the river. As a result it was built minimising the gradient to cater for non-mechanised traffic and includes sharp, nearly right-angled bends at certain points which prevented horses from seeing daylight at the end of the tunnel and bolting for the exit. Now the tunnel is clogged with traffic and though it is not a steep gradient it is a long polluted cycle along the pavement to the fresh air back at Limehouse Basin.

Ride Log

0.0 From Branch Rd turn left into Limehouse Basin. Follow line of DLR viaduct. Cross Regents canal then bear right around the edge of the basin and cross the Limehouse cut canal into a small park. Continue through park around bandstand and exit left onto Narrow St.

1.4 Go right marked 'Thames Path' and follow Thames Path left. Pass the Egyptian style building and before parade of shops there is an elevator on the left. Take this up to Westferry Circus. Go right along Westferry Rd.

4.5 After 3km look for derelict warehouse shell on your left, shortly after this go right up Ferry St.

4.8 Follow the road around left. After 200m you will reach Island Gardens. Go into gardens, dismount and enter foot tunnel.

The view across the Thames to Christopher Wren's Old Naval College buildings

5.3 On the other side turn right along the Thames Path.

5.8 The path leaves the Thames to Cross Deptford Bridge. On the other side rejoin the Thames Path.

6.5 After another 200m the path leaves the river again directing you right onto Borthwick St. Continue to follow blue signs for 'Route 4', left then right to busy Evelyn St.

7.2 Turn right down Grove St. Then third right down Bowditch. At the end rejoin Thames Path to Greenland Dock.

9.0 At the dock cross over Southsea St Bridge then bear left then right over cycleway into Elgar St. At the end bear left across Salter Rd into Shipwright Rd.

9.6 Go through the end of the cul-de-sac and turn right at the cycleway crossroads. Continue going straight on and after 700m take path left through sports ground emerging onto Rotherhithe St.

10.7 Turn left on Rotherhithe St. Continue for 1km.

11.7 Turn left just before the church onto Marychurch St. At the end turn right on Brunel Rd. Then left onto pavement by bus stop. Bear left on path over grass to the entrance of Rotherhithe Tunnel.

13.0 Pass through the tunnel on the pavement back to Limehouse on the other side.

15.4 On the other side of the tunnel is the end of the route.

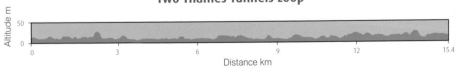

Two Thames Tunnels Loop

Altitude m

Distance km

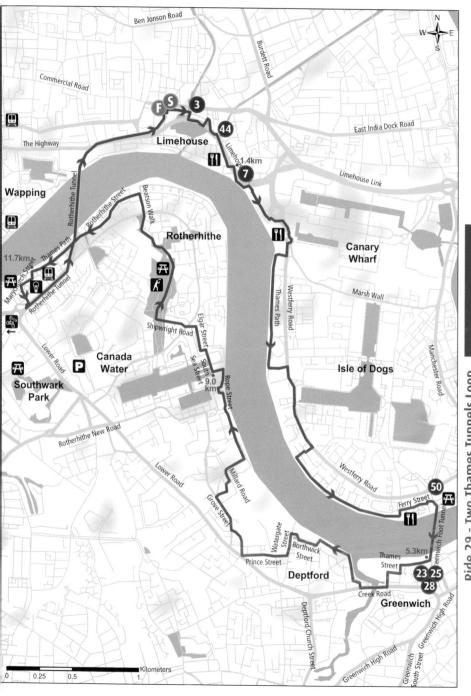

Ride 29 - Two Thames Tunnels Loop

North London

The urban area north of the Regents Canal has grown organically with little planning. The fields between the existing medieval towns and villages were gradually built over, so contrasting styles of housing gradually fused together into a carpet of suburban streets and estates punctuated only by the occasional cherished common and park or bustling town centre, each with an individual identity.

The districts closest to the city centre are Islington in the east and Camden in the west. These older neighbourhoods share the same classic London architecture of 18th century Georgian terraces however, socially, Camden has developed a more anarchistic streak centred on music venues and bars around the colourful ethnic market that attracts Punks, Goths and hoards of tourists. Islington on the other hand has an established antiques market and a strong literary community. Just north of Islington is bohemian Stoke Newington. Tatty shops have been spruced up into 'fair trade' cafes and whole food markets. Nearby is Finsbury Park; the area around this 45 hectare green space has a strong Islamic community while neighbouring Highbury is home to Arsenal, one of the capital's biggest football clubs. West are the affluent 18th century villages of Highgate and Hampstead. Hampstead Heath is a huge emotive green space stretched out over the side of a large hill, from its top there are magnificent views towards the city.

Slightly further out is Alexandra Palace Park and Muswell Hill. Beyond, suburban roads begin to give way to countryside and the open areas of Totteridge Common and Trent Country Park.

Ride 35 transects many of the districts covered in the chapter, starting just south of the Thames and travelling northwards to Alexandra Palace. Rides 30, 32 and 34 are loops around the middle of the district taking in Hampstead Heath, Highgate Village and Finsbury Park while rides 31, 33 and 36 are more geared towards mountain bikes, making use of the off-road trail through the open countryside around London's protected green belt.

Sunset from the old rooftops of North London

Typical London Georgian houses along Grove Terrace in Highgate

At a Glance

Distance 5.8km   **Total Climbing** 108m

Terrain
Half the route is up along surfaced roads the other half down gravel tracks or surfaced paths.

Traffic
Light traffic on road sections. Half the route is car free.

How to Get There
Hampstead Heath Overground Station or West Hampstead Thames Link is just under 2km west of the start of the route; car parking at the top of the hill at Jack Straws Castle.

Food and Drink
Plenty of pubs and cafés around Hampstead Village and Highgate. The Freeman's Arms is just at the start of the big hill.

Side Trip
Kenwood House (daily 11.30am-4pm; free) boasts sumptuous interiors. Brewing magnate, Edward Cecil Guinness, bought the House in 1925. Thanks to him, you can admire masterpieces by Rembrandt, Turner, Reynolds, Gainsborough and Vermeer.

Links to (other rides) 32.

Bike Hire
There is no local cycle hire but for service try Simpson Cycles, 114 Malden Rd, Kentish Town.

Where to Ride Rating

About...

Hampstead Heath is one of London's most popular open spaces, situated six kilometres from Trafalgar Square. The unkempt hilly meadows and woodland are an island of beautiful countryside, with a rich mosaic of flora and fauna, accessible to millions of people. Hampstead has inspired intellectual, liberal, artistic, musical and literary associations. It is also home to some of the most expensive housing in the London area, or indeed anywhere in the world.

The open grassy spaces of Hampstead Heath

This short but surprisingly hilly ride starts at Hampstead Heath Station bearing westwards around the bottom of the heath towards Hampstead Village. After 100m the route passes Keats House (May-Oct Tue-Sun, Nov-Apr Fri-Sun, 1pm-5pm; adult £5, child free) where the poet John Keats lived from 1818 to 1820, and is the setting which inspired some of Keats's most memorable poetry. The building is now a museum exhibiting books, manuscripts, letters, prints, paintings and artefacts relating to the life of the poet. The ride continues past the parade of Georgian white stucco buildings turning onto Devonshire Hill before passing the Freeman's Arms, a popular pub for its beer garden and proximity to the heath. Before reaching the heath however the route turns up pretty Willow Road. The road follows the western boundary of the heath as it climbs past Hampstead Village. Further along the climb gets steeper up to Flask Walk where there is a short respite along Wells Walk before turning upwards again up Christchurch Hill climbing ever upwards to Heath Street. Use the shared footpath along this busy road at the top of the common for the short section to Vale of Heath and the entrance to the meadows.

Cycling is strictly controlled in the heath. There are

only two cycle paths where riding is permitted. The area is London's largest ancient parkland, covering 790 acres. This grassy public space sits astride a sandy ridge, one of the highest points in London, running from Hampstead to Highgate, which rests on a band of London clay. From here there are protected views across to St Paul's Cathedral and the city. The path descends through the hedgerows and ancient trees that provide a home to kingfishers, reed warblers and all three species of British woodpecker. Towards the bottom of the hill the route swings left at a junction of paths towards the eastern perimeter. Here there are a chain of ponds - including three open-air public swimming pools - which were originally reservoirs for drinking water from the River Fleet. Past the ponds the ride exits the heath at Highgate re entering at Parliament Hill fields. This section of the path can be busy at weekends. On the left is Parliament Hill itself, considered to be the focal point of the heath, with the highest part of it nicknamed "Kite Hill" due to its popularity with kite flyers. The hill is around 98m high and has amazing views towards the London skyline. The path ends at Nassington Road leading back to the station.

North

Ride Log

A chain cog on a courier's light weight fixed wheel bike

0.0 Coming out of Hampstead Heath Station use the pedestrian crossing to go up South End Rd opposite. The road winds up to Devonshire Hill, turn right here.

0.6 Turn first left, just after pub onto Willow Rd. Continue to the end.

1.1 Turn right down Well Walk then first left up Christchurch Hill.

1.4 At the end turn left onto Cannon Pl and bear right through No Entry onto Ford Rd.

1.6 At the end turn left and at the top, cross straight over busy Heath St onto West Heath Rd.

1.8 Take first right down Whitestone Walk. Turn left along Heath St. Then bear right at the roundabout using shared use path along Spaniard Rd. The entrance to the heath is 100m on your right.

2.0 Follow the path down staying to cycle trail. After the bridge the path reaches a small section of grassland on the left before plunging back into the forest. A further 100m after going back in the forest there is a left turn for cyclists, take this. This leads to the Highgate Ponds, go between the pond and exit heath right onto Millfield Ln.

4.3 At the end of Millfield Ln turn right onto West Hill. Cross straight over roundabout onto Highgate Rd then after 100m right into the heath once again at Parliament Hill Fields.

4.7 Continue straight on through the heath. The path leads into Nassington Rd.

5.8 At the end bear left back to South End Rd. The station is on your left.

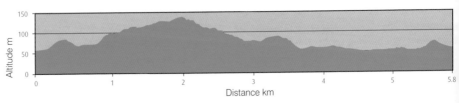

Hampstead Heath Loop

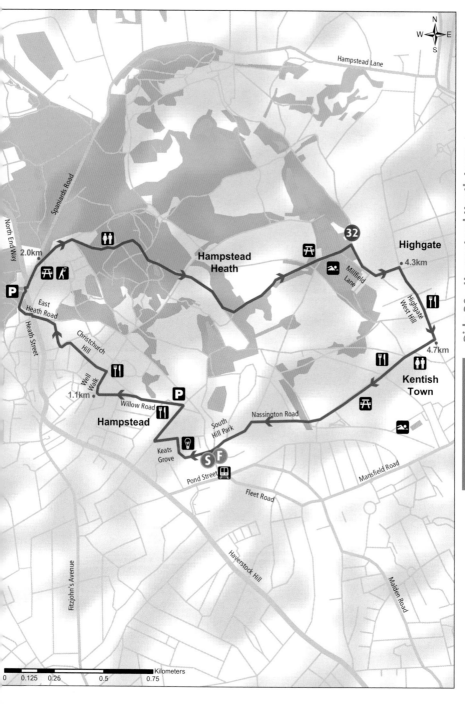

The open green spaces of Totteridge Common

At a Glance

Distance 16.0km **Total Climbing** 121m

Terrain

Surfaced roads and un-surfaced MTB trails.

Traffic

Equally divided between moderately busy country roads with fast moving traffic, quiet country lanes and car free mountain bike trails; be aware that in places it is necessary to lift your bike over stiles. The paths may be muddy after heavy rainfall.

How to Get There

Official start Totteridge and Whetstone tube station, otherwise Oakleigh Park Station in the east or Mill Hill Broadway Station in the west are both close to the route; free parking on residential roads around Woodside Park and around Chipping Barnet.

Food and Drink

The Orange Tree in Totteridge is a popular pub.

Side Trip

For the history buffs, just north of the route off May Lane is the site of the Battle of Barnet. You will simply see an area of fields but in 1471 is was a decisive battle in the War of the Roses.

Links to (other rides) 33, 38.

Bike Hire

No hire; service at Cyclelife, 8 Bittcay Hill near Mill Hill East tube.

Where to Ride Rating

About...

Totteridge is an area of the borough of Barnet. It is a mixture of suburban development and open land including farmland. The boundary to the north and east is the Dollis Brook and the boundary to the south is that river's tributary, the Folly Brook. The route takes in Dollis Brook as it weaves beside country paths and small roads. Starting near its source at Moat Mount open space the ride passes the streams confluence with Folly Brook before reaching Finchley. Here it leaves the river to cut across the suburb of Mill Hill looping back to the source of the brook. You will need to be able to lift your bike clear over your head to pass through some of the stiles along this route.

Bridleway along the disused railway near Mill Hill

Starting at Totteridge and Whetstone Station the route heads southwards towards Finchley following the course of the Dollis Brook, first along the riverside walk and then along quiet suburban roads through Woodside Park and West Finchley until the river meets Finchley golf course. Here the path passes through woodland and crosses the stream on an old wooden bridge before emerging onto Frith Lane in Mill Hill. On the other side of the bridge the route negotiates its way up through a new housing development and around the Inglis Military barracks before joining a bridleway along a section of a long abandoned railway line that used to run from Mill Hill to Edgware. The path along the track bed is shaded with self seeded ash trees and deep green ivy has enveloped the bridges along the route. At the end the path joins a network of suburban lanes leading to the open green space of Mill Hill Park. The route cruises down a hill past playing fields. At the end there is a short section of busy roads gently climbing up Hammers Lane to Highwood Hill. Be careful of fast moving traffic along this section.

At the junction with Hendon Wood Lane is a footpath leading into Hendon Open Space on the corner of Totteridge Common. By law you should walk this section as it crosses the fields to Mays Lane. It is a beautiful rural part of the ride with meadows of cows divided by hedgerows teaming with wildlife and small coppices of trees. Be aware that between fields it will be necessary to lift your bike over stiles. The path criss-crosses the Dollis Brook as it winds eastwards through the fields. After crossing the stream a third time the path leaves the river heading northwards to Mays Lane. After 1km this quiet county road leads to the edge of Chipping Barnet. Here, at Ducks Island recreation ground, the route rejoins the riverside walk passing through playing fields and open space as the brook leads back to Totteridge and Whetstone Station.

Parked bikes outside Oakleigh Park Station

Ride Log

0.0 Turn right out of Totteridge and Whetstone Station and left down Riverside Walk.

1.0 Turn left onto Laurel Way and right onto Holden Rd. Continue going straight on for 2km. The route crosses other roads and changes name ending in Brent Way. At the end of Brent Way the road stops but the cycleway continues. Turn right here on the path leading down hill through woods. Cross the river and follow the path which joins the lane to the golf course car park.

3.6 Go right along this lane and then right when it emerges at Frith Ln. On the left there should be a cycle path through a new housing estate to join Drew Ave (at the time of writing this was still being built – if the path is not finished turn left down Partingdale Ln. then left down Reading Way and left again down Lidbury Rd).

5.3 At the end turn left onto Ridgeway Bittacy then right onto Saunders Ln.

5.7 At the end of the lane is a bridleway. Join the right hand path after the allotments leading down to the disused railway. Go straight along this path to the end.

6.9 At the end turn right on Page St. Go straight over roundabout and at the end left onto Wise Ln. After 200m turn into Mill Hill Park. Follow right hand path along the top of the hill on the eastern edge of the park.

7.9 When it reaches the corner go down the hill exiting the park onto Daws Ln. Turn left up Marion Rd then right and left onto busier Hammers Ln. Continue up hill and at the end bear left onto The Ridgeway. As the road bears right turn left down Combe Hill. At the end of the path turn left then right onto Lawrence Gardens. At the end, turn left onto busy Highwood Hill then bear right to continue along Highwood Hill.

10.7 Right after/on the next junction with Wood Ln take the footpath into the fields on the left. Cross diagonally on path over first field, stay to right of second field. Continue through woodland by the playing field then bear right into third field staying on left edge.

11.7 Cross into fourth field and as path bears right take bridge to left across the stream up through field to Mays Ln.

12.1 Turn right along Mays Ln. Continue for 2km. Turn right down Connaught Rd and at the end left crossing into Dollis Brook Walk. At the end continue straight on along the riverside walk path. Keep going straight on over Barnet Ln.

14.9 Three hundred and fifty metres after crossing Barnet Ln the main path bends left. Go right here. Continue straight along this path for almost 2km until it reaches Totteridge Ln.

16.0 Turn left on Totteridge Ln back to the station.

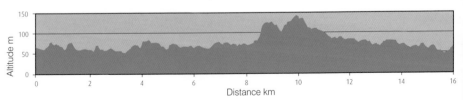

Totteridge Common Loop

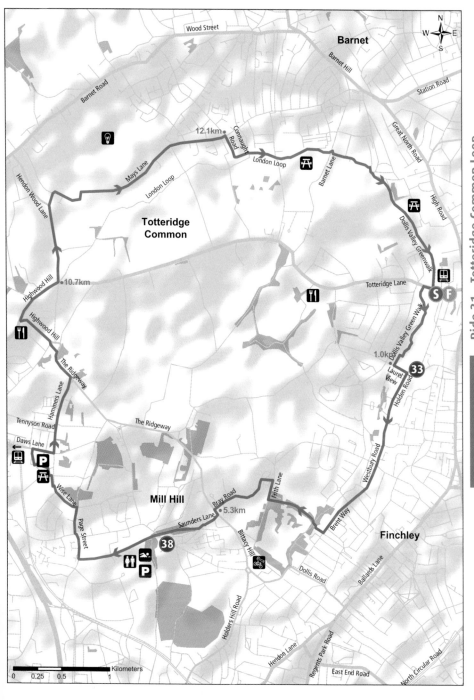

Checking the map near Highgate

At a Glance

Distance 11.4km   **Total Climbing** 138m

Terrain
Mostly surfaced roads, some surfaced paths.

Traffic
Light traffic on predominantly residential streets, some busier crossings over main roads.

How to Get There
Finsbury Park Train Station; parking in pay and display bays around Finsbury Park is around £1.40 per hour.

Food and Drink
Plenty of pubs, cafés, chicken shops and health food stores along the route.

Side Trip
Try returning via route 34 Parkland Walk, a disused rail line.

Links to (other rides) 30, 34, 35.

Bike Hire
No hire; service try Finsbury Cycles at 185 Seven Sisters Road, Cycle Surgery at 70 Holloway Road

Where to Ride Rating

About...

A gentle route along North London lanes, taking in the suburbs of Highbury, Holloway, Archway and Tufnell Park between the green areas of Finsbury Park, Clissold Park and Hampstead Heath. At the end there is a brutal never ending hill up to the pretty shops and cafes of Highgate Village. This urban ride takes in the impressive Arsenal Football Ground and has plenty of watering holes along the route. It can also be used as a return for Ride 34 - Parkland Walk to form a loop.

Highbury Park is a typical terrace of Georgian houses

Starting at Finsbury Park Station the ride crosses into the open grassland of Finsbury Park itself before almost immediately bearing eastwards back out of the park and across busy Seven Sisters Road. Here a series of residential roads through Browswood Park lead to Clissold Park on the borders of Stoke Newington. The park was formed in the grounds of Grade II listed Clissold House, nowadays the popular Clissold Park Café is housed in a former 1790s mansion.

From here the route swings westwards through Arsenal Football Club territory first passing close to the old historic Highbury Ground, now luxury flats, before reaching the new, 60,000 seat, Emirates Stadium. The path passes between the giant letters spelling out "Arsenal" before going over a wide footbridge towards the base of the impressive glass and metal bowl. On a match day the concourse will be awash with red and white but the rest of the time the open space is deserted save a few admirers of the ground.

Beyond the stadium the route passes under a railway to the shops along busy Hornsey Street. Half way along the high street the ride breaks left, leaving the fast food chicken outlets to weave through the quiet residential terraces and local playing fields of

Holloway and Tufnell Park. After around 2km the itinerary reaches the edge of Highgate. Here the ride turns northwards along the cobbles of Georgian Grove Terrace before arriving at the entrance to Hampstead Heath and gently winding its way along the edge of the heath up Highgate Road.

Just beyond the roundabout, encircled by smart cafes and restaurants, the road begins to climb steeply up Millfield Lane. First along the edge of the heath and then passing the mansions along leafy Fitzroy Park on the long hill up to Highgate Village at the top. The route leads away from the pretty but busy high street, teaming with smart boutiques and florists, down Park Walk and down the steep hill to Archway Road and the start of Parkland Walk on the other side.

North

Ride Log

0.0 Turn left out of Finsbury Park Station and cross pedestrian crossing into the park.

0.2 Once in the park bear right on the paths leaving the park again. Cross at pedestrian crossing to go down Finsbury Park Rd opposite you. Take first left down Somerfield Rd and at the end go right along Queens Dr.

1.5 At the end of Queen Dr turn right then left into Clissold Park. After 100m turn right onto cycleway leading to the corner of the park.

2.0 Leave the park and cross over busy Green Ln using the pedestrian crossing. On the other side go down Collins Rd and continue over into Kelross Rd.

2.6 At the end cross straight over busy Highbury Park Rd bearing slightly right into Aubert Park.

3.1 At the end, at the bottom of the hill, turn left then after 100m turn right through the large 'Arsenal' letters. Follow the path over the bridge and down the ramp left of the stadium.

3.7 At the bottom turn right on the roundabout along Hornsey Rd. At the second signalled crossroads turn left onto Seven Sisters Rd then immediately right onto Sussex Way.

5.6 At the end do not follow cycleway over railway but turn left down Hatchard Rd. At the end bear left down Kiver Rd then second right down Davenant Rd.

6.1 At the end use the bike lights to cross into Whittington Park and follow the cycleway to the other

side. Turn right then left down Foxham Rd. At the end pass into the sports ground. Continue on path keeping fields on left. The path brings you out onto Huddelston Rd, turn right through bollards then left along Station Rd.

7.1 At the end cross over busy Junction Rd bearing slightly right into Wyndham Cres.

7.3 At the end cross straight over Park Hill into Spencer Rise and at the end turn right then left into Chetwynd Rd.

7.9 Just before the end, cross over the right hand pavement into Grove Terrace. Continue to the end and turn right on Highgate Rd.

8.5 Go straight over roundabout and then turn left up Millfield Ln. After 1km bear right into Fitzroy Park.

10.2 At the top turn left, then right, then left again onto Busy North Rd.

10.7 After 350m turn right down Park Walk; it is to the right of Kiplings Restaurant (you will have to dismount and walk down pedestrian footway).

10.9 At the end turn right then immediately sharp left down Jacksons Ln. Then take the first right down Southwood Lawn Rd and then left down Southwood Ave.

11.2 At the end go left onto busy Archway Rd then first right down Holmesdale Rd.

11.4 On your left is the entrance to Parkland Walk.

Finsbury to Highgate Route

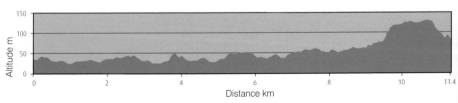

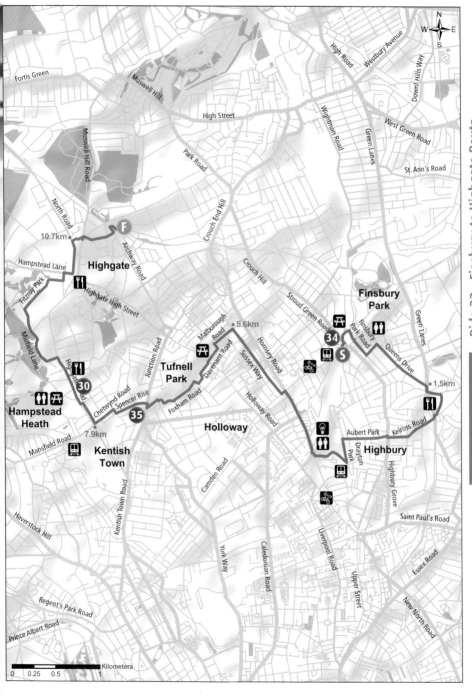

Fortis Green

Muswell Hill

High Road
Westbury Avenue

Downl Hills Way

High Street

Park Road

West Green Road

Wightman Road

Green Lanes

St. Ann's Road

10.7km

Hampstead Lane

Highgate

Archway Road

Crouch End Hill

Crouch Hill

Stroud Green Road

Finsbury Park

Fitzroy Park

Highgate High Street

Millfield Lane

Junction Road

Malborough Road

• 5.6km

Davenant Road

Hornsey Road

Finsbury Park Road

34

Green Lanes

Queens Drive

35

Highgate Road

Chetwynd Road

Spencer Rise

Tufnell Park

Foxham Road

Sussex Way

Holloway Road

30

Hampstead Heath

7.9km

Mansfield Road

Kentish Town

Kentish Town Road

Holloway

Camden Road

York Way

Caledonian Road

Liverpool Road

Drayton Park

Aubert Park

Kelross Road

Highbury

Highbury Grove

• 1.5km

Saint Paul's Road

Essex Road

Haverstock Hill

Regent's Park Road

Prince Albert Road

Upper Street

New North Road

Kilometers
0   0.25   0.5   1

'She loves me ... she loves me not'; a dandelion at Brook Farm open space

At a Glance

Distance 15.7km   **Total Climbing** 49m

Terrain

Surfaced roads, surfaced paths.

Traffic

Light traffic on residential roads.

How to Get There

Alexandra Palace is the nearest station to the start of the route. Alternatively New Southgate Station and Oakleigh Park Station are both along the route; free street car parking can be found on the residential streets around Oakleigh Park and there is metered street parking around Muswell Hill. There is also parking just off the North Circular at Friern Bridge Retail Park.

Food and Drink

There are lots of cafés and restaurants in Muswell Hill.

Side Trip

Visit Alexandra Palace just east of the starting point for fantastic views south towards the city.

Links to (other rides) 31, 34, 35, 36.

Bike Hire

For service there is a Sportsdirect at the Friern Bridge Retail Park or try The Cycle Store at 201 Woodhouse Road in Friary Barnet.

Where to Ride Rating

About...

A pleasant ride through the North London suburbs of Muswell Hill, New South Gate, Friern Barnet, Whetstone and Oakleigh Park between the green spaces of Alexandra Park, Brook Farm Open Space, Oak Hill Park and Brunswick Park. The route is gentle and mostly down hill following the weaving streams of Dollis Brook northwards and Pymme's Brook southwards with a section of meandering suburban back roads in between.

Relaxing in a café near Muswell Hill

Starting at the top of Muswell Hill, with views across to the centre of London, it's mostly downhill as you head northwards away from the city through the affluent terraces around Alexandra Park. The route passes Muswell Hill Golf course along pretty wooded Forest Walk before crossing the busy North Circular into new Southgate. Here a green cycleway bypasses the out-of-town shopping area to New Southgate Station. From here the ride climbs Beaconsfield Road before crossing a recreation ground and a park enroute to Dollis Brook.

The cycleway follows the stream northwards on a smooth cycle path through fields and open space towards the stream's source. Known as Brook Farm Open Space it is remnant countryside, made up of a mosaic of small fields bounded by ancient hedgerows. Fields have been cut for hay over the years creating a grassland habitat where wild flowers and insects thrive. At a large tree the route turns away from the stream and up the gentle valley side eastwards past the recreation ground and adjoining pavilion before reaching suburban streets leading to Oakleigh Park Station.

The ride passes through the station and on to Oak Hill Park, a large informal landscaped area with an open aspect and pretty views towards Oak Hill Woods, a 15 acre ancient woodland home to many fine mature trees and several bat species. The area is a Local Nature Reserve managed in partnership with the London Wildlife Trust. Once through the park the ride enters the suburbs of South Barnet before joining Waterfall Walk cycleway which follows Pymme's Brook, one of the tributaries of the River Lea, as it flows down towards London over a weir and through established woodland.

The route leaves the brook passing Arnos Grove tube station and continuing down the Limes back to New Southgate. From here you can either trace the route uphill back to Muswell Hill or take the train one stop south to Alexandra Palace and cycle back through Alexandra Park to Muswell Hill.

North

Ride Log

0.0 Starting at the big roundabout at the top of Muswell Hill turn right along Dukes Ave then first left down Wellfield Ave. Cross over Muswell Rd bearing slightly right into Muswell Ave, at the end cross over the busy Alexandra Park Rd to continue along Muswell Ave.

1.1 At the end there is a junction of roads, continue straight on down Forest Walk and continue along cycleway bringing you out onto Alexandra Rd. Continue to the end.

2.1 When the road bends left, turn right and turn right again up cycleway alongside Orion Rd. Turn left at roundabout and straight over the next roundabout turning left almost immediately after into a cycleway leading around and down to New Southgate Station.

3.3 At the end cross over busy Friern Barnet Rd into Beaconsfield Rd. Look out for open grassland on the left. Continue and when the grassland comes to an end there is a cyclepath to the left along the side of the grassland. Take this to the end and turn left onto Manor Dr.

4.7 Turn left down Friern Barnet Ln and then right onto a cycleway through Friary Park green space.

5.3 At the end turn right then right again onto Friary Way.

5.6 At the end go left along Friary Rd then first right along Mayfield Ave.

6.4 At the end cross over busy High Rd bearing slightly right into Highwood Ave. Follow the road round then turn left onto Woodside Grove and at the end turn right then left onto Woodside Ln. The road crosses the railway and bears left.

7.4 Just after the road bends left turn right onto Laurel Way then right again onto the Riverside Walk cycle way. Follow the route over Totteridge Ln. After 200m turn right by a big tree up towards a pavilion. Follow the small road around the back of the pavilion over the railway and up to Whetstone High Rd.

9.8 Cross over the busy High Rd bearing slightly right into Buckingham Ave. At the end go left then right then left into Oakleigh Park Station. Walk through the station and turn right on the other side onto Alverstone Ave. Take the first left down Cedar Ave and cross Hill Rd onto Oak Hill Park cycleway. Bear right on the path through the park.

12.1 At the end of the park cross the road into East Walk Rd. At the end, cross the road into Waterfall Walk cycleway along Pymme's Brook.

14.0 Just before the end of the park turn right over bridge into Pimmes Grove. At the end go left and then bear left over busier Waterfall Rd into Broodale.

15.0 At the end cross Bowes Rd bearing left into Palmer's Rd then take first right along The Limes Ave.

15.5 At the end turn right along High Rd then left along Woodland Rd.

15.7 At the end of the road is New Southgate Station. From here you can cycle back the way you came towards Muswell Hill or catch a train.

Muswell Hill Loop

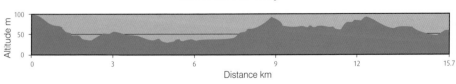

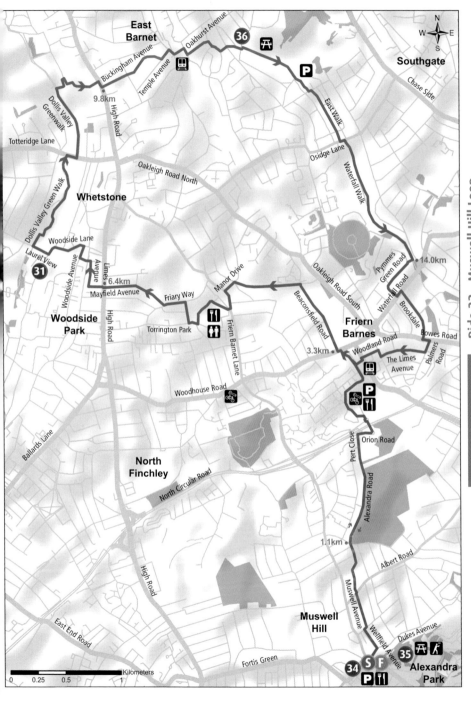

East
Barnet

36

Southgate

Chase Side

Buckingham Avenue

Oakhurst Avenue

Temple Avenue

9.8km

High Road

Dollis Valley
Greenwalk

Totteridge Lane

East Walk

Osidge Lane

Waterfall Walk

Oakleigh Road North

Whetstone

Dollis Valley Green Walk

Woodside Lane

Laurel View

31

Woodside Avenue

Limes Avenue

6.4km

Mayfield Avenue

Friary Way

Manor Drive

Oakleigh Road South

14.0km

Pymmes Green Road

Waterfall Road

Brookdale

Bowes Road

Palmers Road

**Friern
Barnes**

**Woodside
Park**

High Road

Torrington Park

Friern Barnet Lane

Beaconsfield Road

Woodland Road

3.3km

The Limes Avenue

Ballards Lane

Woodhouse Road

**North
Finchley**

North Circular Road

Orion Road

Pert Close

Alexandra Road

1.1km

Albert Road

High Road

Muswell Avenue

**Muswell
Hill**

East End Road

Fortis Green

Wellfield Avenue

Dukes Avenue

35

34 S F

**Alexandra
Park**

Kilometers

0   0.25   0.5   1

A Parkland Walk sign at the Highgate entrance of the local nature reserve

At a Glance

Distance 5.4km   **Total Climbing** 51m

Terrain

Mostly unsurfaced path, some surfaced road sections.

Traffic

Mostly car free, moderately busy on road sections.

How to Get There

Alexandra Palace Station in the north or Finsbury Park Station in the south.

Food and Drink

Plenty of cafés around Muswell Hill, nothing along Parkland Walk itself but there are more eateries around Finsbury Park.

Side Trip

Visit Alexandra Palace at the northern end of the route for stunning views towards the centre of London.

Links to (other rides) 32, 33, 35.

Bike Hire

Service at Two Wheels Good, 143 Crouch Hill or Girls Bike 2 at 228 Archway Road.

Where to Ride Rating

About...

Parkland Walk is a 7.2km narrow, linear, greenway stretching through North London as it follows the track bed of the disused Great Northern suburban branch line railway. It runs gently down hill from Alexandra Park to Highgate Wood in the north and from Highgate Station to Finsbury Park in the south passing through Stroud Green, Crouch End, Highgate and Muswell Hill along the way. Regardless of its short distance, this ride takes in all that is enjoyable of the Parkland Walk.

Many trees have quickly established themselves along the disused line

The disused railway, known as the 'Northern Heights', was constructed in 1867, with the short branch to Alexandra Palace being added in 1873, however the line hasn't seen a passenger for over half a century. The Parkland Walk was created as a green corridor, and opened in 1984 after extensive resurfacing and access improvements were made. The area now supports a huge range of habitats and wildlife and is billed as London's longest Local Nature Reserve.

Clearly, vegetation wasn't allowed to grow on the line when the railway was operational, making the current range of trees all the more remarkable. Oak, ash, birch, cherry, apple, holly, rowan, sycamore and yew have all arrived naturally while the maple, hazel and poplars have been planted. Amongst the rich animal and insect wildlife recorded are 22 species of butterfly; mammals include hedgehogs, squirrels, foxes and the occasional muntjac, a small non-native deer.

The walk begins along Muswell Hill where the first section crosses over the span of the seventeen-arch viaduct over St James's Lane. Its high elevation gives views southwards and eastwards over London

as it skirts the hill. This short section ends at Muswell Hill Road. The old line continued through what is now Highgate Wood but this is not open to cyclists so the route heads southwards, along Muswell Hill Road, to Highgate where it rejoins the Parkland Walk. The path descends a steep cutting where to the left you'll see the entrance to the now blocked off, long Highgate tunnels that link with Highgate Wood. A slightly creepy dead end that thankfully is avoided as the ride goes right. Look out for a man sized green spriggan sculpture by Marilyn Collins, placed in one of the alcoves of the wall on the left. This was thought to be a tribute to a ghostly 'goat-man' who is said to have haunted that particular area. Beyond this the cutting emerges onto an embankment passing through the partly overgrown platforms of Crouch End before reaching Finsbury Park.

The route is now part of the Capital ring of walking trails around London and there have been calls to prevent cyclist from using this route. Please make sure this doesn't happen by being considerate to other users at all times.

North

Ride Log

0.0 From Muswell Hill roundabout, walk on the right hand pavement down the A4504 Muswell Hill.

0.1 After 100m a path leads down to the right signposted Parkland Walk. Take the path and continue to the end.

0.8 Turn left down Muswell Hill Rd.

1.8 At the junction turn left down busy Archway Rd. Take the left after the next junction down Holmesdale Rd.

2.2 After 50m there is an entrance on the left to Parkland Walk, take this and go right along the walk.

5.2 Continue along the path for 4km until you reach Finsbury Park. At Finsbury Park turn right along the edge of the park bearing southwards.

5.4 Exit the park and cross the road to Finsbury Station. This ride can either link in with Ride 32 Finsbury to Highgate to create a loop or you can take a train from Finsbury Park Station to Alexandra Palace Station and cycle back through Alexandra Park to return to the start of the route.

Parked bikes near Finsbury Park Station

Parkland Walk Trail

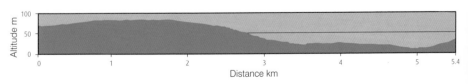

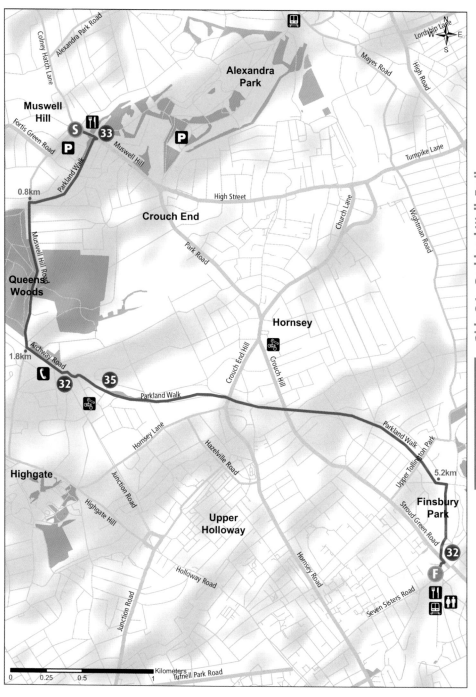

The covered courtyard of the British Museum

At a Glance

Distance 15.1km   **Total Climbing** 168m

Terrain
Surfaced roads and surfaced paths, a short section of unsurfaced path.

Traffic
Light traffic on secondary roads, some busy crossings in central London.

How to Get There
Waterloo Station in the south, Alexandra Palace Station in the north; pay and display parking bays in Kennington near War Museum and there is a large 'pay and display' car park at Alexandra Palace.

Food and Drink
There are restaurants and cafés all along the route. St Pancras Station has bakeries and cake shops while Camden Lock market has sizzling street food stalls.

Side Trip
Just off the route is Covent Garden Market. The iron and glass Victorian arcades used to house the city's main fruit and veg market, today it is bustling area of shops and cafes.

Links to (other rides) 2, 5, 6, 8, 32, 33, 34, 36.

Bike Hire
TFL cycle hire points around central London, however these end at the edge of Zone 1; for service try Evans Cycles at 178 High Holborn or Two Wheels Good, 143 Crouch Hill.

Where to Ride Rating

About...

Sights come thick and fast along this urban route as it climbs from the heart of London to the heights of Alexandra Palace. The reward for the tough ascent to Highgate is the views back across the London valley. There is plenty to break the journey up, from numerous places to eat and drink to museums and churches. The scenery gradually changes once you leave the centre as grand regimented squares and tall municipal buildings give way to more rambling back streets and quiet suburban roads.

The journey starts at the Imperial War Museum. This grand Victorian building houses displays of military vehicles, aircraft, equipment and other artefacts. It also has a moving Holocaust exhibition. The two huge 15" guns pointing away from the building were taken from World War II battleships. From here the route heads along quiet back streets past Waterloo East Station to the National Film Theatre, part of the South Bank cultural space. The theatre is now part of the British Film Institute (BFI) and screens over 1,000 films a year, from rare silent comedies to cult movies and archive television. Winding round onto Waterloo Bridge you pass the modern BFI Imax cinema showing films that are especially made for the giant screen. From Waterloo Bridge the views, across the Thames to the Houses of Parliament and London Eye to the west and towards the city in the east, are fantastic. On the other side the route passes close to Covent Garden and the Royal Opera House. The Victorian Market is now a pedestrian area of shops and cafes surrounded by many of the West End's theatres. Next is the mighty British Museum, its vast collections from antiquity are world famous and would need half a day to do justice. Behind this is Russell Square, a typical example of the West end's Georgian architecture.

From here a cycleway leads to busy Euston Road, opposite is the red brick British Library containing, in its archives, a copy of every book ever published. Beyond this is the side entrance to St Pancras Station. Its stunning train shed is home to Eurostar and international services to Europe. Behind is the St Pancras Chapel and the Hardy Tree, its neatly piled tombstone comes from the graves moved when the railway was built. North is Camden, famous for its colourful ethnic market and food stalls, popular with Goths and punks. Here the ride begins to climb steeply up to Highgate Cemetery. One of the magnificent seven Victorian cemeteries around London its most famous occupant is probably Karl Marx. Take a break from the climb here and have a wander. Beyond this the route descends passing Parkland Walk (Ride 34) before entering Queens Wood. The ancient woodland is inhabited by oak and hornbeam. On the other side are a series of suburban streets leading to the entrance of Alexandra Park. The ride climbs through the park to Alexandra Palace built in 1873 as a public centre of recreation, education and entertainment. The Palace now hosts concerts and houses an ice rink beneath its glass canopy.

Ride Log

0.0 Turn left out of the front gates of the imperial War Museum then first right onto King Edward Walk. Cross straight over using the bike lights onto Morley St and at the end cross busy Waterloo Rd into Gray St.

0.7 Take the first left up Webber. Cross over The Cut onto Cornwall Rd. Pass under the railway and over the next busy road.

1.4 At the end turn left on Upper St. Pass under the bridge and take the second left just before the railway arches up Concert Hall Approach. Turn left on the big roundabout with the Imax in the middle and take the first left across Waterloo Bridge.

2.5 On the other side of the river go straight across at the lights up the 'bike only' route. Watch out for

North

Ride Log

pedestrians here. Take the second right down Tavistock St and then second left up Drury Ln. Continue going straight on across all the roads until the road ends at the British Museum.

3.5 Turn right here onto Russell St then first left up Montague St. Continue straight on along the left side of Russell Square and then up Thorn St straight ahead. Continue straight on past SOAS onto Woburn Square and at the end turn right onto the separated cycleway along Gordon Square.

4.8 Cross straight over at the lights and then take the first left up Marchmont St. At the end use the bike crossing to cross over busy Euston Rd bearing slightly right into Ossulston St.

5.5 Take the first right down Brill St then first left along Purchesse St. At the end follow Goldington Cres around to the left and use the bike lights to cross onto to the cyclepath running along side College St opposite.

6.8 Turn right down Randolph St. (It's after crossing the canal and the turning before the lights and railway bridge).

7.0 Cross straight over at the lights and after 50m look out for a cycleway on the left which crosses the curb bearing right into Stratford Villas. Cross into Camden Square and continue straight up. Just after the road bends right turn left up South Villas. Follow the road around to the left and at the end turn right up North Villas.

7.8 Cross straight over at the bike lights and follow the cycleway up Cliff Rd. Cross straight over at the lights into Hungerford Rd and take the second left down Middleton Grove.

8.4 At the end cross straight over at the lights onto Hilldrop Rd. The road bends around to the left and you pass a school. Just after the school take the narrow passage on the right leading onto Carleton Rd. Cross over the road following the blue sign bearing slightly right into Huddleston Rd. Continue straight on through the bollards.

9.4 At the end turn left into Tufnell Park Rd. At the end bear right up Dartmouth Park Hill (not the hard right up busy Junction Rd, but the smaller road to the left of the Boston Pub). Continue up the steep hill to the top.

11.1 At the lights at the top, cross straight over into Cromwell Ave and at the end left along busy Archway Rd.

11.6 Take the first right down Northwood Rd and left at the end around Stanhope Gardens. Follow the road around and take the first left up Stanhope Rd. Turn left at the end and then right into Priory Gardens.

12.7 As the road bends left there is a path to the right. Take this straight through the wood. On the other side cross over Causton Rd and continue through the wood. After 50m take the path to the right to exit the wood. Turn left along Wood Vale and then left and right at the end down The Chine.

13.7 Take the first right along Etheldene Ave. At the end turn left. Cross straight over the busy junction at the lights into Alexandra Palace Way and then bear right onto the yellow road through the iron gates into the park.

14.5 Once in the park take the first path bearing left. Take the next path left leading onto Palace Way. Follow the road around to the right to the front of the palace.

15.1 Enjoy the views back towards London.

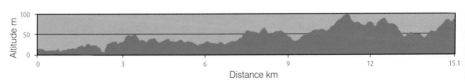

War Museum to Ali Pali

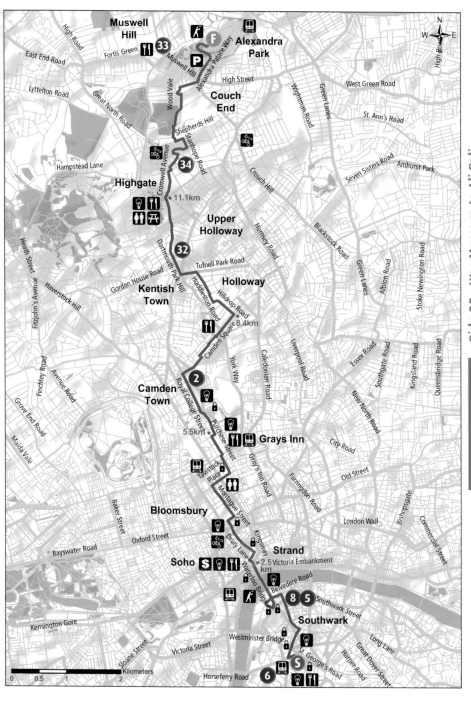

Muswell
Hill

Fortis Green

Alexandra
Park

East End Road

Lyttelton Road

High Road

Great North Road

Hampstead Lane

Wood Vale

Muswell Hill

Alexandra Palace Way

High Street

Couch
End

Shepherds Hill

Stanhope Road

Cromwell Avenue

Highgate

• 11.1km

Dartmouth Park Hill

Heath Street

Fitzjohn's Avenue

Haverstock Hill

Gordon House Road

Kentish
Town

Huddleston Road

Upper
Holloway

Hilldrap Road

Tufnell Park Road

Holloway

Camden Square   8.4km

West Green Road

Wightman Road

Green Lanes

St. Ann's Road

Crouch Hill

Hornsey Road

Seven Sisters Road

Amhurst Park

Blackstock Road

Stoke Newington Road

Seven Sisters Road

Green Lanes

Albion Road

Essex Road

Southgate Road

Kingsland Road

Queensbridge Road

York Way

Caledonian Road

Liverpool Road

New North Road

City Road

Old Street

Finchley Road

Avenue Road

Grove End Road

Maida Vale

Camden
Town

Royal College Street

5.5km •

Purchase Street

Tavistock
Place

Bloomsbury

Oxford Street

Soho

Montague Street

Kingsway

Drury Lane

Waterloo Bridge

Grays Inn

Gray's Inn Road

Farringdon Road

London Wall

Bishopsgate

Commercial Street

Baker Street

Bayswater Road

Strand

2.5 Victoria Embankment
km

Belvedere Road

Southwark Street

8 5

Southwark

Kensington Gore

Sloane Street

Victoria Street

Westminster Bridge

Horseferry Road

St. George's Road

6

5

Long Lane

Great Dover Street

Harper Road

WhereToRide London   179

Beautifully bleak; Hadley Common's winter mist

At a Glance

Distance 16.4km   **Total Climbing** 140m

Terrain

Half the route is on MTB trail – unsurfaced path and the other half on surfaced roads.

Traffic

Half car-free, the other half is either on moderately busy country roads with some fast moving traffic, or on country lanes with light traffic.

How to Get There

Route starts at Oakleigh Park Station, alternatively Oakwood tube and rail station are along the route. Car parks at Monken Hadley and Trent Country Park.

Food and Drink

The Cock & Dragon pub at 9 Chalk Lane is a traditional pub and acclaimed Thai restaurant.

Side Trip

Visit MoDA (Museum of Domestic Design and Architecture) (Tue-Sat 10am-5pm, Sun 2pm-5pm; free) situated at Middlesex University's Cat Hill Campus. The museum has two permanent exhibition galleries which tell the story of ordinary homes in the 20th century.

Links to (other rides) 33, 35.

Bike Hire

Be prepared - there are no bike shops in this area.

Where to Ride Rating

About...

This rolling leafy ride follows the route of Greater London's northern boundary with Hertfordshire. Here the suburbs of East Barnet give way to the fields, forest and common ground around Monken Hadley and Trent Park. There are some excellent mountain bike trails but also some long sections of quite busy road to link them and some of the hills require fitness and determination. Sights along the route include the Wilbraham's Almshouses, Trent Park Mansion House, Hadley Wood and Pymme's Brook.

In summer a butterfly perches on lavender outside a suburban front garden

Starting at Oakleigh Park Station the route heads down the valley side passing briefly into Oak Hill Park and crossing Pymme's Brook. Climbing up the other side of the valley the ride travels through the suburbs of East Barnet and Cockfosters. Past the Cock & Dragon pub you enter Beech Hill Park where the route drops down through woodland to cross back over Pymme's Brook. On the other side the rugged path climbs Newman's Hill, crossing a footbridge over the railway, before rejoining a lane rising to Monken Hadley. Here large stately homes, built by rich London merchants during the 18th and 19th centuries line the road. Among them are the older Wilbraham Almshouses, founded in 1612 by Roger Wilbraham, Solicitor General for Queen Elizabeth I, to provide for six 'poor decayed housekeepers'.

Travellers have passed along the Great North Road, which runs past Monken Hadley, since the Middle Ages. As the volume of coach travel increased the road was lined with inns, taverns and alehouses offering hospitality to travellers and stabling for horses. As you would expect in an area so steeped in history the ancient common land of Monken Hadley and village are all within a conservation area.

The route continues along Camley Way down through the suburb of Hadley Wood before climbing again up Ferny Hill and the entrance to leafy Trent Park Country Park. The green space was formed from the grounds of a mansion house that still stands in the centre of the park. The house currently forms the Trent Park campus of Middlesex University, however during World War II Trent Park was used as a special prison for captured German generals and staff officers. Many of the rooms inside the mansion had been bugged thus the British military were able to gather important information from the German military elite.

The country park includes publicly accessible countryside, farmland, a golf course and an equestrian centre. Features of the original landscaping include an impressive avenue of lime trees, an obelisk, ornamental lakes and a water garden. The route crosses back to Oakleigh Station through the suburb of Oakwood.

North

Ride Log

0.0 Turn right out of the station down Alverstone Rd, then first left down Cedar Ave. At the end cross over into the park.

0.7 Once over the stream bear left up the hill. Cross over the road and up the alley and turn left up Ridgeway.

0.9 At the end continue straight on, over busy Cat Hill, into Belmont Ave, then take first left up Norry's Rd. At the end go left along Mount Pleasant and then first right down Bevan Rd.

2.5 At the end cross through white bollards and turn left along Chalk Ln.

2.8 At the end bear left into Games Rd. The road curves around to the right and through a white gate. Go to the end and then take the path down through the forest. Keep to the left and the path joins Hadley Wood Rd.

5.7 After 1.9km take the right turn onto Camlet Way. Continue straight for 2km.

8.3 At the mini roundabout turn right onto Cockfosters Rd then at the next mini roundabout left up Ferny Hill for 1.5km.

9.8 The road noticeably bends around to the right. Just after this there is an entrance to Trent Park on the right with a brown sign marked Hadley Road Gate. Go

through here and bear right onto the track through the woods.

10.8 Pass the lakes and continue.

11.2 Where the path joins the road turn left past the monument then right up Snakes Ln. After 1.3km the lane brings you out of the park opposite Oakwood Station.

12.6 Turn right here using the shared use path along Bramley Rd. Continue straight on at the lights. Follow bike path round until it reaches Bramley Rd then cross at the zebra crossing into Reservoir Rd.

13.0 Turn right down Green Rd and just before the end left down De Bohun Ave.

14.0 Turn right onto Monkfrith Ave. At the end turn left onto Chase side and after 100m right onto Monkfrith Way.

14.9 At the bottom go right along Brookside and then first left down Parkside Gardens.

15.2 Turn right into Oak Hill Park and go through the car park onto the cycleway and bear left over the bridge. Once over the bridge stay on left hand path.

16.0 Exit the park and go up Cedar Ave opposite. Follow the road up and around to Alverstone Ave. Turn right here and the station is on the left.

16.4 You have reached your destination.

Hadley Common Loop

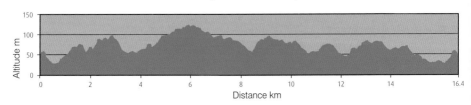

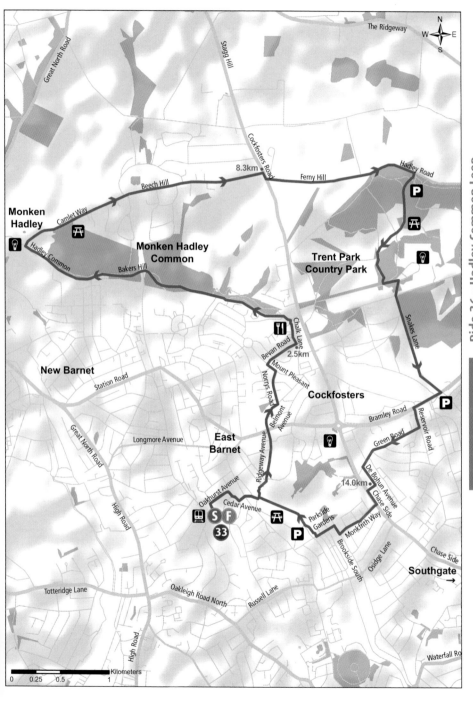

The Ridgeway

Great North Road

Stagg Hill

Cockfosters Road

8.3km

Beech Hill

Ferny Hill

Hadley Road

Monken Hadley

Camlet Way

Hadley Common

Monken Hadley Common

Bakers Hill

Trent Park Country Park

Snakes Lane

New Barnet

Station Road

Chalk Lane

2.5km

Bevan Road

Mount Pleasant

Norrys Road

Cockfosters

Bramley Road

Reservoir Road

Green Road

Longmore Avenue

Belmont Avenue

East Barnet

Ridgeway Avenue

De Bohun Avenue

14.0km

Chase Side

Great North Road

High Road

Oakhurst Avenue

Cedar Avenue

S F

33

Parkside Gardens

Monkfrith Way

Brookside South

Osidge Lane

Chase Side

Southgate

Totteridge Lane

Oakleigh Road North

Russell Lane

High Road

Waterfall Ro

Kilometers

0   0.25   0.5   1

West London

West London stretches from Paddington to Heathrow. The area has grown up as a transport hub, being the point at which a number of London's main transport arteries converge. The area is still dominated by residential housing but there is a high concentration of warehouses and light industry not only confined to industrial parks but following the course of the busy roads, canals and railways as they cut through the district.

It was the arrival of the railways, and after that, air travel, that became the catalyst to drive west London's fortunes; in the 100 years from 1801 to 1901, the area saw its population jump from just 10,000 to 250,000. Today the densely populated mesh of suburbs still thrives on the jobs created around the airport.

Closest to the centre are the affluent suburbs of Notting Hill and Holland Park. Bustling Portobello market attracts visitors and shoppers alike, while Holland Park is a tranquil retreat. Further west are the riverside towns of Hammersmith and Chiswick, both with pretty waterfronts teaming with pubs that overlook the Thames Path. Inland is the shopping area of Shepherds Bush and the nearby BBC studios at White City. Further west are the residential areas of Acton and Ealing. Closest to the western edge of London are Southall and Hounslow, both have a strong vibrant Indian culture thanks to the high proportion of South Asians living in the area.

The rides in the west are predominantly centred around the region's magnificent waterways. Ride 39 follows the towpath of the Grand Union canal around the entire area and it is practically car free. Ride 37 follows the River Brent while Ride 40 follows the Thames Path. Ride 42 is the most central ride and has the most sights but if you're after a spin through quiet parks, then Ride 28 is the one for you.

Peeling paint on Golborne Road

Cycling along Wembley's roads

At a Glance

Distance 13.5km   **Total Climbing** 67m

Terrain

Surfaced roads and surfaced paths.

Traffic

Light traffic on road sections however please be careful of lorries and vans around the small lanes of the Wembley Industrial Estate.

How to Get There

Willesden Junction Overground Station at the southern end of the route and Hendon Station at the northern end of the route. Free street parking on residential streets around Hendon. Car park near Brent Reservoir off Cool Oak Lane.

Food and Drink

Ace Café, Ace Corner, North Circular Road; a bustling, boisterous old transport café. Opened in 1938 and popular with Rockers in the 1950/60s, it is refurbished in this style and popular with bikers of the Harley kind.

Side Trip

If you fancy a bit of retail therapy you can visit Brent Cross Shopping Centre just south of Park Road.

Links to (other rides) 38, 39, 41.

Bike Hire

No hire but for service you can try Broadway Bikes at 250 West Hendon Broadway or Cycle King 173 Hillside, both are close to the route.

Where to Ride Rating

About...

A largely car free route linking rides 37 and 38. Through the tangle of railways at Willesden Junction the ride takes in a section of the Grand Union Canal before crossing the busy North Circular Road. At Stonebridge you join the riverside walk along the Brent as it weaves its way up to Wembley and Hendon. You will pass by some bleak industrial estates and areas of depravation but highlights include Wembley Stadium and Welsh Harp Nature Reserve around the Brent Reservoir.

Looking down Olympic Way towards Wembley Stadium

From Willesden Junction Station the route joins the Grand Union Canal heading westwards past warehouses and power stations. This section of the canal was created in 1801 and became part of the Grand Union in 1929 in response to the decline in traffic due the construction of the roads and railways. The canal runs 137 miles northwest to Birmingham and it is now used by leisure traffic including barges, canoeists and rowers. Just before the Abbey Road bridge the ride climbs away from the canal northwards through an industrial park and over a cycle suspension bridge that crosses the North Circular highway.

On the other side the path passes under mighty Victorian railway arches near auto workshops and a bus depot before crossing the busy Harrow Road at the bike lights to join the River Brent walk. The walk follows the course of the stream northwards through a corridor of parkland and then woodland. Ignore the obligatory submerged shopping trolleys and the car free route is quite pleasant as is winds along the river edge.

The path ends abruptly in the Wembley industrial estates. Though the roads are not busy please be careful of heavy goods vehicles around the park as you negotiate your way to Olympic Way. This pedestrian brick path has good sightlines back to the national football stadium; the iconic 1923 arena, venue for the 1948 Olympics was demolished in 2003 and work was not finished on the new stadium until 2007, the cost of which was £800 million. The mighty white steel arch is used to support the retractable roof. It is lit when events are being held at the arena.

The ride passes Wembley tube station and weaves through 1990s housing before entering Welsh Harp Nature Reserve. The trees and grassland boarder the Brent Reservoir used to feed the Grand Union Canal. The lake is used by a flotilla of small sailing boats and is an important site for breeding water birds such as the Great Crested Grebe. The route then enters the terraces of West Hendon, near Brent Cross, crossing the M1 motorway before reaching Hendon Park. It is possible to get a train from Hendon Station back to Willesden Junction.

West

Ride Log

0.0 Turn right out of Willesden Station along Station Approach. At the end turn left onto Old Oak Ln. Cross the bridge and take the pedestrian ramp to the left immediately after to join the canal towpath.

0.6 Turn left along the canal and continue for 2km.

2.6 Exit the canal just before the Abbey Road bridge then turn right along Abbey Rd. Take the first right after the roundabout and join the cycleway crossing the motorway. On the other side bear right and follow the path beneath the railway arches.

3.7 Turn left up signposted Stonebridge Park Station and then right at the roundabout in front of the station.

4.1 At the end use the pedestrian lights to cross over busy Harrow Rd and join the River Brent walk opposite. Continue along the path until it ends.

6.1 Turn left on Atlas Rd then dismount and walk down the one-way Fifth Way. At the junction turn right down Fulton Rd and then third right onto the brick surfaced Olympic Way. Please be careful of HGVs in this area – walk on pavement if necessary.

7.2 At the end of Olympic Way continue through tunnel and then take the ramp to the left in front of the station to join Bridge Rd. Turn left and walk bike on pavement along Bridge Rd until the first right down Chalkhill Rd.

7.6 Continue bearing right down Bowater Rd and across the end into Barnhill Rd where the road bears left to busy Blackbird Hill.

8.9 Cross straight over bearing slightly right into Birchen Grove. Continue to the end and take the right hand path along the edge of the reservoir until you join Cool Oak Ln.

11.0 Turn right along the lane and over the bridge. At the top dismount and cross at pedestrian lights to your left. Go on pavement along The Broadway and then second right up Park Rd (first right being a car park). To reach Hendon Station take the first left after crossing the motorway otherwise continue straight on.

12.5 At busy Hendon Way dismount and use the subway to your left to pass under the road into Beaufort Gardens. At the end turn right down Cheyne Walk and at the roundabout left to Hendon Park.

13.5 Once in the park you are at the end of Ride 37 and the start of Ride 38.

River Brent Route

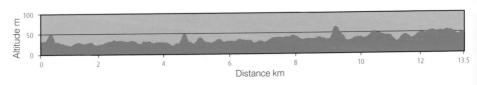

Altitude m / Distance km

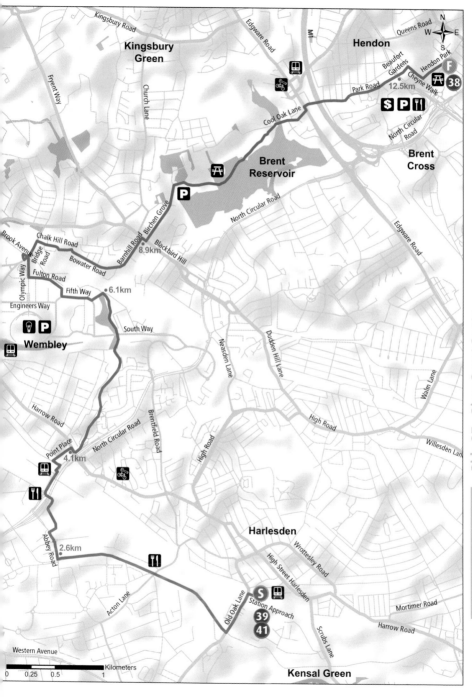

Kingsbury Road

Kingsbury
Green

Edgware Road

M1

Queens Road

Hendon

Beaufort
Gardens

Hendon Park

12.5km

Cheyne
Walk

F
38

Fryent Way

Church Lane

Park Road

North Circular
Road

Cool Oak Lane

Brent Cross

Brent
Reservoir

North Circular Road

Brent
Cross

Edgware Road

Chalk Hill Road

Brook Avenue

Bridge
Road

Bowater Road

Barnhill Road

Birchen Grove

Blackbird Hill

8.9km

Olympic Way

Fulton Road

Fifth Way

6.1km

Engineers Way

South Way

Wembley

Neasden Lane

Dudden Hill Lane

Walm Lane

Harrow Road

North Circular Road

Brentfield Road

High Road

High Road

Willesden Lane

Point Place

4.1km

Harlesden

Wrottesley Road

High Road

High Street Harlesden

Mortimer Road

Abbey Road

2.6km

Acton Lane

Old Oak Lane

Station Approach

S

39
41

Scrubs Lane

Harrow Road

Western Avenue

Kilometers

0   0.25   0.5   1

Kensal Green

Looking up toward the forest canopy

At a Glance

Distance 9.6km   **Total Climbing** 71m

Terrain

Surfaced roads, surfaced paths and other sections of unsurfaced paths.

Traffic

Largely car free sections of quiet suburban roads.

How to Get There

Hendon Station. Free parking on residential streets or car park in Sunny Hill Park.

Food and Drink

Sunny Hill Park Café is a popular spot to stop, alternatively there are many shops and restaurants along Brent Street.

Side Trip

From Church Road head westwards under the M1 motorway. After passing the police training centre turn right at the roundabout and you will reach the RAF Museum Hendon. The museum houses over 100 aircraft in five halls with a large display on the battle of Britain. (daily, 10am-6pm; free).

Links to (other rides) 31, 37.

Bike Hire

Evans Cycles have a branch at 250 Watford Way or Cyclelife at 8 Bittacy Hill.

Where to Ride Rating

About...

A great short ride around Hendon in North West London. Home of the Metropolitan Police Training College and several small undulating parks including Hendon Park, Sunny Hill Park and the open spaces around Hendon Golf Course. This ride returns southwards along the banks of Dollis Brook completing the mostly traffic free hilly loop.

A cheeky squirrel in Hendon Park

Starting in Hendon Park, a short ride from Hendon Central tube station and Hendon Station, the path leads northwards on smooth bitumen path, passing football fields on the left. Beyond the pitches you can see the hedges of an Edwardian memorial garden containing a pond, opposite this there is a cafe that was originally built as a World War II bomb shelter. The rest of the park is mainly covered by wild Cat Grass and local strains of Wheat Grass. The path exits the park crossing Queens Road into West View Way. This narrow pedestrian back alley leads behind the houses to busy Church Road, be careful of walkers and use your bell. The route crosses through an estate emerging into the top of Sunny Hill Park. From here there are views northwards to Totteridge Common and Westwards over the M1 motorway to the modern 60s building of the Police Academy and beyond. The path continues northwards through the park and down the hill past the cricket pitch on your right.

At the end is the Great North Way. A subway takes you under the ugly highway and into Barnet Copthall Sports Centre. Along quiet Greenlands Lane you pass an athletic track and a golf course before passing through the swimming pool car park and onto a cycle path. As the ride enters the wood there is a crossroads of paths, here you turn right along the bed of a disused rail track which once ran from Mill Hill East to Edgware. The woodland corridor now has a great bridleway for cycling and is home to an abundance of wildlife.

The route leaves the bridleway up steps just before a short tunnel, taking you to Sanders Lane leading to Ashley Lane and a cycle way through Hendon Golf Course. Watch out for golfers and buggies crossing the bridleway. From here the route joins the back roads past suburban houses to Dollis Brook. As you go down Holders Hill look out for the hidden foot passage on the right leading to the stream. The ride follows the course of the brook as it trickles down through Brent Park towards the Brent Reservoir. The route leaves the river at Golders Green road to loop back to Hendon Park at the start of the route.

West

Ride Log

0.0 From the Shire Hall Ln entrance to Hendon Park head northwards along the edge of the park. At the end of the park continue over Queens Rd into West View Way.

1.2 At the end turn left along Church Rd and then right along Church End. Then take the first right down Prince of Wales Close and bear left into Church Terrace.

1.6 At the end continue straight on into the park keeping to the right-hand edge. Drop down the hill and exit the park.

2.5 Cross under the subway beneath the busy Great North Rd and turn right along the cycleway.

3.0 Take the first left down Greenlands Ln. At the end continue straight on through the swimming pool car park and onto the cycle track.

3.8 At the crossroads of paths turn right.

4.3 Just before the tunnel take the path scaling the bank on the right and turn right along Sanders Ln.

4.6 Take the first right down Ashley Ln and continue onto the cycleway at the end.

5.7 When you come back out onto the road continue straight on then take the first left down Manor Hall Ave. At the end turn left down Holders Hill.

6.7 After passing Rydal Cl on the left look out for a hidden footpath on the right. You can identify it by the protective metal barriers between its entrance and the road. Dismount and walk down the footpath. Saddle-up and turn right along the stream.

7.6 Continue following the stream over Waverley R• and Brook Dale's Bridge Ln into Brent Park.

9.1 At the end of the park exit the river walk turning right onto busy Brent St. Take the second left dow• Shire Hall Ln and look out for the park entrance o• your right.

9.6 Enter the park.

The blue metropolitan police lanterns can be foun•
outside police stations all over Londo•

Hendon Parks Loop

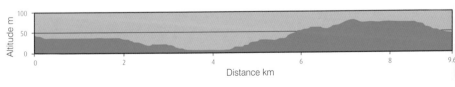

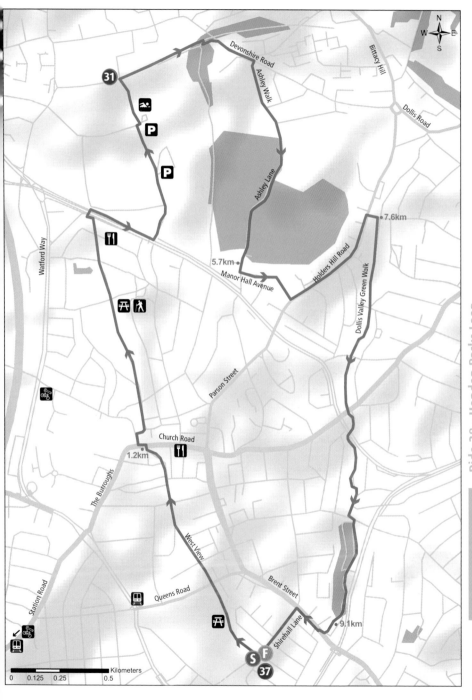

Devonshire Road

Bittacy Hill

Ashley Walk

Dollis Road

Ashley Lane

7.6km

5.7km

Manor Hall Avenue

Holders Hill Road

Watford Way

Dollis Valley Green Walk

Parson Street

Church Road

1.2km

The Burroughs

West View

Queens Road

Brent Street

Shirehall Lane

9.1km

Station Road

N
W   E
S

Kilometers
0   0.125   0.25   0.5

A bridge on the Paddington branch of the canal

At a Glance

Distance 28.3km   **Total Climbing** 53m

Terrain

Sections of surfaced and unsurfaced canal towpath.

Traffic

Almost completely traffic free, a short section at the start of the route along suburban roads to reach the start of the canal.

How to Get There

Gunnersbury Station at southern end and Willesden Junction at northern end are both on the Overground.

Food and Drink

There are plenty of pubs with canal views including The Black Horse, Oldfield Rd, Greenford; The Grand Junction Arms near the Paddington branch turn; The Old Oaktree Inn past the Hanwell Locks and the Weir Pub in Brentford.

Side Trip

Venture into Southall for a fantastic curry and a Bollywood film at the Himalaya Cinema.

Links to (other rides) 14, 37, 40, 41.

Bike Hire

No hire, service at WiZZBiKE, 113-114 High Street, Brentford.

Where to Ride Rating

About...

This 28 kilometre ride of car free, flat gravel, riverside paths is a calm oasis of ever changing scenery along the water's edge. Starting at the Grand Union Canal's locks with the Thames at Brentford, the route travels westwards to Bulls Bridge where the trail leaves the main canal and uses the Paddington branch canal to return north and eastwards towards the city. An overground train from Willesden Junction to Gunnersbury will complete the loop.

Houseboats moored beneath autumnal trees just north of Bulls Bridge

Suburban roads lead the 2km from Gunnersbury to the start of the canal at Brentford Dock. The basin was originally built as part of a freight terminus of the Great Western Railway by Isambard Brunel. The dock was used to transfer goods from the railways to barges however the area was recently redeveloped as flats and little industrial archaeology remains. The important transport infrastructure was located here as Brentford is the terminus of the Grand Union Canal and while the waterway is still used for leisure traffic the barges have long gone. The trail squeezes between houseboats and apartment blocks and then through a spooky disused covered loading area before passing beneath the Great Western Road and the green girders of the M4 motorway. From here the path becomes less urban through the meadows and scrubland of Brent River Nature Reserve.

Apart from the numerous herons, swans and rowers the next built sight is Hanwell. Here you climb past a flight of six locks which raise the canal by 20 metres and represent the only real height change along the route. It's a great spot to have a picnic and be a gongoozler, the name given to observers standing on the towpath. Further along the towpath reaches Bulls

Bridge, the main Grand Union continues the 137 miles northwest to Birmingham, however our route travels northwards along the Paddington Branch leading towards the Regents Canal.

Along this quiet stretch you get a real sense of the seasons as the trees drop into the water reflecting their leaves and branches. There is a quiet stillness broken only by kingfishers and herons. The canal slowly meanders eastwards passing the Willow Tree Marina, a mooring for houseboats created from one of the many factory wharfs that used to branch into the canal.

Further along is a short section following the edge of Perivale Wood Nature Reserve. The oaks are home to over 500 species of moth. From here countryside begins to cede to industry for control of the banks. The path becomes a hard surface and the trees give way to factories, warehouses and estates. After passing on an aqueduct over the North Circular Motorway the ride leaves the canal at Old Oak Lane to finish at Willesden Junction Station. Here trains return to Gunnersbury to complete the loop.

West

Ride Log

The weaving Grand Union canal towpath

0.0 Turn right out of Gunnersbury Station along Wellesley Rd. At the end turn left along Chiswick High Rd and at the lights just past Kew Bridge Station bear right down Kew Bridge Rd.

1.1 Take the first right up Dragon Ln then after 500m turn left along Clayponds which become Netley Rd. Cross straight over busy Ealing Rd into Braemer Rd.

2.4 At the end it's a quick left then right in Latewood Rd leading in to St Paul's. At the end it's left and right again into Lion Way. At the end you'll see the busy high street. Turn right into the high street crossing over the River Brent.

3.6 Once over the river turn right onto the canal towpath and continue for 8.8km to Bull's Bridge.

12.4 At Bull's Bridge turn right along the Paddington Branch Canal and continue for 15.5km.

27.9 Exit the canal at Old Oak Park Ln and turn right along the road. Take the first right down Station Approach.

28.3 Take a southbound Overground train from Willesden Junction Station back to Gunnersbury and the start of the route.

The Grand Union Canal Loop

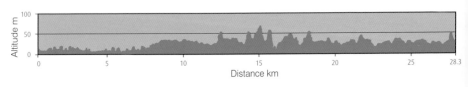

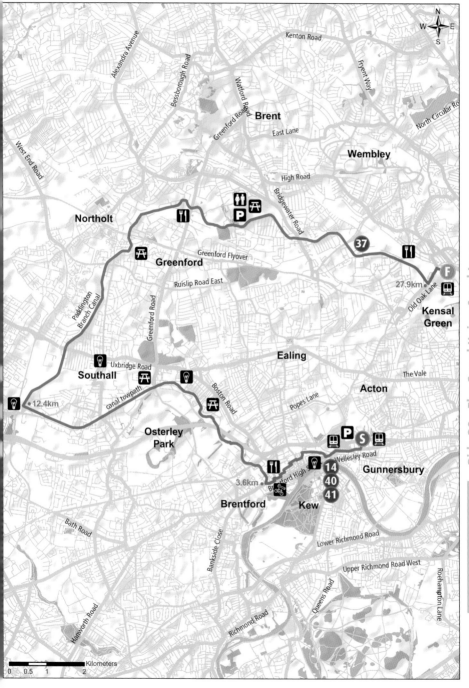

This flat area is well suited to cycling

At a Glance

Distance 9.9km   **Total Climbing** 47m

Terrain

Unsurfaced Thames Path and surfaced roads.

Traffic

Quiet residential roads and car free paths.

How to Get There

Kew Bridge or Putney Stations. You can park in most residential roads in Barnes for free.

Food and Drink

There are several lovely riverside pubs around Strand on the Green such as The City Barge and The Bulls Head.

Side Trip

Chiswick House was designed by the Third Earl of Burlington, and built for him in 1726–9 as an extension to an earlier Jacobean house (subsequently demolished in 1788); it is considered to be among the finest surviving examples of Palladian architecture in Britain, with superb collections of paintings and furniture. Its surrounding grounds constitute one of the most important historical gardens in England and Wales, and mark a significant step on the road to the picturesque aesthetic in garden design.

Links to (other rides) 14, 39, 41.

Bike Hire

No rental but for service try Bikes & Bits at 62 Mortlake High Street.

Where to Ride Rating

About...

Taking in two large bends of the mighty Thames as it weaves its way towards the centre of London through the riverside suburbs of Kew, Barnes and Chiswick, these quiet well-heeled villages have gastro pubs along the river banks with great views of the championship rowing course running from Mortlake to Putney. The whole stretch is popular with rowers and professional clubs and much of the ride is along the Thames Path just above the course.

Spring daffodils in Chiswick

Starting at Barnes Station the ride travels eastwards through the woods of Barnes Common. To the north is the acclaimed Barnes Wetland Centre, home to a huge array of waterbirds. Barnes village is built around a pond near the original Norman chapel of St Mary's built at some point between 1100 and 1150. The route passes south of this but emerges onto the waterfront on a road lined with Georgian mansions known as the Terrace. Some of the houses date from as early as 1720 and are amongst the oldest houses in London.

The route scales a significantly long set of steps to Barnes Bridge Station and crosses the river on a footbridge attached to the iron lattice railway bridge. On the north bank is Chiswick, the old English word for "Cheese Farm" originating from the riverside meadows and farms that are thought to have supported an annual cheese fair on Dukes Meadows up until the 18th century. The path follows the rail line along the edge of Dukes Meadows to Chiswick railway station.

From here quiet suburban roads pass in front of Edwardian houses before rejoining the river front along Thames Road. The Chiswick reach of the Thames is heavily used for competitive and recreational rowing, and Chiswick itself is home to several clubs because of its position at the upriver end of the championship course from Mortlake to Putney. The most known contest is the Oxford vs. Cambridge University boat race, which takes place annually in spring. A Café Rouge restaurant facing the river has the perfect view from its iron balcony, over the stretch of grass on the bank known as Strand on the Green, towards Oliver's Island, one of several islands in the river.

Further along, the route crosses back to the south bank across busy Kew Bridge. On the right are the Royal Botanical Gardens (see Ride 14). However the route goes left following the refurbished Thames Path to Mortlake passing under Chiswick Bridge cutting away from the river between the Ship Inn Pub and the huge Budweiser brewery before crossing Mortlake Green and following the railway line back to Barnes Common to complete the loop.

West

Ride Log

0.0 Turn left out of Barnes Station on the cycleway past the cricket ground. At Vine Rd turn left across the railway line and then right into the recreation ground.

0.3 Follow the path along the right edge of the ground. On the other side dismount and walk bike through foot tunnel beneath the rail line. Once through turn left and cycle down Cleveland Gardens. At the end turn left on the river front and take the cycleway on your side of the rail bridge. Beware there are around 40 steps up.

1.4 Once across turn left along Promenade Rd passing in front of a fitness centre. Continue straight onto a shared footpath keeping the rail line on your left.

2.6 When the path emerges onto Burlington Ln turn left and follow the road around as it becomes Sutton Court Rd.

3.0 Just after the road bends around to the right take the first sharp left doubling back over the railway over Grove Park Bridge. Once over the bridge turn sharp right down Grove Park Gardens.

3.5 At the end cross straight over Grove Park Terrace into the cycleway leading into Riverview Grove. The road bends left and then right into Thames Rd. Keep going straight on down Thames Rd.

4.7 At the end turn left up and over Kew Bridge using the shared use pavement.

5.0 On the other side take the first left down Thames Bank and then left again doubling back around to the base of the bridge to join the Thames Path.

5.3 Continue along the Thames Path eastwards for 2.3km.

7.6 Shortly after the path passes under Kew Bridge it becomes a small lane. Turn right here up Ship Ln. At the end use bike lights to cross into The Green and cycle across the green towards the station opposite. Cross Sheen Ln and turn down North Worpole Way just before the level crossing.

8.9 Turn right over the next level crossing and then second left down Rosslyn Ave. Continue over the cycleway at the end into Woodlands Rd and at the end cross straight over Vine Rd into a footpath through Barnes Common.

9.9 The footpath ends at Barnes Station to complete the loop.

A Moorhen in the Barnes Wetland Centre

Barnes and Chiswick Loop

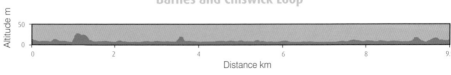

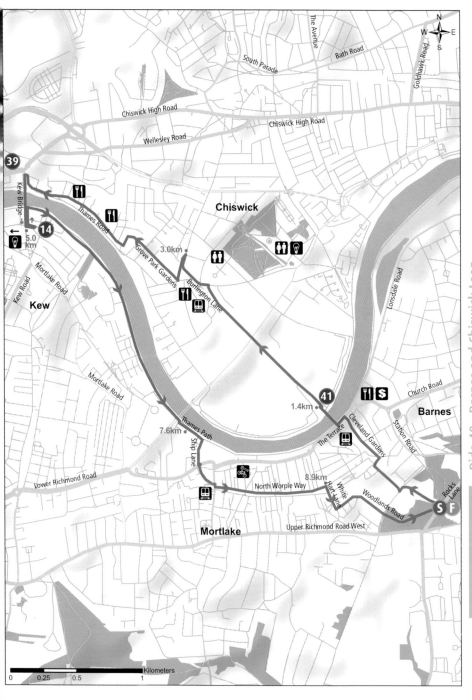

Chiswick

Kew

Barnes

Mortlake

West

5.0 km

3.0km

1.4km

7.6km

8.9km

Café Rouge on the Chiswick riverfront

At a Glance

Distance 31.5km   **Total Climbing** 60m

Terrain

Sealed towpaths and sealed roads.

Traffic

Half car free, the rest is mostly on quiet roads, however there are some busy roads that have to be crossed.

How to Get There

Willesden Junction Overground Station, alternatively Shepherds Bush Overground and Gunnersbury Overground are both close to the route as is Kew Bridge Station. Multistorey car parks at Westfield and in Hammersmith. Free street parking on residential streets around South Ealing and Cleveland Park.

Food and Drink

The Dove or The Ship on Hammersmith Waterfront both ooze charm. Alternatively for chain fast food devoid of character try the halls of Westfield Shopping Centre.

Side Trip

Take a detour past the Ealing Studios where they have been making films for 100 years from the famous Ealing comedies to present day blockbusters. Sadly the studios are not open to the public. But Walpole Park behind the studios is a good spot for a picnic.

Links to (other rides) 14, 15, 37, 39, 40.

Bike Hire

Richmond Cycles, 145-155 Kings Street, Hammersmith W8 or Ealing Cycles, 9 Bond Street, W5 both offer service.

Where to Ride Rating

About...

Bound to the north by the Grand Union Paddington Branch Canal and to the south by the river Thames this ride takes in the west London suburbs of Chiswick, Ealing, Shepherds Bush and Hammersmith. The route passes near many sights including Chiswick House, Kew Gardens, Ealing Cemetery, Wormwood Scrubs Prison, Shepherds Bush Green, the Westfield Shopping Centre and the Hammersmith Riverside. It is quite a long ride but has plenty to keep you entertained along the way.

We start at the transport hub of Willesden Junction however you can start anywhere along the route. The first section of the ride is industrial and bleak, passing through Wormwood Scrubs Park, neighbouring infamous Wormwood Scrubs high security prison. The route passes beneath the high austere perimeter wall topped with watchtowers and barbed wire. From here you'll travel beneath the concrete supports of the Westway motorway, there is an unlikely climbing wall and riding centre here. On the other side the route briefly passes through industrial units and housing before crossing back over the main road into the Westfield shopping complex. Opened in 2008 the 150 000 m2 of retail make up the largest urban area indoor shopping centre in Europe with crowds to match.

Just to the south is Shepherds Bush Green. This triangle of grass and trees is surrounded by busy roads, shops, pubs, cinema and concert venue. The cyclepath skirts around the green and down to the more sedate Brook Green to the south. From here it's a matter of negotiating through the Hammersmith one-way system and under the flyover before emerging a world away at the Thames Path. It is necessary to dismount along the front for short sections where the pubs' tables and chairs spill out onto the footpath. This is the prettiest part of the ride as the route follows the river along ancient terraces, alleys and parks passing The Dove, the oldest surviving riverside pub in London with, reputedly, the smallest bar in the world, frequented in the past by Ernest Hemingway and Graham Greene. The narrow alley in which it stands is the only remnant of the riverside village of Hammersmith.

Further along the path enters Chiswick. The Chiswick reach of the Thames is heavily used for competitive and recreational rowing, and Chiswick itself is home to several clubs because of its position at the upriver end of the championship course from Mortlake to Putney. Here is the venue for the famous Oxford vs. Cambridge University boat race, which takes place annually in spring. At Kew Bridge the route trail turns northwards passing through South Ealing Cemetery. Ealing is best known for its film studios, which are the oldest in the world and are known especially for the Ealing comedies, including Kind Hearts and Coronets, and Passport to Pimlico. The route passes Ealing Broadway Station and continues northwards along suburban roads before crossing Ealing Golf Course to join the Grand Union Canal Paddington Branch. The towpath then leads back to Willesden.

Ride Log

0.0 Turn right out of Willesden Station up Station Approach. At the end turn left along Old Oak Ln. After passing over the canal take the first left down Old Oak Common Ln.

0.7 Pass under the railway and bear left down Braybrook St. At the corner of the prison turn left into the park and follow the cycleway around the athletic track.

3.7 At the end cross over busy Wood Ln into North Pole Rd. Pass under the railway and take the first right down Latimer Rd. At the end continue as the road bends around to the left. Just after the bend take the cycleway on the right beneath the Westway fly over emerging onto Freston Rd.

4.5 Go straight down Freston Rd, bear right at the T-junction to continue down Freston Rd. At the end bear right into Hunt Cl. At the back take the cycleway scaling the bank in front of you. Cross over bearing right of the shopping centre down Ariel Way.

5.7 At the end turn left along Wood Ln. At the lights cross over into the cycleway around Shepherds Bush Green.

Ride Log

Continue round as the path bends left then use the bike lights to cross right over busy Bush Green into Rockery Rd. At the end bear right into Lakeside Rd and then left into Blythe Rd.

7.4 Take the first right down Dunsany Rd and at the end cross straight over Brook Green. Once through the green dismount and walk left along Brook Green Rd then cycle down the first right, Luxemburg Gardens. At the end turn left down Bute Gardens and then right down Wolverton Rd.

8.3 At the end join the cyclepath left and take first right down Shortlands. At the end cross the road onto the right-hand pavement and use the brown segregated cycle route going against the flow of traffic. At the end of the cycle lane use the bike lights to cross the road. Bear right on shared use pavement beneath the flyover.

8.8 Use the subway in front of you to pass under Fulham Palace Rd. Pass in front of the Apollo and turn left down Queen Caroline St. At the end dismount and walk along the Thames Path going right under Hammersmith Bridge. Walk along the path on the other side until you pass Furnival Gardens then cycle along Upper Mall. At the end of this stretch there is another short section of walking to reach Chiswick Mall. Continue following the river. Ignore the 'No Entry' as cyclists are allowed. Keep going straight on at the end, past the church, onto Pumping Station Rd.

11.5 At the roundabout take the second exit through the gate posts down Thames Cres and continue onto the cycleway at the end. Follow the path right and turn left under the railway in front of the fitness centre and continue round crossing straight over busy Great Churtsey Rd into Hartington Rd. At the end the road bears left into Grove Park Rd. Continue to Kew Bridge.

16.6 At the busy junction cross straight over into Kew Bridge Rd then take the first right up Dragon Ln. After 500m

take the green cycleway right leading over the railway then under the motorway straight on along Clayponds Ave. At the end continue straight on through the cemetery.

18.5 Cross straight over busy Popes Ln using the lights into Olive Rd. At the end continue straight on along the footpath over the railway. Continue up the alley and behind the church. When it ends turn right onto Ranelagh Rd and at the end left onto Ascott Ave. Continue straight on to The Mall.

20.7 Dismount here and cross road using lights. Walk up The Broadway and in front of Ealing Broadway Station. Cycle up the Haven Rd and then immediately left into a cyclepath across the green. On the other side use the bike lights to cross over Spring Bridge Rd into Gordon Rd.

22.0 At the end turn right along The Avenue. Continue straight on around the church into North Ave and at the end turn left into Cleveland Rd before taking the first right up Kent Ave.

23.3 At the end continue straight over into the park. Follow the path straight on past football fields. Continue over triangle of gravel and path bends right around the back of the football pitches. Just after a small pavilion on the left there is a crossroads of tracks. Go left here. The path emerges on Perivale Ln.

24.2 Cross over bearing slightly left into Old Church Ln. At the end use the cycle bridge to cross the busy road. Exit the bridge ramp turning left and then left again up Horsenden Lane South.

25.3 At the lights as the road narrows to cross the canal turn right onto the footpath leading down to the canal towpath. Turn right along the towpath and continue for 6km to Old Oak Ln (road name marked on the bridges). Turn right onto Old Oak Ln and then right into Station Approach.

31.5 This completes the loop.

Willesden to Kew Bridge Loop

Altitude m

Distance km

 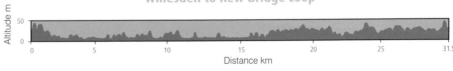

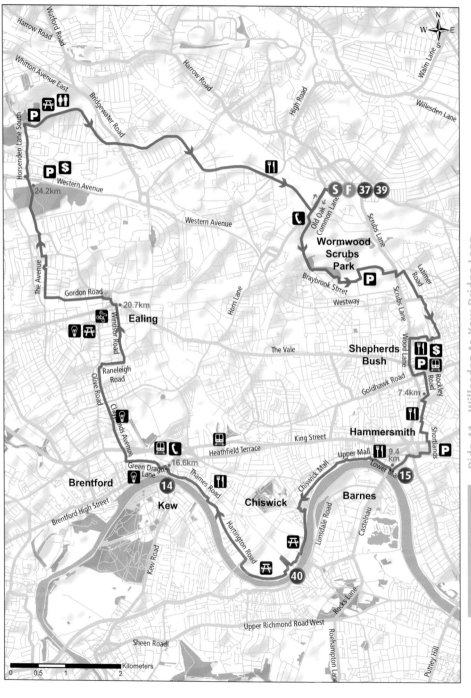

Paint textures on the railway bridge along Golborne Road

At a Glance

Distance 13.5km **Total Climbing** 62m

Terrain

Surfaced roads, surfaced canal towpath and surfaced paths.

Traffic

Around a third of the route is car free, the rest is on quiet city streets designated as cycle routes.

How to Get There

South Hampstead Overground is near the northern start of the route and Imperial Wharf Overground at the end of the route; metered street parking around Primrose Hill, multistorey car park at Earls Court.

Food and Drink

Primrose Hill has plenty of cafés, there are market stalls and eateries around Portobello Road including the Electric Brassiere. In Holland Park there is the Castle Pub while further south both the Fulham Road

and Kings Road have plenty of gastronomic delights.

Side Trip

Holland Park is a great place to stop for a picnic.

Links to (other rides) 1, 2, 20.

Bike Hire

TFL cycle hire points around Kensington and Notting Hill, however you will need to return your bike to Zone 1 after you finish the route; for service try Cyclopedia at 262 Kensington High Street, Cyclecare 54 Earls Court Road, EJ Barnes at 285 Westbourne Grove and Half Pipe at 40 Golbourne Road.

Where to Ride Rating

About...

A pleasant ride taking in many of West London's, indeed the country's, most affluent residential areas from the pop star's houses at Primrose Hill to the Middle Eastern mansions around Regents Park; the rich kids of Notting Hill and the expatriates in Holland Park, the old money in Kensington and the new money in Imperial Wharf. Sights along the route include the Regents Canal, Portobello Market and West Brompton Cemetery. There are plenty of great places to stop and eat along the way including The Prince of Wales Pub in Holland Park and the Electric Brassiere in Notting Hill.

Stencil graffiti

The ride starts at the edge of grassy Primrose Hill, a 78m mound on the northern side of Regents Park with views of the City. Bearing north along Regents Park Road you'll pass the pastel coloured regency houses, little boutiques and cute cafés that make this area so popular with its celebrity residents such as model Kate Moss. Here we join the Regents canal as it winds its way into Regents Park beneath the netted aviary of London Zoo and behind the back gardens of some of the most expensive mansions in the country including Grove House previously owned by Robert Holmes à Court, the Australian businessman. The house has one of the largest gardens in central London after Buckingham Palace and borders the canal. The route leaves the towpath for a short section rejoining at Maida Vale. The basin in known as Little Venice due to the concentration of pretty coloured houseboats moored up along the banks, their decks covered in potted geraniums and the odd old bicycle.

The path finally leaves the Canal at Golborne Road. The bridge passing over the railway line has views back to the Trellick Tower, the 31-storey block designed in the Brutalist style by architect Ernno Goldfinger, some of the flats are regarded as highly desirable residences and the building is Grade II listed. Beyond this is the start of

Portobello Market, originally an antiques market there are now also stalls selling food and fresh produce. The area was changed by the 1999 film 'Notting Hill', since then the white washed regency terraces have become an increasingly desirable place to live and visit. The route climbs up and over Notting Hill before descending into Holland Park. This affluent leafy neighbourhood is home to many Embassy staff and expats working in London. The Avenue has a parade of boutiques and an excellent ice-cream parlour. From here a cycleway climbs the short but steep Holland Walk which runs up the east side of Holland Park. Cycling is not allowed in the park but the Japanese Garden and Dutch Gardens complete with peacocks are well worth visiting. The ride crosses the posh shopping destination of High Street Kensington before winding through Kensington's terraces to West Brompton Cemetery opposite the Earl's Court Exhibition Centre. The cemetery is one of the magnificent seven created in Victorian times, its mausoleum and skyward gazing angels covered in creeping ivy are very emotive. The ride ends at the New Imperial Wharf Overground Station near a group of luxury riverside flats. You can return by train from Imperial Wharf Station changing at Willesden Junction for trains back to Camden Road Station.

West

Ride Log

0.0 At the corner of Primrose Hill Park turn left along Regents Park Rd. At the end turn right along Gloucester Ave. After 200m on the left there is a small shop called Melrose and Morgan. Take the passageway here leading right to join the canal. Turn right along the canal for 2.5km.

2.7 At the end exit the towpath over the footbridge and continue on the opposite bank crossing Lisson Rd into Frampton St. Take the second right along Fisherton St and continue as road bends left.

3.6 At the end turn right along Lyons Pl and then left into cycleway along Aberdeen Pl. Cross Edgware Rd at bike lights into Blomfield Rd.

4.3 Just after the basin on your left turn left over the bridge and then right into Delamere Terrace. Take the cycleway through the park to rejoin the canal towpath.

6.0 After just under 2km exit the canal towpath turning left down Kensal Rd. Cross over the rail line and take the fourth left down Portobello Rd. Dismount and walk down the one-way beneath the motorway.

6.8 On the other side turn left up Tavistock and then right down Basing St. At the end go right down Westbourne Park cross back over Portobello Rd then take first left along Kensington Park Rd.

7.7 Turn right opposite the church down Stanley Gardens and at the end left along Stanley Cres. At the

end bear right into Crescent Park Gardens and then left down busy Ladbroke Grove. Cross the road at the lights onto the pavement and walk right for 40m to Holland Walk. Pedal furiously up the hill and then cruise down to Kensington High St.

9.5 Cross the road and continue straight on down Earls Court Rd. Take the first left down Pater St and then right down Abingdon Rd. Turn left along Stratford Terrace then right at the end along Marloes Rd. Cross straight over the busy Cromwell Rd in an alley on the other side leading into Kenway Rd.

10.7 Turn left along Earls Court Rd and then third right down Earls Court Square crossing straight over Warwick Rd and then Lille Rd into the cycleway through West Brompton Cemetery.

11.4 Follow the path around to the left and exit crossing straight over the busy Fulham Rd into Hortensia Rd. At the end cross over the Kings Rd into an alley leading into a small park. Cross through this into Upcerne Rd.

12.9 At the end turn right along Lots Rd and at the mini roundabout left passing under the rail line and through the barriers.

13.5 Once through turn right into Imperial Wharf Station to complete the route. You can return by train from Imperial Wharf Station changing at Willesden Junction for trains back to Camden Road Station.

Camden to the Thames Route

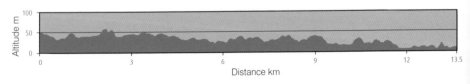

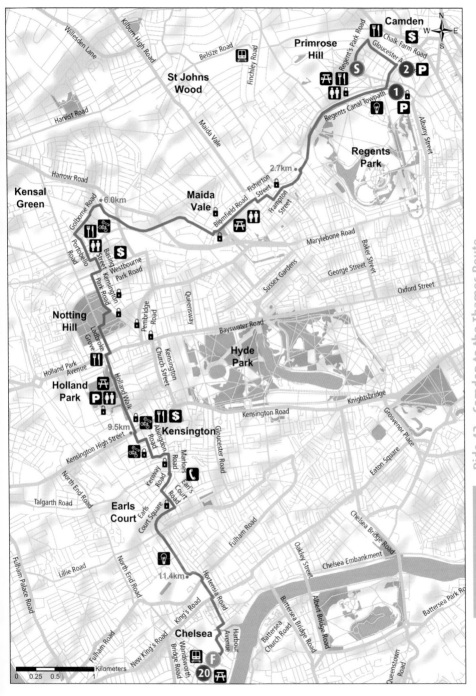

Camden

Primrose
Hill

St Johns
Wood

Regents
Park

Kensal
Green

Maida
Vale

Notting
Hill

Holland
Park

Hyde
Park

Kensington

Earls
Court

Chelsea

2.7km

6.0km

9.5km

11.4km

West

East London

The districts north and east of The City include Hackney, Mile End and Stratford, due east are Whitechapel, Wapping, Canary Wharf and the Royal Docks. Like most of London, the districts of the east-end are a hotchpotch of industry and housing, with pockets of both deprivation and wealth interwoven into the mix of cultures and identities running through the area.

Traditionally east London has been associated with industry, manual work, factories and poor housing. It was where many migrants to London first landed at custom's house and due to cheap rents, where many still choose to settle. Today the area is shaking off this run-down image thanks to billions of pounds of investment.

On the edge of The City Shoreditch's abandoned warehouses evolved from artists' squats to smart loft apartments. One of London's most fashionable neighbourhoods, the scene is fast spreading northwards to Hoxton and Hackney. Hackney's Victoria Park borders both the Regent Canal to the west and the Lee River to the east. The Lee River towpath runs north to the small market town of Waltham Abbey and south, past the developing 2012 Olympic Park, onto Canary Wharf. This large office development on the Isle of Dogs is built around disused docks. Many banks are relocating here where they get more flexible office space than in The City and the area is now bristling with skyscrapers. Northeast of Stratford's Olympic Park, a thin strip of ancient woodland leads to the wilds of Epping Forest and due east a car free greenway runs to the Royal Docks.

Rides 43 and 49 are off-road mountain bike trails through the woods. Rides 44, 46 and 48 are predominantly gentle, car free riverside paths. Rides 47 and 50 are fairly industrial routes while Ride 45 takes you through Hackney's parks, market and residential areas. In short, a little of everything for those looking for the full London cycling experience.

East End Graffiti

The white-washed Tudor Queen Elizabeth hunting lodge

At a Glance

Distance 19.5km   **Total Climbing** 151m

Terrain

MTB – unsurfaced paths and tracks and can be muddy after wet weather.

Traffic

Car free.

How to Get There

Chingford Station; car park off Rangers Road opposite Queen Elisabeth's Hunting Lodge or at the Epping Forest Visitor Centre in High Beech.

Food and Drink

The Owl, Lippits Hill, Loughton or Kings Oak Hotel, Paul's Nursery Road, High Beech; there is also a tea hut at Hill Wood.

Side Trip

If you're swept away by the forest tracks and want to do more, try getting in touch with Epping Forest Mountain Bike Riders, information at www.epping-forest-mbc.co.uk.

Links to (other rides) 49.

Bike Hire

For service try Ash Auto-parts & Cycles, 94 Station Road, Chingford, unfortunately there is no bike hire.

Where to Ride Rating 

About...

An undulating, adventurous mountain bike ride through the wilds of Epping Forest, the ancient woodland where Henry VIII and Queen Elizabeth I hunted for deer. The vales of oak, beech and hornbeam make up the largest area of forest within M25. The trees are criss-crossed by a maze of tracks and bridleways. A compass is essential equipment if you are not to get lost as the falling leaves can cover the trails and it is easy to lose one's sense of direction on this exciting but demanding trail.

Inside the hunting lodge is a Tudor food display

Starting at the brilliant white, lime-washed Queen Elizabeth's Hunting Lodge (Mar-Sep Wed-Sun 12-5pm, Oct-Feb Fri-Sun 12-3pm; free) the route heads down a vale before climbing gently up to the forest. The Hunting Lodge was originally known as the Great Standing and was built for Henry VIII in 1543. It was constructed as a grandstand to allow guests to view the hunt from a high vantage point. It also served as a venue for royal Tudor 'corporate hospitality' to show off the wealth and power of the king. On the ground floor, there is a colourful display of Tudor foods and replica kitchenware while the upper floors have great views over Chingford Plain and Epping Forest.

Once in the forest, the wide path heads northwards through woodland, grassland and heath, passing rivers, bogs and ponds towards the Epping Forest Visitor Centre containing maps, books and items carved with wood from the forest. Staff are on hand to answer your every query about the woodland (daily, Mar-Sep 10am-5pm, Oct-Feb 10am-3pm; free). From here the path continues northwards along the ridge between the valleys of the rivers Lea and Roding. The elevated, thin, gravely soil are the result of retreating glaciations and this poor soil has historically made the area unsuitable for agriculture resulting in the, 19 kilometres long but never more than four kilometres wide, forest we now know.

The narrowing path crosses a few roads before reaching the embankments of the Iron Age Ambresbury Banks. The banks and ditch remaining are protected so please only visit on foot to avoid damaging the ancient fortified site. Further north a brick parapet marks the entrance to the M25 motorway into a cut-and-cover tunnel that runs beneath the cricket pitch. Here the path returns southwards along the Green Ride following the eastern edge of the forest over rolling hills past the earth works of Loughton Camp, a second iron age settlement dating from around 500BC, before returning to the hunting lodge to complete the loop. A number of clubs organise rides, particularly on Sunday mornings. The forest is also used as a training area for many national level mountain bike racers as it is highly regarded for its fast and tight flowing single track trails known as cross country.

East

Ride Log

0.0 Starting at the Queen Elizabeth Hunting Lodge 800m east of Chingford Station. Go eastwards along Rangers Rd for 50m turn left just past a building that was formally Butler's Retreat tea room. The path leads down through grassland into a vale. At the bottom bear right onto a track until you reach the surfaced 'Green Ride'. Turn left and continue along this for 1.7km.

1.9 Here the route bends sharp right (eastwards). On the bend take a left turn into a clearing to join a path that continues the original bearing northwards. The path continues through woods to another clearing.

2.0 Ignore the bridleways left and right and continue on the principal surfaced path as it bears right then left before re-entering the forest.

3.0 After 1km the path emerges onto Cross Roads Rd. Cross straight over and continue back into the forest and behind the Epping Forest Visitor Centre. Cross over the Pillow Mounds car park approach road and bear right onto another surface forest path called the General's Ride. This path crosses over Claypit Hill Rd and continues north eastwards along the Forest Way path.

5.6 At the end cross the busy A121 Woodridden Hill and bear right on the other side along a track parallel with the road. Then head around the back of a riding school. bearing left onto a track now parallel with busy B1393 Epping Rd.

7.3 Cross straight over the small Lodge Rd and follow the path straight across the busy Epping Rd, please be aware of fast traffic here.

7.4 On the other side take Forest Rd. After a short distance there is a junction of rides. Bear left here along the Green Ride (northwards) and continue for 500 undulating metres. The embankments of Amesbury Banks lie in the trees to the left.

7.6 The next junction marks the start of a 3km loop which you can cut out if you wish. Following the loop anticlockwise continue for another 1km. At the end of the forest the path curves left past a cricket pitch on the right before descending back into the forest and between a few ponds before bearing left to rejoin the main path.

10.6 Turn right on the main Green Ride path. After 600m cross straight over the B172 road into Ditches Ride crossing straight over Golding Hill A121 Rd.

13.3 After this the path then goes down, then up, then down again and up again before crossing Earls Path Rd near the Strawberry Hill Ponds. Continue southwards through clearing before crossing over the corner of Warren Hill and Nursery Rd. The path undulates again through the forest emerging onto Manor Rd. Cross over and follow the path into the forest before bearing right into a clearing.

18.5 On the other side cross Epping New Rd and follow the grassy path westwards back to the hunting lodge.

19.5 You are at the start.

Epping Forest Loop

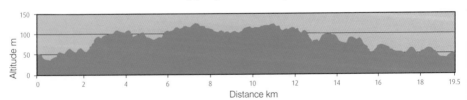

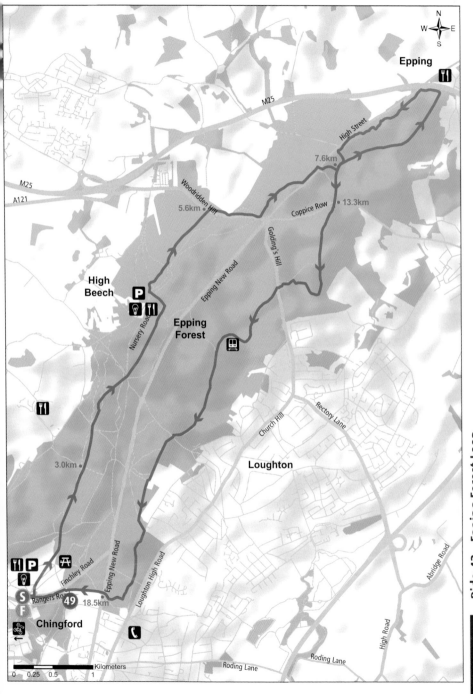

Epping

N
W — E
S

M25

A121

M25

High Street

7.6km

Woodridden Hill

5.6km

Coppice Row   • 13.3km

Golding's Hill

High
Beech

P

Epping New Road

Epping
Forest

Nursery Road

3.0km •

Loughton

Church Hill

Rectory Lane

Finchley Road

Epping New Road

Loughton High Road

High Road

Abridge Road

S
F

Rangers Rd   49   18.5km

Chingford

Roding Lane   Roding Lane

Kilometers
0   0.25   0.5   1

Cyclepath going south looking towards Canary Wharf from Three Bridges

At a Glance

Distance 16.0km **Total Climbing** 35m

Terrain

Surfaced roads and surfaced paths with a short 50m section of cobbles.

Traffic

Almost all this route is car free, only the first two kilometres are on quiet roads.

How to Get There

Woolwich Arsenal Station at the eastern start, Shadwell Overground at the western end; car parking at the ExCel exhibition centre.

Food and Drink

There is a café at Three Mills and riverside eateries and pubs around Limehouse; for Chinese try Yi Ban on Dockside Road overlooking Royal Albert Dock.

Side Trip

Take a detour down the Olympic greenway and turn southwards along the Lee River to rejoin the main route, check out London's progress on the 2012 Olympic Park.

Links to (other rides) 3, 7, 22, 23, 28, 29, 47, 50.

Bike Hire

Station Cycles, Arch 1-4 Upper Walthamstow or Evans Cycles Canary Wharf.

Where to Ride Rating

About...

A varied and interesting ride from seafaring Woolwich in the east through the regenerating royal docks to the start of the East London Greenway. This strip of green runs on top of the Northern Outfall Sewer through the heart of East London to the evolving Olympic Park in Stratford. From here the route follows a towpath along the canalised River Lee as it flows southwards before branching onto the Limehouse Cut beneath iron bridges and floating walkways, emerging at the Limehouse basin and Canary Wharf. From here a ferry can take you back to the start.

Green hand painted on one of the colourful houseboats

Starting at Woolwich Arsenal Station the route crosses through the historic Royal Arsenal. The warehouses used for armaments manufacture are now being converted into apartments but the Firepower Museum (Wed-Sun, 10.30am-5pm; adult £5, child £2.50) charts the area's history. From here the trail follows the Thames Path to the Woolwich Ferry. The free boat across the Thames runs about every 15 minutes carrying cars and lorries. On the other side the route passes alongside the creepy disused railway in the shadow of the mighty Tate & Lyle sugar factory. The acrid smells of refinement fill your lungs before the route peels away around London City Airport and between the royal docks. The huge disused Victorian docks are being surrounded by regeneration schemes. On the left is the white box of the ExCel exhibition space while on the right you'll see the small planes taking off and landing at London's business airport. In front is the modern London Regatta centre who use the docks for rowing and sailing.

The route follows a greenway through Beckton to the start of the East London Greenway constructed on the embankment containing the Northern Outfall Sewer (NOS). The NOS is a major gravity sewer which runs from Wick Lane in Hackney to Beckton Sewage Works

in east London (east of Stratford); most of it was designed by Joseph Bazalgette after an outbreak of cholera in 1853 and "The Big Stink" of 1858. It is still a little pongy around here but the greenway is a fantastic car free route above the rooftops of East Ham, Plaistow and West Ham. At the other end is Stratford and opposite is the emerging Olympic Park being built for the 2012 games.

Here the route turns southwards between the canalised Lee River and Three Mills Green. The House Mill remains the largest tidal mill in the world and though no longer used for bottling and warehousing by Bass Charrington, the original buildings are used for educational projects. From here the trail follows a narrow island between the Lee and the Limehouse Cut beneath lattice iron railway bridges and a cobbled path over the Bow Creek locks recently refurbished by British waterways to keep the tide out of the canal system thereby preventing silt build-up in the channel. As part of the works a floating cyclepath was constructed on the canal under the A12 leading to the towpath along the edge of the cut all the way back to the Limehouse Basin. From here the route joins the Thames Path to the edge of the Canary Wharf development where river boats depart for Woolwich and central London.

Ride Log

0.0 Turn right out of Woolwich Arsenal Station onto New Rd. At the end use the pedestrian lights to cross over the busy Plumstead Rd into the Royal Arsenal. Cycle down to the Thames Path and turn left along the river.

1.2 When you reach the ferry use the ferry approach road to access.

1.7 On the other side take the first left off the ferry approach ramp onto Pier Rd. Follow the road around to the right and at the end turn left along Factory Rd. At the end continue straight onto the cycleway.

3.6 At the roundabout turn right staying on the right hand shared use path as it leaves the edge of road and bends right passing a car park. Cross Hartmann Rd and take shared use path left following the City Airport perimeter fence. The path leads beneath the road and onto a dedicated cycle bridge across the wharf.

4.2 On the other side turn right along the wharf pedestrian area then turn left after the Regatta Centre buildings under the DLR line and straight across Dockside Rd. At the end turn right along the path. Cross over Stansfeild Rd and continue straight on.

6.0 At busy Woolwich Manor Way turn left on cycleway. Follow the cycleway around the outside of the roundabout using bike lights to cross Tollgate Rd. Turn left off the path before it passes under Woolwich Manor, instead rising back to the shared use pavement parallel with Woolwich Manor Way.

6.7 At the busy junction as the cyclepath bears left, use the bike lights to cross right under the A13 flyover. On the other side continue up High St South for 20m before the turning left onto the clearly marked Greenway.

6.8 Follow the Greenway straight on across several roads for almost 5km.

11.6 At the busy High St turn left along shared use pavement. Twenty metres after crossing Abbey Ln turn left down onto canal towpath.

11.7 Follow the towpath along the edge of the canal to Three Mills Ln. Turn right through the Mill and then left on the other side to resume the route along the towpath between the Lee River and the Limehouse Cut Canal. The route passes under railway bridges and over a set of locks before plunging beneath the A13 on a cycle boardwalk floating along the edge of the canal.

13.3 On the other side follow the towpath southwards for 2km.

15.3 Exit left through a small park just before a footbridge and the Limehouse Basin.

15.5 On the other side of the park cross over Narrow St and follow signs for Thames Path. Turn left along the Thames Path to the parade of waterside restaurants.

16.0 This is the end of the route. You can take a riverboat from the pier back to Woolwich or return via another route.

East London Greenway

Distance km

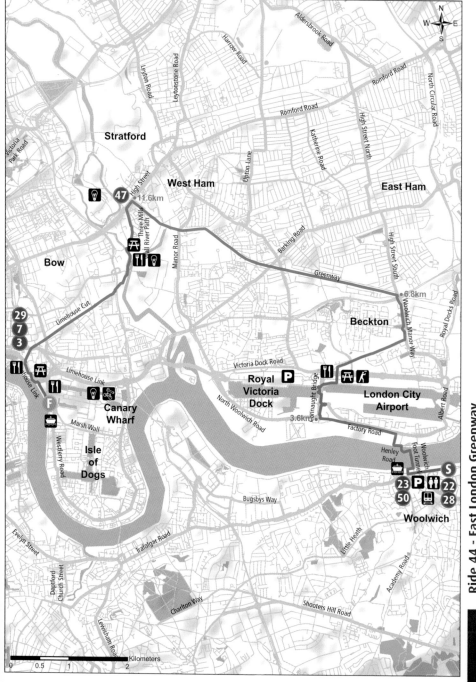

Stratford

West Ham

East Ham

Bow

Beckton

Canary
Wharf

Royal
Victoria
Dock

London City
Airport

Isle
of
Dogs

Woolwich

Hackney Parks Loop

A peloton streams through Victoria Park

At a Glance

Distance 10.2km   **Total Climbing** 59m

Terrain
Surfaced roads and surfaced paths.

Traffic
Quiet residential roads designated as cycle routes, some busy crossings.

How to Get There
London Fields Station, alternatively Hackney Central Overground; metered street parking on residential streets around London Fields.

Food and Drink
Stalls along Broadway Food Market or Lock 7 Cycle Café, 129 Pritchards Road.

Side Trip
Middlesex Filter Beds are a nature reserve in the Lee Valley Regional Park. They are home to all sorts of different plant and animal life and are a tranquil place for a picnic.

Links to (other rides) 2, 3, 47, 48.

Bike Hire
Lock 7 Cycle Café, 129 Pritchards Road or London Fields Cycles 281 Mare Street.

Where to Ride Rating

About...

Hackney not only has the highest percentage of people cycling to work in London, but also the UK's largest increase in cycling from 1991-2001. So the area can rightfully claim to be the capital's cycling borough. In fact 8% of all journeys in the borough are by bicycle, which is four times the Greater London average. Our 'Tour de Hackney' pays tribute to this achievement taking in the borough's pretty parks between the hubbub of vibrant streets.

Colourful graffiti in Hackney and the east end is common

Starting in London Fields, once the traditional grazing ground for animals going to nearby Broadway Market, now a pleasant open space home to one of the capitals few 50m lidos, the route bears northwards along Victorian terraces before arriving at Hackney Downs. The trail takes a diagonal direction across the wide grassy open space before leaving into a maze of suburban roads through Clapton leading up to North Mill Fields recreation ground. Here the ride joins the towpath along side the Lee Navigation, a canalised river used for transporting grain from Hertfordshire down to the city mills but is mainly used today by rowers and houseboats. The canal is only a brief distraction before the route heads away from the water through South Mill Fields. At the end Powerscroft Road leads all the way to the busy shopping streets around Hackney Central with vibrant ethnic shops sharing the pavements with cafes and greasy spoons. The route passes through pretty early Victorian Clapton Square before crossing the busy lower Clapton Road into Churchwell Path past the churchyard gardens of St John at Hackney. The pretty and tranquil graveyard is a nice place for a rest. On the left is the National Trust run Sutton House (Feb-Dec

12-4.30pm; adult £2.90, child 80p). One of the oldest houses in East London, the building contains five centuries of family history showing changing styles and tastes through the ages while the authentic Tudor kitchen has objects to touch and smell. From here you duck beneath the railway line to yet more quiet residential streets leading to Well Street Common in south Hackney of which George Grocott wrote in 1846 "the undesirable characters who frequented it were a source of annoyance to the residents of the superior class houses abutting thereon". Fortunately this was all remedied when the annoying characters moved into the superior class houses in the 1960s and the place now has a laid back casual atmosphere. On the other side of the common the ride passes through Victoria Park. Laid out in 1842 it is the oldest municipal park in the world and the fine mature plain trees and wide avenues provide lots of beautiful cycling. On the western edge is Regents canal. The towpath leads to Lock 17 bike café on the edge of the busy Broadway Food Market, here barrow boys still sell everything from bacon to beans to an increasingly gentrified clientele. It may be necessary to dismount to reach the far end of the market and London Fields to complete the loop.

East

Ride Log

0.0 Starting at London Fields Station turn right onto Martello Terrace and at the end bearing right onto Martello St. After 50m enter park on left and follow cyclepath past play area. Cross Richmond Rd into Eleanor Rd.

0.7 At the end go left then right into Navarino Rd crossing straight over busy Dalston Ln into Wayland Ave.

1.3 At the end it's a right then left into Amhurst Rd followed by second right along Down Park Rd.

1.8 As soon as you've passed under the railway, turn left into Hackney Downs and cross the open space diagonally towards the opposite corner. Here turn right along Downs Rd. At the junction turn left to continue along Downs Rd.

2.5 At the end turn left along busy Lower Clapton Rd and then first right, doubling back in front of a row of terraced houses also called Lower Clapton Rd.

2.8 Take the first left along Newick Rd and at the end right then left into Fletching Rd.

3.4 At the end turn left along Chatsworth Rd. Cross over the busy road at the end and follow the cycleway right, parallel with Lee Bridge Rd. Before the bridge bear off left and follow green signs right following the canal route under the cycle and road bridge. Continue along the path on the other side. After 80m take the right turn into South Mill Fields and follow the cycleway diagonally through the open space.

4.6 Exit crossing straight over the junction to continue on the same trajectory along Powerscroft Rd.

5.3 At the end cross straight over busy Lower Clapton Rd into narrow pedestrianised Clapton Passage and at the end bear left along Clapton Square.

5.6 Cross straight over the busy Lower Clapton Rd into the Churchwell Path cycleway. Continue straight on under the railway and across Morning Ln into Chatham Pl finally bearing left into Elsdale St.

6.6 At the end of Elsdale St turn right then left into Cassland Rd. Take the first right down Meynell Rd and enter Well Street Common. Follow the cycleway in front of you and after 70m at the junction of paths bear left towards the eastern corner of the open space. Here bear right onto St Marks Gate and pass into Victoria Park at the end.

7.4 Turn right along the northern edge of the park continuing straight across Grove Rd. Continue as the path bears left around the edge of the park and exit bearing right onto the Regent Canal in front of you. Follow the canal towpath.

9.6 Come off the towpath at the second road bridge signposted Broadway Market. Turn right (northwards) through the market (it may be necessary to dismount if busy). And at the end cross into London Fields using the bike lights.

10.2 Follow the cycleway through the park to the start of the route.

Hackney Parks Loop

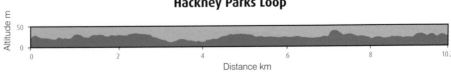

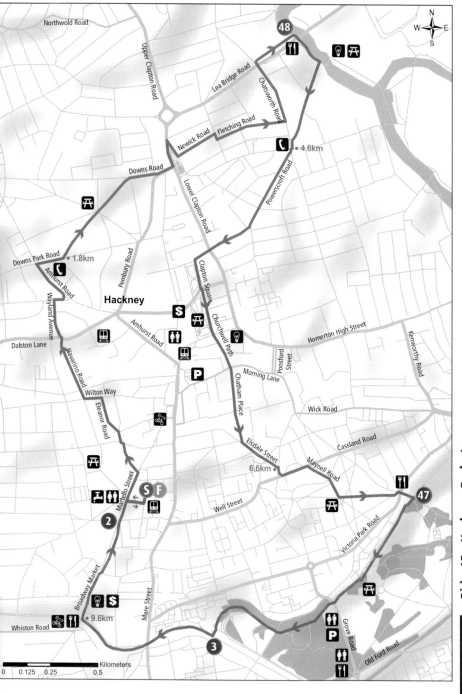

Northwold Road

Upper Clapton Road

48

Lea Bridge Road

Chatsworth Road

Newick Road   Fletching Road

Downs Road

4.6km

Lower Clapton Road

Powerscroft Road

Downs Park Road   1.8km

Pembury Road

Amhurst Road

Hackney

Wayland Avenue

Dalston Lane

Navarino Road

Amhurst Road

Clapton Square

Churchwell Path

Homerton High Street

Kenworthy Road

Wilton Way

Eleanor Road

Morning Lane

Ponsford Street

Chatham Place

Wick Road

Martello Street

Elsdale Street

Cassland Road

6.6km

Maynell Road

S F

2

Well Street

Victoria Park Road

Broadway Market

47

Mare Street

9.6km

Whiston Road

3

Grove Road

Old Ford Road

0   0.125   0.25   0.5   Kilometers

Ride 45 - Hackney Parks Loop

East

Waltham Abbey's Saturday village market

At a Glance

Distance 14.7km   **Total Climbing** 37m

Terrain

Surfaced and unsurfaced canal towpath, short cobbled sections.

Traffic

Almost all car free except for the last 800m through Waltham Abbey.

How to Get There

Stoke Newington Rail Station, South Tottenham Overground and Tottenham Hale are all within 2km of the start of the route, Waltham Cross Rail Station is near the northern end of the route.

Food and Drink

Plenty of pubs and tea rooms in Waltham Abbey as well as a market. Otherwise try the Ferry Boat, Ferry Lane near Tottenham Hale.

Side Trip

Epping Forest is only a few kilometres away if you fancy heading back to London through the trees.

Links to (other rides) 48.

Bike Hire

Cyclone Cycles, 15 Market Square, Waltham Abbey

Where to Ride Rating

About...

A route from Clapton through Walthamstow, Tottenham and Edmonton to Waltham Abbey just beyond the M25 may sound like a white-knuckle ride through the grimmest estates in north-east London, that is until you discover the River Lee. The Lee Navigation is a canalised river flowing from Hertfordshire to the Thames at Bow Creek. Along its edge are a chain of nature reserves, quiet parks and reservoirs forming the Lee Valley Regional Park. The route follows the towpath northwards past houseboats and rowers before arriving at the traditional market town of Waltham Abbey in the shadow of the 1000 year old church.

Waltham Abbey

Starting at Springfield Park, easily accessed from Stoke Newington Station and surrounding stations, the route heads due north along the towpath on the western edge of the Lee Navigation canal. This part of the ride forms a section of National Cycle Route 1 stretching from Dover to the Shetland Islands! To the right the high grass banks contain the lakes belonging to the Lee Valley Reservoir Chain with the 13 reservoirs that supply drinking water to London and on the left are the Tottenham Marshes, home to many kingfisher and butterflies. After Stonebridge locks the path enters an industrial area of warehouses and workshops before passing beneath the grim north circular flyover. Beyond this is Pickets Lock. From here you could almost be in Norfolk with all greenery and gaily-painted barges. Only the enormous network of electricity pylons remind you that you're still in London.

The towpath continues northwards and the scenery remains unchanged until you reach Enfield Island Village created in the 1990s after closure of a small arms factory. Here the route joins quiet Government Row passing in front of factory workers cottages before rejoining the towpath through Rammey Marsh. At the edge the ride passes under the M25 Motorway

before leaving the canal at Station Road and heading eastwards into the medieval market town of Waltham Abbey. The town takes its name from the Abbey Church of Waltham Holy Cross, which was prominent in the early history of the town. Founded in 1030 to house a Holy Rood, a large black flint crucifix from Glastonbury, Harold Godwinson (later King Harold II) rebuilt, re-founded and richly endowed the church in 1060. He stopped to pray at Waltham on his way to fight William of Normandy, and the battle-cry of the English troops at Hastings was "Holy Cross". The later Augustinian abbey was a popular place for overnight stays with kings and other notables who were hunting in Waltham Forest. As a result it was the last abbey in England to be dissolved by Henry VIII and the Holy Cross disappeared without trace at this time. After its destruction the remnant of the nave became the town's parish church that still stands today.

Ride Log

0.0 From Springfield Park head north along the western towpath following the signs for National Cycle Route.

1.0 The blue arrows are very clearly positioned at the occasional junction along the towpath.

13.0 Continue on the towpath beneath the wide concrete bridge carrying the M25 motorway.

13.7 Look out for an exit from the towpath leading up to Highbridge St. Here you leave National Cycle Route 1 and turn right onto Highbridge St.

14.0 At the large roundabout take the third exit to continue along Highbridge St leading to the back of Waltham Abbey in front of you.

14.7 Waltham Abbey is the end of the route.

Neatly arranged Bream decorate a fishmonger's stall at the Saturday market

Lee Valley Regional Park Trail

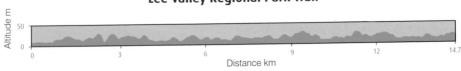

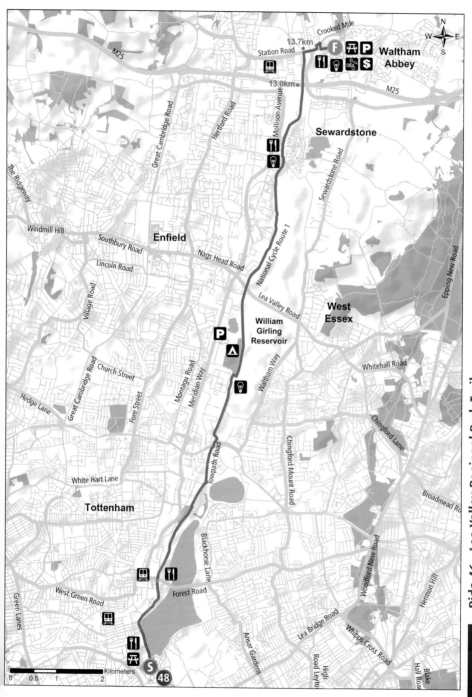

Ride 46 - Lee Valley Regional Park Trail

East

The old post office on Cadogan Terrace next to Victoria Park

At a Glance

Distance 12.1km   **Total Climbing** 62m

Terrain

Surfaced roads and surfaced greenway path.

Traffic

Around half the route is car free, however there are some sections on busy roads particularly around the northern edge of the Olympic Park where large works vehicles are circulating.

How to Get There

Stratford Station and Stratford Overground; parking at Stratford shopping centre.

Food and Drink

The Pavilion Café Victoria Park.

Side Trip

Broadway Market near London Fields has great food stalls and cafes or visit the Lee Valley Cycle Circuit just north of the route on Quartermile Lane where there is 3km of smooth track.

Links to (other rides) 3, 44, 45, 48, 49.

Bike Hire

Bikeworks, Unit 8 Gun Wharf, 241 Old Ford Road.

Where to Ride Rating

About...

The ever-changing London 2012 site is turning a largely derelict area of the lower Lee Valley Regional Park into sports stadiums and parkland. Some of the surrounding roads have heavy plant traffic delivering building materials to the park and the routes around the park may change as construction progresses, however this route allows you to access the centre of the giant building site where a viewing pod overlooks the main Olympic stadium and iconic wave-like aquatics centre.

The 2012 London Olympic Stadium

From Stratford Station the route heads along the north edge of the park. The road between the Hackney Marshes and the Olympic Park is congested with building trucks and diverted traffic so be careful along this section. Once past the contractors' entrance the route becomes calmer before passing through the scrapyards of twisted metal and broken cars between the Hackney Wick warehouses.

From here a cycle bridge crosses over the busy A12 to the edge of Victoria Park. The mature London plane trees and areas of open grassland and ponds were laid out by James Pennethorne between 1842 and 1846 are a fantastic place to picnic and relax. The area is the world's first public park and the Olympic park will be the world's newest inner urban public park. The route passes around the outside of Victoria Park and joins the Regents Canal that runs along the western edge of the park. Heading southwards along the popular towpath past houseboats and walkers you'll eventually branch off up the quieter Hertford Union Canal. At the end are disused warehouses and squats being converted into a modern apartment block. The colourful hoardings around the Olympic Park reflect in the water while the red brick walls are covered in graffiti.

The trail crosses over to the opposite bank near the confluence of the Hertford Canal and Lee Navigation before continuing southwards on the towpath in the shadow of the white tubular Olympic stadium. After 500m the route turns off onto the main Olympic Greenway rising on a cutting that slices through the park. Park you bike and visit the yellow containers of the 'view tube' for a panorama over the construction site with the Olympic stadium on the left and the wave-like aquatic centre designed by Zaha Hadid on the right. In the distance you can see the arching roof of the velodrome behind Stratford Station, the new Eurostar station and Westfield Shopping Centre. The greenway ends at the busy High Street leading northwards to Stratford, however the route weaves along back streets past new apartments and estates before crossing over a pedestrian bridge crossing the tube to avoid the traffic.

East

Ride 47 - Olympic Greenway Loop

Ride Log

Graffiti is a familiar sight along the walled sections of the Lee canalised river

0.0 Turn left out of Stratford Station along the shared cycle pavement running next to busy Great Eastern Rd. Take the first left up Angle Ln and continue straight on into Leyton Rd.

1.2 At the end turn left along Temple Mill Ln. Please be aware of heavy plant traffic in this area associated with the Olympic development. Continue round as the road bears right before passing under the A12.

2.4 At the end turn left along Ruckholt following the shared use pavement and cycle signs back under the A12 and past the Olympic Park plant access point. Continue on the green cyclepath over the canal and straight on at the lights before following the road around as it bears left along Eastway.

4.0 At the next set of lights bear left into the cycle lane and into Chapman Rd passing under a rail line before turning right immediately after a car breakers yard to join a footbridge passing over the busy A12.

4.6 On the other side enter Victoria Park and turn right on the surfaced path around the northern edge of the park. Continue as the path swings westwards crossing straight over Grove Rd.

6.0 After crossing Grove Rd take the wide path left and follow this around until you can access the Regents Canal.

6.7 Turn left along the canal towpath. After 100m there is a rise, turn left here onto the Hertford Union Canal towpath and follow this to the end.

8.8 Emerging up onto White Post Ln turn right and then right again down onto the towpath along the eastern edge of the Lee Navigation. Go southward back towards the junction of canals.

9.5 After a lock, pass over a footbridge. At the next bridge turn left off the canal onto the Olympic Greenway passing right through the Olympic Park and emerging onto the busy High St.

10.6 Turn left here and then second left along Carpenters Rd. Take the right before the railway bridge along Gibbins Rd. Follow the road around and look left for a footbridge over the rail line.

12.1 Once over this, turn left back to Stratford Station.

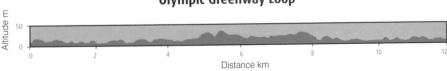

Olympic Greenway Loop

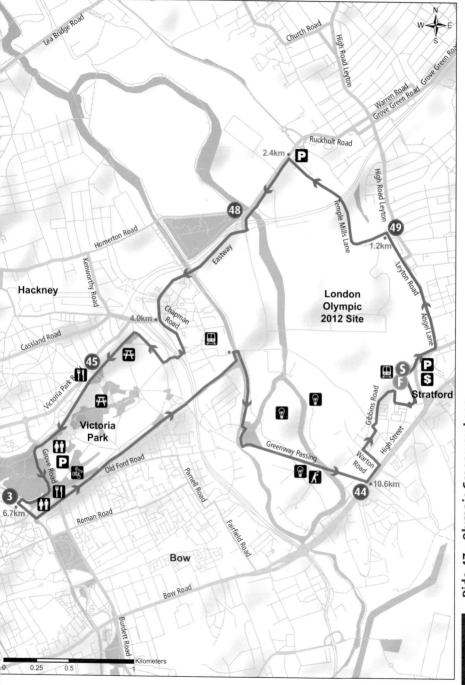

Ride 47 - Olympic Greenway Loop

A route sign marking the Lee Valley walk; there are plenty of cycle route signs too

At a Glance

Distance 11.0km   **Total Climbing** 24m

Terrain

Surfaced and unsurfaced towpath; beware that some parts of this route can become unpassable after heavy rain.

Traffic

Car free.

How to Get There

Hackney Wick Overground Station; free parking on industrial roads around Hackney Wick Station.

Food and Drink

The Riverside Café, Spring Hill.

Side Trip

The Olympic Greenway and Victoria Park are both worth a detour.

Links to (other rides) 45, 46, 47.

Bike Hire

No hire, service at AS Cycles, 1 Chatsworth Road, Clapton.

Where to Ride Rating

About...

From Hackney Wick Station there is a brief assault course through skanky scrapyards until you reach the Lee Navigation. This canalised river incorporating the River Lee runs from Hertford Castle Weir all the way to the River Thames at Bow Creek and was used to transport grain from the rich arable lands of Hertfordshire through to the mills around the marshes. Though commercial traffic has all but ceased, the waterway is popular with leisure boats rowers and canoeists.

Graffiti around the canal is a familiar sight

From here the towpath blazes northwards passing the colourful hoarding of the Olympic construction site before ducking under a grim flyover carrying the A12. On the other side you enter the semi-rural vista that is Hackney Marsh and the first time you feel truly within the Lee Valley Regional Park, a 42km long linear reserve, much of it green spaces following the course of the River Lee. Keep left before crossing the river on an old bridge opposite the Middlesex filter beds. Just after Springfield Park the shingle track reaches Lee Valley Marina, popular with rowing clubs. Here the route crosses an iron bridge, just below the reservoirs at copper mill, through a community of gaily-painted barges before ducking low beneath a rail line. The claustrophobic passage is susceptible to flooding and can become impassable in wet weather.

On the right is the entrance to the pretty nature reserve that is Walthamstow Marshes, home to cows, geese and ducks. From here it gets seriously bucolic: huge skies and lush greenery, punctuated only by the odd high-rise and the occasional burst of graffiti. The marshes contain several species of rare insects and marshland birds including reed bunting, sedge and willow warblers plus a variety of wintering birds. At

the end are the Middlesex filter beds, built in 1852, three years after London's worst Cholera outbreak in response to the consequent demand for cleaner water. After more than 100 years in operation, the Middlesex Filter Beds had become outdated but each disused filter bed is now managed so as to provide a variety of habitats for wildlife. The wetland areas are ideal for amphibians such as toads, frogs and newts all of which breed here.

From here a new bridge crosses to Hackney Marsh. It was originally a true marsh, but was extensively drained from medieval times and rubble was dumped here from buildings damaged by air raids during World War II and is now occupied by playing fields. At the southern end past the recreation fields is the Temple Mills. These water mills belonged to the Knights Templar, and were used mainly for grinding corn. Beyond A12 the park continues but is currently closed for construction of sites hosting the 2012 London Olympic Games. It is hoped that the park will eventually extend three kilometres further south to the Thames. The route crosses the busy roads to rejoin the towpath back to Hackney Wick completing the nearly all off-road loop.

East

Ride Log

0.0 From Hackney Wick Station turn left out of the station and left along White Post Ln. Cross the canal and join the towpath going northwards back under the bridge you passed over.

0.4 Continue following the river for 2.5km staying to the edge of the canal until the path crosses a bridge at the Middlesex Filter Beds Nature Reserve.

3.0 Continue along the west bank under Lee Bridge Rd.

4.8 Just past Springfield Park cross back over the canal using High Bridge. On the other side pass through the boat park and bear left on the surfaced path under the rail line.

5.4 As soon as you pass under, turn right. After 600m this leads under another rail line. Continue to follow the path straight southwards.

7.2 Just after passing through the Middlesex filter beds the path bends left. At this point take the path bearing right across the River Lee. On the other side turn left to go around the eastern edge of the playing fields.

9.4 When the path ends turn left onto Homerton Rd. Cross straight over the busy junction using the bike lights and pass under the A12 flyover on the shared use pavement.

9.6 On the other side turn right along East Way passing in front of the contractor's entrance to the Olympic Park. After 400m there is a path signposted with a green footpath marker to the left. Take this to rejoin the Lee canal. Head southwards back to Hackney Wick Station along the path you came.

11.0 Once back at the station you have completed the loop.

Rowing boats neatly stacked at the Lee Valley Marina near Springfield Park

River Lee South Trail

Altitude m

Distance km

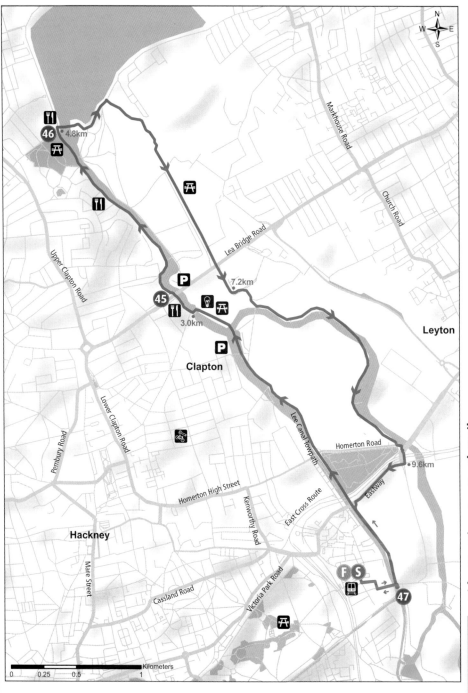

Leyton

Clapton

Hackney

4.8km

7.2km

3.0km

9.6km

Markhouse Road

Church Road

Lea Bridge Road

Upper Clapton Road

Lower Clapton Road

Pembury Road

Homerton High Street

Kenworthy Road

Lee Canal Towpath

East Cross Route

Homerton Road

Eastway

Mare Street

Cassland Road

Victoria Park Road

F S

N
W—E
S

Kilometers
0   0.25   0.5   1

A dusty bike in a Stratford back alley

At a Glance

Distance 13.3km   **Total Climbing** 68m

Terrain

MTB, rough unsurfaced tracks and paths.

Traffic

Mostly car free, the last section through Stratford is along quiet residential roads, there are some busy crossings.

How to Get There

Chingford Railway Station at the northern start of the route and Stratford Overground Station at the southern end of the route; parking opposite Queen Elizabeth's Hunting Lodge on Ranger Road, multistorey car park in Stratford shopping centre.

Food and Drink

There are no cafés or tea huts along the route however there are plenty of good picnic spots.

Side Trip

Cross over and return via the Lee River or extend your route up through Epping Forest.

Links to (other rides) 43, 47.

Bike Hire

Ash Auto-parts & Cycles, 94 Station Road, Chingford or Bike Trax, 3 Cambridge Park, Wanstead. Both offer sales and service, no hire.

Where to Ride Rating

About...

A 13km path heading due south from the wilds of Epping Forest to the chaos of Stratford and the Olympic construction site. The route makes use of an ancient green chain of forest, open common land and parks that cut through the urban sprawl. Never a long way from suburbia but far from the maddening crowds. Dirt tracks and grassy bridleways add to the adventure.

Double yellow lines

Starting just up the road from Chingford Station at the Tudor Queen Elizabeth's Hunting Lodge (Mar-Sep Wed-Sun 12-5pm, Oct-Feb Fri-Sun 12-3pm; free). The lodge was originally known as the Great Standing and was built for Henry VIII in 1543. The wooden framed and white lime-washed house was constructed as a grandstand to allow guests to view the hunt from a high vantage point, however it was also used as a venue for royal Tudor 'corporate hospitality' to show off the wealth and power of the king or queen. On the ground floor, there is a colourful display of Tudor foods and replica kitchenware while the upper floors have great views over Chingford Plain and Epping Forest.

Leaving the lodge the route bears southwards through the car park and around Warren Pond before blazing a trail through the thin sliver of Epping Forrest. Here the trail joins a bridleway following the banks of the River Ching. The stream springs in Epping Forest and flows into the Lee River near Banbury Reservoir and the trail follows the course of the brook for several kilometres before reaching the boating lake in The Highams Park. The pond was created by the damming of the river and provides a habitat for birds; watch out for protective nesting swans. The path continues back into the trees before emerging at a footbridge crossing the unsightly North Circular. On the other side there is a covered reservoir mound and a terrace of council allotments. From here the path gets narrower crashing through the trees before reaching Gilberts Slade, a stretch of open grassland in an otherwise mainly wooded part of the forest.

The white tipped posts, marking the continuation of the bridleway lead to the Hollow Pond boating lake used by locals for fishing and rowing. South again and the network of tracks weave to a surfaced cycleway under the grim A12. On the other side the route blazes through Bush Wood to an avenue of lime trees leading past playing fields before leaving the tranquillity of the forest and negotiating a way through the quiet suburban back streets of Leytonstone to Stratford Station next to the mighty 2012 Olympic construction site.

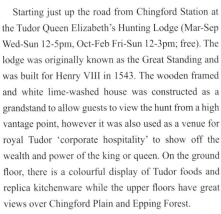

East

Ride Log

0.0 Turn right along Warren Pond Rd. Just after the pond bear left onto a dirt path through the forest. After 400m the path meets another path. Turn right here. Cross straight over Whitehall Rd continuing southwards.

1.9 After another kilometre bear around the right side of the golf course but continue southwards ignoring paths left and right. Follow the white-topped wooden posts marking the bridleway.

2.4 Cross Chingford Ln into the next section of forest. You pass around the left side of the boating lake before crossing The Charter Rd back into the forest. After 1.5km the path bends slightly right into a small open space before crossing Oakhill into dense forest. Continue southwards bearing left for 1km until you reach another open space. Stay on the right edge back into the scrub before a footbridge passing over the north circular. Continue straight on the other side to the next footbridge over Forest Rd.

5.4 Pass around the left side of the allotments before bearing left just after the boating lake and over Woodford New Rd. Take the narrow footpath on the other side until you reach open space then bear along the path on the right edge of the open space around the school and back into the trees.

6.9 At the end cross over Snaresbrook Rd through a small car park and back onto the path. Bear left around the lake but continue on a southerly heading. At the far corner of the open ground take the surfaced cycleway beneath Greenman roundabout. Ignore cyclepath left and right but when the cyclepath ends turn left along Bush Rd.

8.5 Turn right back into the open ground just beyond the junction with Browning Rd. The path goes back into the trees.

9.1 On the other side of the trees bear right onto a path along a grassy avenue with playing fields on the left.

9.6 Just past the playing fields turn right out of park onto Briscoe Cl. Pass under the railway and take the second left down Cecil Rd. At the mini roundabout turn right along Harrow Rd and then first left down Matcham Rd. Take the first right down Napier Rd and follow to the end.

11.0 Turn right on Ranelagh Rd and left onto High Rd. At the lights turn right into Crownfield Rd crossing straight over busy Leyton Major Rd leading into Temple Mill Ln. Take the first left down Leyton Rd.

13.0 At the end bear right onto the cycleway following busy Great Eastern Rd to Stratford Railway Station.

13.3 The station is the end of the route.

Epping to Stratford Trail

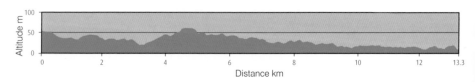

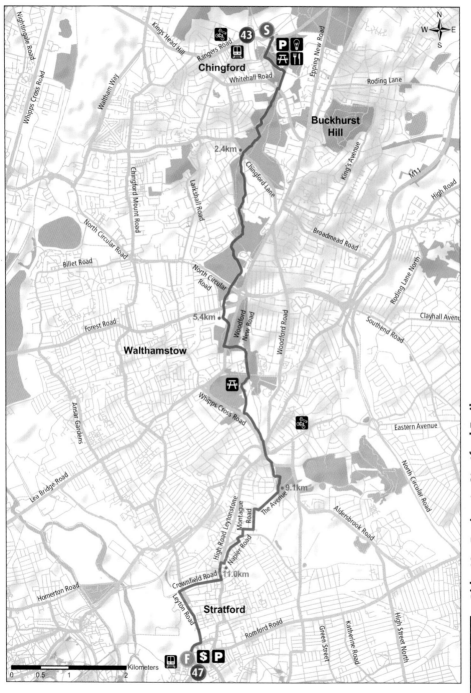

Looking towards the O2 entertainment arena from Orchard Place

At a Glance

Distance 8.9km   **Total Climbing** 26m

Terrain
Surfaced roads.

Traffic
Quiet industrial roads, though be aware that there are sections on dedicated cycle ways next to busy roads, there may also be some busy crossings.

How to Get There
Woolwich Arsenal Station, Greenwich Station; Thames riverboat points at Canary Wharf, Woolwich and Greenwich; street parking around Silvertown and at the southern end of the Isle of Dogs.

Food and Drink
Fat Boys Diner at Orchard Place or the Park Café at Island Gardens.

Side Trip
Both the Thames Barrier Park and Fat Boys Diner at Orchard Place are well worth the detours.

Links to (other rides) 22, 23, 28, 29, 44.

Bike Hire
Evans Cycles have a branch at Canary Wharf for sales and service only.

Where to Ride Rating

About...

This industrial trail takes in the factories and docks of the east end, passing the abandoned warehouses and dilapidated workshops lying beneath the new concrete viaducts of the Dockland Light Railway (DLR) as it bisects the Silvertown Peninsular, the land bridge between the empty Royal Docks and the River Thames. Beyond are the gleaming glass towers of Canary Wharf and the rest of the changing Isle of Dogs. Principal sights en route include Fat Boys Diner at Orchard Place, the manicured gardens and maze of the Thames Barrier Park and the Canary Wharf skyscrapers.

Cycling through a modern pavilion in the Thames Barrier Park

Starting on the south side of the river at Woolwich Arsenal Station the route heads northwards through the historic Royal Arsenal, the warehouses used for armaments manufacture are now being converted into apartments but the Firepower Museum (Wed-Sun, 10.30am-5pm; adult £5, child £2.50) charts the area's history. From here the trail follows the Thames Path to the Woolwich Ferry. The free boat across the Thames runs about every 15 minutes carrying cars and lorries. On the other side the route passes alongside the creepy disused railway in the shadow of the mighty Tate & Lyle sugar factory so be ready to fill your lungs with the acrid sting of refinement. On the other side of the railway you see the small aircraft taking off and landing at London's city airport, the runway having been built on a strip of land between two of the disused Royal Docks.

A little further along, next to Pontoon Dock DLR station, are the modern architectural gardens and walkways of the Thames Barrier Park. Maybe stop here for a picnic to admire the sleek beaten metal dome protruding from the river, between each one an individually controlled wall can be rotated into place protecting London from tidal flooding. Here the cycleway ends and the route continues along Dock Road passing warehouses, workshops and industrial units before reaching the flyover of the lower Lee crossing. Here a cycleway passes high above the river and the East India dock basin. On the other side a worthwhile detour to Orchard Place brings you to the mouth of the Lee. Here colourful shipping containers make up artist studios. There is an exhibition space and the berth of the Thames Clipper boats that operate the commuter services on the river. In the creek are disused lighthouse boats in front of Fat Boys Diner (Tue-Sun, 10am-5pm) a wonderful gleaming 1940s American style restaurant serving milkshakes, hamburgers and full-on American breakfast. There are fantastic views towards the O2 Arena and Canary Wharf. From here the route passes more new apartment developments bordering the Thames before passing over on an old iron bridge into the Isle of Dogs. On the right are the skyscrapers of the Canary Wharf business district. The route continues to the end of the island through Mudchute Park to Island Gardens. This pretty square of grass, next to the northern entrance of the Greenwich foot tunnel, looks over the river towards the beautiful Royal Naval College and maritime Greenwich.

East

Ride 50 - Woolwich to Isle of Dogs

Ride Log

0.0 From the Woolwich Arsenal Pier face inland and turn right along the waterfront keeping the river on your right. At the ferry use the ferry approach road to board.

1.3 On the other side take the first left off the pier along Pier Rd and at the end right along Henley Rd and left along Factory Rd.

2.6 At the end continue along the cycleway, crossing Thames Rd to a cycleway parallel with North Woolwich Rd.

4.2 Just after West Silvertown DLR Station turn left down Dock Rd. At the end bear left onto the cycleway up and over the lower Lee crossing. Continue to the big roundabout and go left here.

6.0 At the next smaller roundabout go right along Blackwall Way and continue as the road bears left. At the end turn right along Yabsley St and then left along Preston Rd.

7.4 Pass over the iron bridge and at the roundabout take the second exit down East Ferry Rd.

8.1 When the road bends sharply left turn right over the pavement crossing left onto another East Ferry Rd.

8.6 Just after passing Mudchute Park Station on the right look out for a turning left into Mudchute Park. Follow the cyclepath through the park keeping to the right edge.

8.8 At the end cross over Manchester Rd and take path ahead past the artificial playing field to Island Gardens.

A honey bee pollinates one of the many colourful flowers found in the Thames Barrier Park

8.9 This is the end of the route but if you want to return to the start you should cross to Greenwich via the foot tunnel and either get a river boat to Woolwich from the pier or cycle to Greenwich Station and get a train back to Woolwich. Alternatively cycle back via Rides 23 or 28 to make the loop.

Woolwich to Isle of Dogs

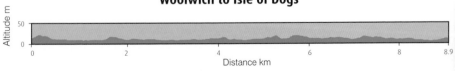

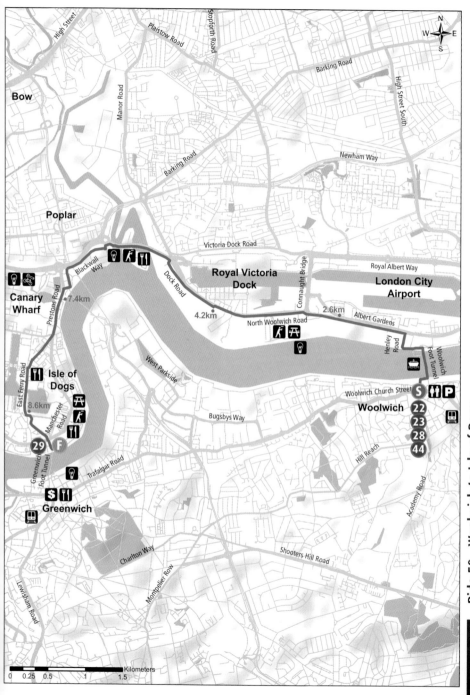

Bow

Poplar

Canary
Wharf

7.4km

Blackwall Way

Prestons Road

Isle of
Dogs

East Ferry Road

8.6km

Manchester Road

29　F

Greenwich Foot Tunnel

Trafalgar Road

Greenwich

Plaistow Road

Stopforth Road

Barking Road

Manor Road

Barking Road

Newham Way

High Street

High Street South

Victoria Dock Road

Royal Victoria
Dock

Dock Road

Connaught Bridge

Royal Albert Way

London City
Airport

4.2km

North Woolwich Road

2.6km

Albert Gardens

Henley Road

Woolwich Foot Tunnel

West Parkside

Bugsbys Way

Woolwich Church Street

Woolwich

S　22　23　28　44

Hill Reach

Academy Road

Charlton Way

Montpelier Row

Shooters Hill Road

Lewisham Road

Kilometers

0　0.25　0.5　1　1.5

Kids' Rides

If you're reading this you are probably a parent so you will understand the importance of teaching children to ride in a safe, interesting environment. Most children can learn to ride a bicycle between the ages of four and six. The secret is not the pedalling but the balancing; a child who can ride a two-wheeled scooter can very quickly learn to ride a bicycle but a child with stabilisers can't begin to learn until the stabilisers are removed because they effectively support the bicycle. Once balancing is learned, everything else is an incremental step: breaking, steering, pedalling and later on changing gear. Once a child is ready to learn it is essential to get the right sized bike. A bike can not be grown into like a school jumper because an oversized bike will be awkward, heavy and difficult to handle, it will likely put the child off or worse still, it could be dangerous; out grown bikes can be sold second hand.

London may not seem at first an obvious place to learn to ride, however when you think of the number of well kept parks and open spaces free from traffic with smooth tracks and plenty of cafes, the prospect of teaching children to ride no longer becomes daunting but appealing. This chapter suggests five places spread about the capital with a safe environment in which to learn. Once they've nailed it, cycling will be an activity the whole family can enjoy. A sunny Sunday trip along a canal for a picnic or pub lunch is a fine way to spend a summer day, however the scope of cycling is much wider than this. Kids can cycle to school or the family can holiday on bikes from one campsite to another. While cycling is a fantastic form of transport later in life, for a child it has an even more significant role being the only form of transport where they are not just a passenger; for them this is a huge boost of independence and a milestone in a child's life and what's more, you never forget. "It's like riding a bike" as the proverbial saying goes.

Impressing mum in Richmond Park

Green deckchairs in neighbouring St James Park

Distance 3.3km

Terrain

A flat circular bike route on sealed car free path inside the park.

How to Get There

Nearby mainline stations include Victoria and Charing Cross. Pay and display street parking in Kensington and there is a large underground car park off Park Lane on the eastern edge of Hyde Park.

Amenities and Things to Do

As well as several cafés and easily accessible public conveniences there is also a gallery, fountains and memorials. Pedalos can be hired to navigate the Serpentine and there is also a solar powered ferry.

About

This green ride follows a dedicated cycle path around the Serpentine in the centre of Hyde Park, one of central London's largest open green spaces. The area may be busy at weekends but there are plenty of extra activities such as pedalos or a ride on the solar boat. There are fountains, memorials galleries and abundant wildlife along the route.

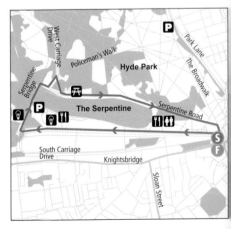

Ride 2 - Wimbledon Common

Distance 3.2km

Terrain

A flat circular route, half on smooth un-surfaced, car free path and half on a quiet surfaced road through common.

How to Get There

The route is up the hill from Wimbledon mainline station. There is a car park at the Windmill on Wimbledon Common.

Amenities and Things to Do

Wimbledon Windmill Museum. There are numerous cafés and child friendly pubs along the route. Home of the Wimbledon Wombles; fictional, furry, pointy nosed creatures that live in burrows.

About

A huge expanse of open ground criss-crossed by bike tracks, bridleways and walking routes. The easy parking and great local pubs and cafes make this a popular spot in summer, however in winter it can seem a little exposed to the weather. Despite the many green spaces to choose from in south west London, Wimbledon Common continues to be one of the most popular spots for parents teaching their kids to ride.

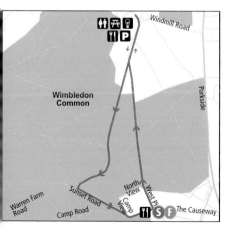

Building confidence

Kids' Rides

Dulwich Village

Distance 1.7km

Terrain

A brilliant flat surfaced car free circular route around the centre of Dulwich Park.

How to Get There

West Dulwich and North Dulwich train stations are close by; there is parking along the access road into the park from College Road though this can become busy at weekends.

Amenities and Things to Do

There is a duck pond, popular park café, a local picture gallery and an equestrian centre and there is also a hut where you can rent recumbent bicycles.

About

Created in 1890 and boarded by ancient oaks, the open lawns and manicured gardens of Dulwich Park are the perfect place to learn to ride. The smooth car free paths and plethora of activities mean parents with children swarm here in droves. The park café is very popular and as many prams as deckchairs cover the grass around the building.

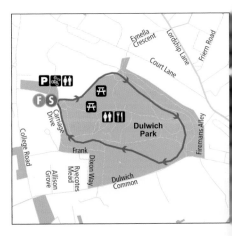

Ride 4 - Hampstead Heath

Distance 800m

Terrain

A smooth straight, flat path running from the Highgate Hill entrance to the Hampstead Heath Station gate.

How to Get There

Hampstead Heath train station; car parking at Hampstead Ponds off Heath Road.

Amenities and Things to Do

There is a park café, acres of grassland and ponds as well as a Lido and tennis courts. There are also several child friendly pubs and restaurants on the edges of the heath.

About

Despite the cycling restrictions, learning to ride on the heath is a right of passage for many north London children. I learnt to ride here in the 70s on an orange Raleigh chopper and at the weekend thousands of young children are doing the same.

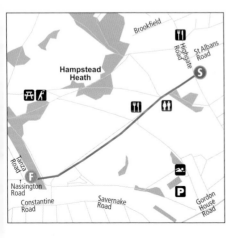

Spring on the heath

Kids' Rides

A family thing...

Distance 3.2km

Terrain

Another fantastic, smooth surfaced, car free path, this time, looping around the centre of Victoria Park in East London.

How to Get There

Cambridge Heath train station. Limited parking along Grove Road.

Amenities and Things to Do

A popular park café overlooking the duck pond; there is also a stretch of the regents canal towpath, a playground, a bandstand and tennis courts.

About

An established Victorian park with mature trees and noble wrought iron gates is an oasis of calm from the thundering buzz of surrounding east London. Bohemian parents bring their children to play and relax while they natter in the park café.

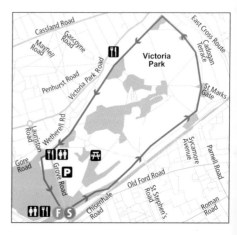

Notes

Notes

Notes

Notes

Notes

Notes

WheretoRide *London*